Cocoa® Programming for Mac® OS X

THIRD EDITION

COCOA® PROGRAMMING
FOR MAC® OS X

THIRD EDITION

Aaron Hillegass

✦✦Addison-Wesley

Upper Saddle River, NJ • Boston • Indianapolis • San Francisco
New York • Toronto • Montreal • London • Munich • Paris • Madrid
Capetown • Sydney • Tokyo • Singapore • Mexico City

Many of the designations used by manufacturers and sellers to distinguish their products are claimed as trademarks. Where those designations appear in this book, and the publisher was aware of a trademark claim, the designations have been printed with initial capital letters or in all capitals.

The author and publisher have taken care in the preparation of this book, but make no expressed or implied warranty of any kind and assume no responsibility for errors or omissions. No liability is assumed for incidental or consequential damages in connection with or arising out of the use of the information or programs contained herein.

The publisher offers excellent discounts on this book when ordered in quantity for bulk purchases or special sales, which may include electronic versions and/or custom covers and content particular to your business, training goals, marketing focus, and branding interests. For more information, please contact:

U.S. Corporate and Government Sales
(800) 382-3419
corpsales@pearsontechgroup.com

For sales outside the United States please contact:

International Sales
international@pearson.com

Visit us on the Web: www.informit.com/aw

Library of Congress Cataloging-in-Publication Data
Hillegass, Aaron.
  Cocoa programming for Mac OS X / Aaron Hillegass. — 3rd ed.
       p. cm.
  Includes index.
  ISBN 978-0-321-50361-9 (pbk. : alk. paper)
 1. Cocoa (Application development environment) 2. Mac OS. 3. Operating systems
(Computers) 4. Macintosh (Computer)—Programming. I. Title.

  QA76.76.O63H57145 2008
  005.26'8—dc22

                                                        2008008239

ISBN-13: 978-0321-50361-9
ISBN-10:   0-321-50361-9
Text printed in the United States on recycled paper at Courier in Stoughton, Massachusetts.
First printing, May 2008

For my sons, Walden and Otto

CONTENTS

PREFACE

If you are developing applications for the Mac, or are hoping to do so, this book is just the resource you need. Does it cover everything you will ever want to know about programming for the Mac? Of course it doesn't. But it does cover probably 80% of what you need to know. You can find the remaining 20%, the 20% that is unique to you, in Apple's online documentation.

This book, then, acts as a foundation. It covers the Objective-C language and the major design patterns of Cocoa. It will also get you started with the three most commonly used developer tools: Xcode, Interface Builder, and Instruments. After reading this book, you will be able to understand and utilize Apple's online documentation.

There is a lot of code in this book. Through that code, I will introduce you to the idioms of the Cocoa community. My hope is that by presenting exemplary code, I can help you to become not just a Cocoa developer, but a stylish Cocoa developer.

This third edition includes technologies introduced in Mac OS X 10.4 and 10.5. These include Xcode 3, Objective-C 2, Core Data, the garbage collector, and CoreAnimation.

This book is written for programmers who already know some C programming and something about objects. You are not expected to have any experience with Mac programming. It's a hands-on book and assumes that you have access to Mac OS X and the developer tools. The developer tools are free. If you bought a shrink-wrapped copy of Mac OS X, the installer for the developer tools was on the DVD. The tools can also be downloaded from the Apple Developer Connection Web site (http://developer.apple.com/).

I have tried to make this book as useful for you as possible, if not indispensable. That said, I'd love to hear from you if you have any suggestions for improving it.

Aaron Hillegass
aaron@bignerdranch.com

ACKNOWLEDGMENTS

Creating this book required the efforts of many people. I want to thank them for their help. Their contributions have made this a better book than I could have ever written alone.

First, I want to thank the students who took the Cocoa programming course at the Big Nerd Ranch. They helped me work the kinks out of the exercises and explanations that appear here. The students' curiosity inspired me to make the book more comprehensive, and their patience made it possible.

By helping me teach and develop materials at the Ranch, Chris Campbell and Mark Fenoglio played important roles in the revisions for this edition. They made great additions and caught many of my most egregious errors. I had the great honor of working for several years with Kai Christiansen. He taught me many things about Cocoa and about teaching. Together, we wrote several courses on OpenStep and WebObjects. For me, writing this book was a natural continuation of our work. Although my hands were on the keyboard, Kai's voice was frequently what came out on the page.

The people at Addison-Wesley took my manuscript and made it into a book. They put the book on trucks and convinced bookstores to put it on the shelves. Without their help, it would still be just a stack of papers in my office.

The final thank-you goes to my family. Some of the attention that would normally be given to my wife, Michele, was diverted into the creation of this book. My sons, Walden and Otto, also deserve thanks for their patience and understanding.

Chapter 1
COCOA: WHAT IS IT?

A Little History

The story of Cocoa starts with a delightful bit of history. Once upon a time, two guys named Steve started a company called Apple Computer in their garage. The company grew rapidly, so they hired an experienced executive named John Sculley to be its CEO. After a few conflicts, John Sculley moved Steve Jobs to a position in which he had no control over the company at all. Steve Jobs left to form another computer company, called NeXT Computer.

NeXT hired a small team of brilliant engineers. This small team developed a computer, an operating system, a printer, a factory, and a set of development tools. Each piece was years ahead of competing technologies, and the masses were excited and amazed. Unfortunately, the excited masses did not buy either the computer or the printer. In 1993, the factory was closed, and NeXT Computer, Inc., became NeXT Software, Inc.

The operating system and the development tools continued to sell under the name NeXTSTEP. Although the average computer user had never heard of NeXTSTEP, it was very popular with scientists, investment banks, and intelligence agencies. These were people who developed new applications every week, and they found that NeXTSTEP enabled them to implement their ideas more quickly than any other technology did.

What was this operating system? NeXT decided to use Unix as the core of NeXTSTEP, relying on the source code for BSD Unix from the University of California at Berkeley. Why Unix? Unix crashed much less frequently than Microsoft Windows or Mac OS and came with powerful, reliable networking capabilities.

Apple has made the source code to the Unix part of Mac OS X available under the name Darwin. A community of developers continues to work to improve Darwin. You can learn more about Darwin at http://macosforge.org/.

NeXT then wrote a *window server* for the operating system. A window server takes events from the user and forwards them to the applications. The application then sends drawing commands back to the window server to update what the user sees. One of the nifty things about the NeXT window server is that the drawing code that goes to the window server is the same drawing code that would be sent to the printer. Thus, a programmer has to write the drawing code only once, and it can then be used for display on the screen or printing. In the NeXTSTEP days, programmers were writing code that generated PostScript. With Mac OS X, programmers are writing code that uses the CoreGraphics framework (also known as Quartz). Quartz can composite those graphics onto the screen, send them to the printer, or generate PDF data. The Portable Document Format is an open standard created by the Adobe Corporation for vector graphics.

If you have used Unix machines before, you are probably familiar with the X window server. The window server for Mac OS X is completely different but fulfills the same function as the X window server: It gets events from the user, forwards them to the applications, and puts data from the applications onto the screen. At the moment, the X protocol has poor support for antialiased fonts and transparency. This is one of the reasons that the Mac OS X window server looks so much better than an X window server.

NeXTSTEP came with a set of libraries and tools to enable programmers to deal with the window manager in an elegant manner. The libraries were called frameworks. In 1993, the frameworks and tools were revised and renamed OpenStep, which was itself later renamed Cocoa.

As shown in Figure 1.1, the window server and your application are Unix processes. Cocoa enables your application to receive events from the window server and to draw to the screen.

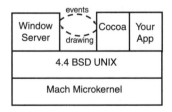

Figure 1.1   How Is Cocoa Used?

Programming with the frameworks is done in a language called *Objective-C*. Like C++, Objective-C is an extension to the C programming language, making it object oriented. Unlike C++, Objective-C is weakly typed and extremely powerful. With power comes responsibility: Objective-C allows programmers to make ridiculous errors. Objective-C is a very simple addition to C, and you will find it very easy to learn.

Programmers loved OpenStep. It enabled them to experiment more easily with new ideas. In fact, Tim Berners-Lee developed the first Web browser and the first Web server on NeXTSTEP. Securities analysts could code and test new financial models much more quickly. Colleges could develop the applications that made their research possible. I don't know what the intelligence community was using it for, but intelligence agencies bought thousands of copies of OpenStep. Because they were so useful, the OpenStep development tools were ported to Solaris and Windows NT, and the NeXTSTEP operating system was ported to most of the popular CPUs of the day: Intel, Motorola, Hewlett-Packard's PA-RISC, and SPARC. (Oddly enough, OpenStep didn't run on a Mac until the first version of Mac OS X Server, known as Rhapsody, shipped in 1999.)

For many years, Apple Computer had been working to develop an operating system with many of the features of NeXTSTEP. This effort was known as Copland. Project Copland gradually spun out of control, and Apple finally decided to pull the plug and buy the next version of Mac OS from another company. After surveying the existing operating systems, Apple selected NeXTSTEP. Because NeXT was small, Apple simply bought the whole company in December 1996.

Where do I fit into this story? I was writing code for NeXT computers on Wall Street until NeXT hired me to teach OpenStep programming to other developers. I was an employee at NeXT when it merged with Apple, and I taught many of the Apple engineers how to write applications for Mac OS X. No longer an Apple employee, I now teach Cocoa programming for Big Nerd Ranch, Inc.

NeXTSTEP became Mac OS X. It is Unix underneath, and you can get all the standard Unix programs, such as the Apache Web server, on Mac OS X, which is more stable than Windows and Mac OS 9. The user interface is spectacular. You, the developer, are going to love Mac OS X because Cocoa will enable you to write full-featured applications in a radically more efficient and elegant manner.

Tools

You *will* love Cocoa but perhaps not immediately. First, you will learn the basics. Let's start with the tools that you will use.

All the tools for Cocoa development come as part of the Mac OS X Developer Tools, and you get them for free with Mac OS X. Although the developer tools will add about a dozen handy applications to your system, you will use primarily two applications: Xcode and Interface Builder. Behind the scenes, the GNU C compiler (gcc) will be used to compile your code, and the GNU debugger (gdb) will help you find your errors.

Xcode tracks all the resources that will go into an application: code, images, sounds, and so on. You will edit your code in Xcode, and Xcode can compile and launch your application. Xcode can also be used to invoke and control the debugger.

Interface Builder is a GUI builder. It allows you to lay out windows and add widgets to those windows. It is, however, much more. Interface Builder allows the developer to create objects and edit their attributes. Most of those objects are UI elements, such as buttons and text fields, but some will be instances of classes that you create.

Language

This book uses Objective-C for all the examples. Objective-C is a simple and elegant extension to C, and mastering it will take about two hours if you already know C and an object-oriented language, such as Java or C++.

It is possible to develop Cocoa applications in Ruby or Python. This book will not cover that technique, but there is plenty of information on the Web. To understand that information, you will still need a working knowledge of Objective-C.

Objective-C has recently undergone a major revision. All the code in this book is Objective-C 2. With Objective-C 2.0, Apple added a garbage collector to the language. The garbage collector is *opt-in*; that is, you can choose to use it or not. The code in this book will be *dual-mode*; that is, it will work whether or not you turn the garbage collector on.

The Objective-C code will be compiled by gcc, the GNU C compiler. The compiler allows you to freely mix C, C++, and Objective-C code in a single file.

The GNU debugger, gdb, will be used to set breakpoints and browse variables at runtime. Objective-C gives you a lot of freedom to do dumb things; you will be glad to have a decent debugger.

Objects, Classes, Methods, and Messages

All Cocoa programming is done using object-oriented techniques. This section very briefly reviews terms used in object-oriented programming. If you have not done any object-oriented programming before, I recommend that you read *The Objective-C Language*. The PDF file for the book is on the Apple Web site (`http://developer.apple.com/documentation/Cocoa/Conceptual/ ObjectiveC/ObjC.pdf`).

What is an object? An *object* is like a C struct: It takes up memory and has variables inside it. The variables in an object are called *instance variables*. So when dealing with objects, the first questions we typically ask are: How do you allocate space for one? What instance variables does the object have? How do you destroy the object when you are done with it?

Some of the instance variables of an object will be pointers to other objects. These pointers enable one object to "know about" another object.

Classes are structures that can create objects. Classes specify the variables that the object has and are responsible for allocating memory for the object. We say that the object is an *instance* of the class that created it (Figure 1.2).

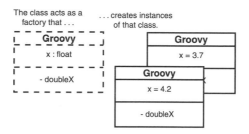

Figure 1.2   Classes Create Instances

An object is better than a struct, because an object can have functions associated with it. We call the functions *methods*. To call a method, you send the object a *message* (Figure 1.3).

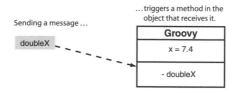

Figure 1.3   Messages Trigger Methods

Frameworks

A *framework* is a collection of classes that are intended to be used together. In other words, the classes are compiled together into a reusable library of code. Any related resources are put into a directory with the library. The directory is renamed with the extension .framework. You can find the built-in frameworks for your machine in /System/Library/Frameworks.

Cocoa is made up of three frameworks:

1. *Foundation:* Every object-oriented programming language needs the standard value, collection, and utility classes. Strings, dates, lists, threads, and timers are in the Foundation framework.

2. *AppKit:* All things related to the user interface are in the AppKit framework. Windows, buttons, text fields, events, and drawing classes are in the AppKit. You will also see this framework called the *ApplicationKit*.

3. *Core Data:* Core Data makes it easy to save your objects to a file and then reload them into memory. We say that Core Data is a *persistence* framework.

Numerous other frameworks handle such duties as encryption, QuickTime, and CD burning, but this book focuses on Foundation, AppKit, and Core Data because they are the most commonly used. Once you have mastered these, the other frameworks will be easier to understand.

You can also create your own frameworks from the classes that you create. Typically, if a set of classes is used in several applications, you will want to turn them into a framework.

How to Read This Book

When I sat down to write this book, I imagined that I was guiding a friend through activities that would help him understand Cocoa programming. This book acts as the guide through these activities. Often, I will ask you to do something and will explain the details or theory afterward. If you are confused, read a little more. Usually, the help you seek will be only a paragraph or two away.

If you are still stumped, you can get help on the Web site for this book: www.bignerdranch.com/products/. Errata, hints, and examples are listed there as well. Also, all the solutions for the exercises can be downloaded from there.

Each chapter guides you through the process of adding features to an application. This is not, however, a cookbook. This book teaches ideas, and the exercises show these ideas in action. Don't be afraid to experiment.

About 300 classes are in the the Cocoa frameworks. All the classes are documented in the online reference (accessed through Xcode's Help menu). Cocoa programmers spend a lot of time browsing through these pages. But until you understand a lot about Cocoa, it is hard to find the right starting place in your search for answers. As this book introduces you to a new class, look it up in the reference. You may not understand everything you find there, but browsing through the reference will give you some appreciation for the richness of the frameworks. When you reach the end of this book, the reference will become your guide.

Most of the time, Cocoa fulfills the promise: Common things are easy, and uncommon things are possible. If you find yourself writing many lines of code to do something rather ordinary, you are probably on the wrong track.

Typographical Conventions

To make the book easier to comprehend, I've used several typographical conventions.

In Objective-C, class names are always capitalized. In this book, I've also made them appear in a monospaced boldface font. In Objective-C, method names start with a lowercase letter. Method names also will appear in a monospaced boldface font. For example, you might see "The class **NSObject** has the method **dealloc**."

Other literals (including instance variable names) that you would see in code will appear in a regular monospaced font. Also, filenames will appear in this same font. Thus, you might see "In MyClass.m, set the variable favoriteColor to nil."

Common Mistakes

Having watched many, many people work through this material, I've seen the same mistakes made hundreds of times. I see two mistakes particularly often: capitalization mistakes and forgotten connections.

Capitalization mistakes happen because C and Objective-C are case-sensitive languages—the compiler does not consider Foo and foo to be the same thing. If you are having trouble making something compile, check to make sure that you have typed all the letters in the correct case.

When creating an application, you will use Interface Builder to connect objects together. Forgotten connections usually allow your application to build and run but result in aberrant behavior. If your application is misbehaving, go back to Interface Builder and check your connections.

It is easy to miss some warnings the first time a file is compiled. Because Xcode does incremental compiles, you may not see those warnings again unless you clean and rebuild the project. If you are stuck, try cleaning and rebuilding.

How to Learn

All sorts of people come to my class: the bright and the not so bright, the motivated and the lazy, the experienced and the novice. Inevitably, the people who get the most from the class share one characteristic: They remain focused on the topic at hand.

The first trick to maintaining focus is to get enough sleep. I suggest ten hours of sleep each night while you are studying new ideas. Before dismissing this idea, try it. You will wake up refreshed and ready to learn. *Caffeine is not a substitute for sleep.*

The second trick is to stop thinking about yourself. While learning something new, many students will think, "Damn, this is hard for me. I wonder if I am stupid." Because stupidity is such an unthinkably terrible thing in our culture, the students will then spend hours constructing arguments that explain why they are intelligent yet are having difficulties. The moment you start down this path, you have lost your focus.

I used to have a boss named Rock. Rock had earned a degree in astrophysics from Cal Tech and had never had a job in which he used his knowledge of the heavens. Once I asked him whether he regretted getting the degree. "Actually, my degree in astrophysics has proved to be very valuable," he said. "Some things in this world are just hard. When I am struggling with something, I sometimes think 'Damn, this is hard for me. I wonder if I am stupid,' and then I remember that I have a degree in astrophysics from Cal Tech; I must not be stupid."

Before going any farther, assure yourself that you are not stupid and that some things are hard. Armed with this silly affirmation and a well-rested mind, you are ready to conquer Cocoa.

Chapter 2
LET'S GET STARTED

Many books start by giving you a lot of philosophy. But doing so would be a waste of precious paper at this point. Instead, I am going to guide you through writing your first Cocoa application. Upon finishing, you will be excited and confused—and ready for the philosophy.

Our first project will be a random number generator application having two buttons: Seed random number generator with time and Generate random number. A text field will display the generated number. This simple example involves taking user input and generating output. At times, the description of what you are doing and why will seem, well, terse. Don't worry—we will explore all this in more detail throughout this book. For now, just play along.

Figure 2.1 shows what the completed application will look like.

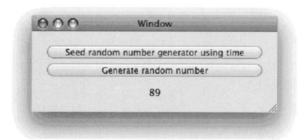

Figure 2.1   Completed Application

In Xcode

Assuming that you have installed the developer tools, you will find Xcode in /Developer/Applications/. Drag the application to the dock at the bottom of your screen; you will be using it a lot. Launch Xcode.

As mentioned earlier, Xcode will keep track of all the resources that go into your application. All these resources will be kept in a directory called the *project directory.* The first step in developing a new application is to create a new project directory with the default skeleton of an application.

Create a New Project

Under the File menu, choose New Project.... When the panel appears (see Figure 2.2), choose the type of project you would like to create: Cocoa Application. Note that many other types of projects are available as well.

Figure 2.2   Choose Project Type

In this book, we discuss the following major types of projects:

- *Application:* A program that creates windows.
- *Tool:* A program that does not have a graphical user interface. Typically, a tool is a command line utility or a daemon that runs in the background.
- *Bundle or framework:* A directory of resources that can be used in an application or a tool. A bundle (also called a *plug-in*) is dynamically loaded at runtime. An application typically links against a framework at compile time.

For the project name, type in RandomApp, as in Figure 2.3. Application names are typically capitalized. You can also pick the directory into which your project

Figure 2.3   Name Project

directory will be created. By default, your project directory will be created inside your home directory. Click the Finish button.

A project directory, with the skeleton of an application inside it, will be created for you. You will extend this skeleton into the source for a complete application and then compile the source into a working application.

Looking at the new project in Xcode, you will see an outline view on the left side of the window. Each item in the outline view represents one type of information that might be useful to a programmer. Some items are files; others are messages, such as compiler errors or find results. For now, you will be dealing with editing files, so select RandomApp to see the files that will be compiled into an application.

The skeleton of a project that was created for you will compile and run. It has a menu and a window. Click on the toolbar item with the hammer and green circle to build and run the project, as shown in Figure 2.4.

While the application is launching, you will see a bouncing icon in the dock. The name of your application will then appear in the menu. This means that your application is now active. The window for your application may be hidden by another window. If you do not see your window, choose Hide Others from the RandomApp menu. You should see an empty window, as shown in Figure 2.5.

It doesn't do much, but note that it is already a fully functional application. Printing even works. There is exactly one line of code in the application. Let's look at it now; quit RandomApp and return to Xcode.

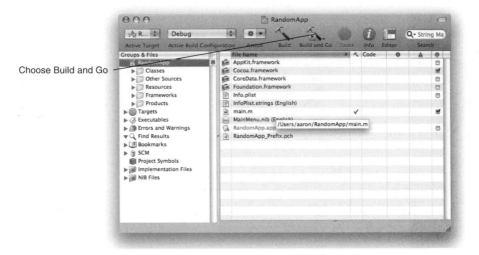

Choose Build and Go

Figure 2.4   Skeleton of a Project

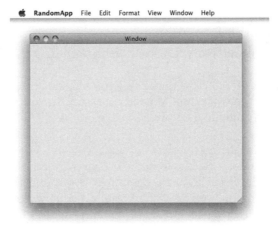

Figure 2.5   Running the Project

The main Function

Select main.m by single-clicking on it. If you double-click on the filename, it will open in a new window. Because I deal with many files in a day, this tends to overwhelm me rather quickly, so I use the single-window style. Click on the Editor toolbar item to split the window and create an editor view. The code will appear in the editor view (Figure 2.6).

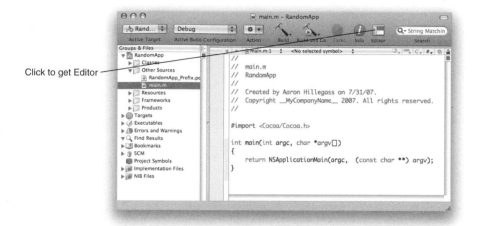

Click to get Editor

Figure 2.6   `main()` Function

You will almost never modify `main.m` in an application project. The default `main()` simply calls **NSApplicationMain()**, which in turn loads the user interface objects from a *nib file*. Nib files are created with Interface Builder. (*Trivia:* NIB stands for NeXT Interface Builder; NS stands for NeXTSTEP.) Once it has loaded the nib file, your application simply waits for the user to do something. When the user clicks or types, your code will be called automatically. If you have never written an application with a graphical user interface before, this change will be startling to you: The user is in control, and your code simply reacts to what the user does.

In Interface Builder

In the outline view under Resources is a nib file called `MainMenu.nib`. Double-click on it to open the nib in Interface Builder (Figure 2.7). Lots of windows will appear, so this is a good time to hide your other applications. In the Interface Builder menu, you will find Hide Others.

Interface Builder allows you to create and edit user interface objects (e.g., windows and buttons) and save those objects into a file. You can also create instances of your custom classes and make connections between those instances and the standard user interface objects. When users interact with the user interface objects, the connections you have made between them and your custom classes will cause your code to be executed.

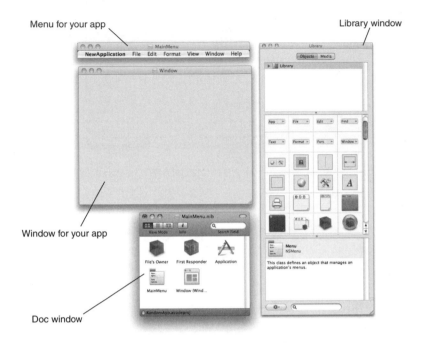

Menu for your app

Library window

Window for your app

Doc window

Figure 2.7   MainMenu.nib

The Library Window

The Library window is where you will find user interface widgets that can be dragged into your interface. For example, if you want a button, you can drag it from the Library window.

The Blank Window

The blank window represents an **NSWindow** class instance that is inside your nib file. As you drop objects from the library onto the window, they will be added to the nib file.

After you have created instances of these objects and edited their attributes, saving the nib file is like freeze-drying the objects into the file. When the application is run, the nib file will be read, and the objects will be revived. The cool kids say, "The objects are *archived* into the nib file by Interface Builder and *unarchived* when the application is run."

Lay Out the Interface

I am going to walk you through it, but keep in mind that your goal is to create a user interface that looks like Figure 2.8.

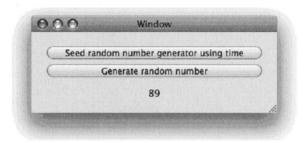

Figure 2.8   Completed Interface

Drag a button from the Library window (as shown in Figure 2.9) and drop it onto the blank window. (To make it easier to find, you can select the Cocoa -> Views & Cells group in the top part of the Library window.)

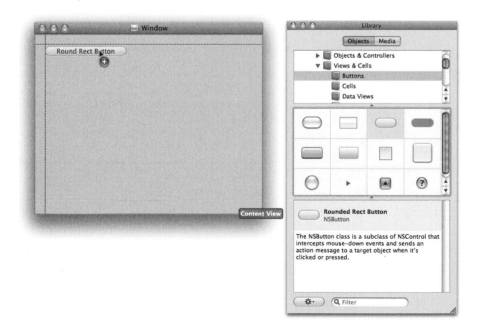

Figure 2.9   Dragging a Button

Double-click the button to change its title to Seed random number generator using time.

Copy and paste the button. Relabel the new button Generate random number. Drag out the Label text field (as shown in Figure 2.10) and drop it on the window.

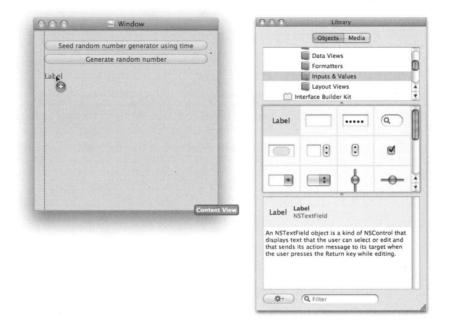

Figure 2.10   Dragging a Text Field

To make the text field as wide as the buttons, drag the left and right sides of the text field toward the sides of the window. (You may notice that blue lines appear when you are close to the edge of the window. These guides are intended to help you conform to Apple's GUI guidelines.)

Make the window smaller.

To make the text field center its contents, you will need to use the *Inspector*. Select the text field, and choose Attributes Inspector from the Tools menu. Click on the center-justify button (Figure 2.11).

Work-flow tip: In the morning, I open up the Inspector window and never close it again.

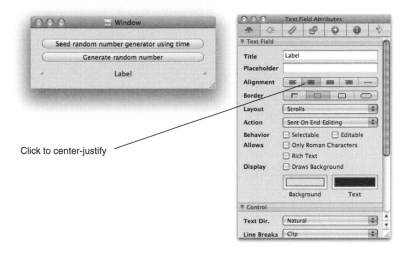

Click to center-justify

Figure 2.11   Center-Justify Text Field

The Doc Window

In your nib file, some objects (e.g., buttons) are visible, and others (e.g., your custom controller objects) are invisible. The icons that represent the invisible objects appear in the *doc window.*

In the doc window (the one entitled MainMenu.nib), you will see icons representing the main menu and the window. First Responder is a fictional object, but it is a very useful fiction. It is fully explained in Chapter 21. File's Owner in this nib is the **NSApplication** object for your application. The **NSApplication** object takes events from the event queue and forwards them to the appropriate window. We discuss the meaning of File's Owner in depth in Chapter 12.

Create a Class

In Objective-C, every class is defined by two files: a header file and an implementation file. The header file, also known as the interface file, declares the instance variables and methods your class will have. The implementation file defines what those methods do.

Go back to Xcode, and use the File->New File menu item to create a new Cocoa -> Objective-C class. Name the file Foo.m. (Figure 2.12).

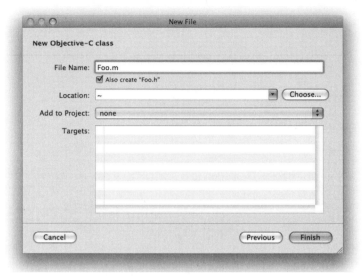

Figure 2.12   Create a New Class

The files Foo.h and Foo.m will appear in your project. If they don't appear in the Classes group, drag them there (Figure 2.13).

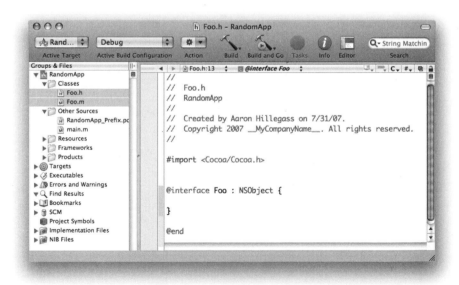

Figure 2.13   Put Foo.h and Foo.m in the Classes Group

In Foo.h, you will add instance variables and methods to your class. Instance variables that are pointers to other objects are called *outlets*. Methods that can be triggered by user interface objects are called *actions*.

Edit Foo.h to look like this:

```
#import <Cocoa/Cocoa.h>

@interface Foo : NSObject {
    IBOutlet NSTextField *textField;
}
- (IBAction)seed:(id)sender;
- (IBAction)generate:(id)sender;
@end
```

An Objective-C programmer can tell three things from this file.

1. **Foo** is a subclass of **NSObject**.

2. **Foo** has one instance variable: textField is a pointer to an instance of the class **NSTextField**.

3. **Foo** has two methods: **seed:** and **generate:** are action methods.

By convention, the names of methods and instance variables start with lowercase letters. If the name would be multiple words in English, each new word is capitalized—for example, favoriteColor. Also by convention, class names start with capital letters—for example, **Foo**.

Save Foo.h.

Create an Instance

Next, you will create an instance of the class **Foo** in your nib file. Return to Interface Builder. From the Library window, drag a blue Object (under Cocoa -> Objects & Controllers). Drop it in your doc window (Figure 2.14).

In the Identity Inspector, set its class to **Foo** (Figure 2.15). (Your actions and outlets should appear in the Inspector. If they do not, check Foo.h. You have a mistake in it, or it hasn't been saved.)

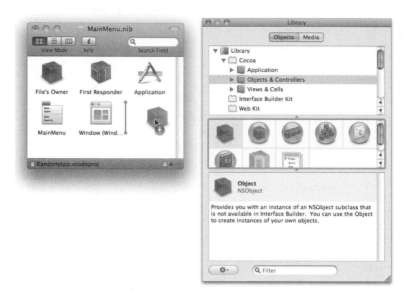

Figure 2.14   Skeleton of a Project

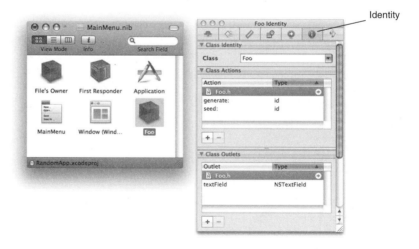

Figure 2.15   Setting the Class

Make Connections

A lot of object-oriented programming has to do with which objects need to know about which other objects. Now you are going to introduce some objects to each other. Cocoa programmers would say, "We are now going to set the outlets of our objects." To introduce one object to another, you will Control-drag *from* the object that needs to know *to* the object it needs to know about. Figure 2.16 is an object diagram that shows which objects need to be connected in your example.

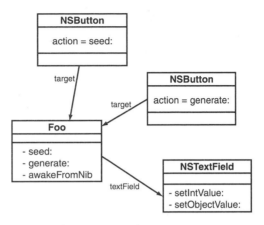

Figure 2.16   Object Diagram

You will set **Foo**'s textField instance variable to point to the **NSTextField** object on the window that currently says Label. Right-click (or Control-click if you have a one-button mouse) on the symbol that represents your instance of **Foo** to the text field. The Inspector panel will then appear. Drag from the circle beside textField to the text field that says Label (Figure 2.17).

This step is all about pointers: You have just set the pointer textField in your **Foo** object to point to the text field.

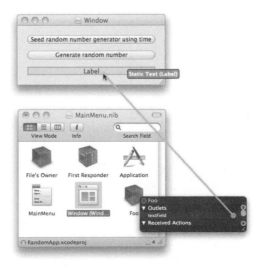

Figure 2.17   Set the textField Outlet

Now you will set the Seed button's `target` outlet to point to your instance of **Foo**. Furthermore, you want the button to trigger **Foo**'s **seed:** method. Control-drag from the button to your instance of **Foo**. When the panel appears, select **seed:** (Figure 2.18).

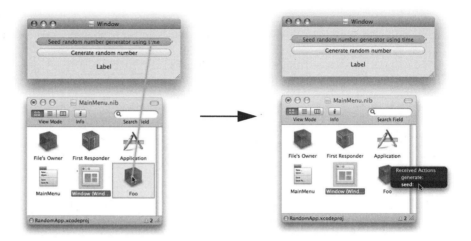

Figure 2.18   Set the Target and Action of the Seed Button

Similarly, you will set the Generate button's `target` instance variable to point to your instance of **Foo** and set its action to the **generate:** method. Control-drag from the button to **Foo**. Choose **generate:** in the Received Actions panel (Figure 2.19).

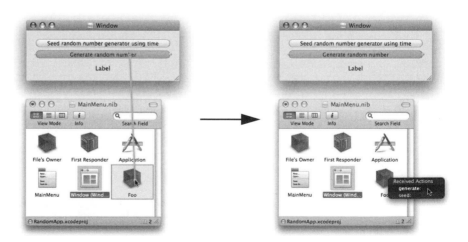

Figure 2.19   Set the Target and Action of the Generate Button

You are done with Interface Builder, so save the file and hide the application. Return to Xcode.

Back in Xcode

If this is the first time that you are seeing Objective-C code, you may be alarmed to discover that it looks quite different from C++ or Java code. The syntax may be different, but the underlying concepts are the same. In Java, for example, a class would be declared like this:

```
import com.megacorp.Bar;
import com.megacorp.Baz;

public class Rex extends Bar implements Baz {
...methods and instance variables...
}
```

This says, "The class **Rex** inherits from the class **Bar** and implements the methods declared in the **Baz** interface."

The analogous class in Objective-C would be declared like this:

```
#import <megacorp/Bar.h>
#import <megacorp/Baz.h>

@interface Rex : Bar <Baz> {
...instance variables...
}
...methods...
@end
```

If you know Java, Objective-C really isn't so strange. Note that like Java, Objective-C allows only single inheritance; that is, a class has only one superclass.

Types and Constants in Objective-C

Objective-C programmers use a few types that are not found in the rest of the C world.

- id is a pointer to any type of object.
- BOOL is the same as char but is used as a Boolean value.

- YES is 1.

- NO is 0.

- **IBOutlet** is a macro that evaluates to nothing. Ignore it. (**IBOutlet** is a hint to Interface Builder when it reads the declaration of a class from a .h file.)

- **IBAction** is the same as void and acts as a hint to Interface Builder.

- nil is the same as NULL. We use nil instead of NULL for pointers to objects.

Look at the Header File

Click on Foo.h. Study it for a moment. It declares **Foo** to be a subclass of **NSObject**. Instance variables are declared inside braces.

```
#import <Cocoa/Cocoa.h>

@interface Foo : NSObject
{
    IBOutlet NSTextField *textField;
}
- (IBAction)generate:(id)sender;
- (IBAction)seed:(id)sender;
@end
```

#import is similar to the C preprocessor's #include. However, #import ensures that the file is included only once. You are importing <Cocoa/Cocoa.h> because that includes the declaration of **NSObject**, which is the superclass of **Foo**.

Note that the declaration of the class starts with @interface. The @ symbol is not used in the C programming language. To minimize conflicts between C code and Objective-C code, Objective-C keywords are prefixed by @. Here are a few other Objective-C keywords: @end, @implementation, @class, @selector, @protocol, @property, and @synthesize.

In general, you will find entering code easier if you turn on syntax-aware indention. In Xcode's Preferences, select the Indentation pane. Check the box labeled Syntax-aware indenting, as shown in Figure 2.20.

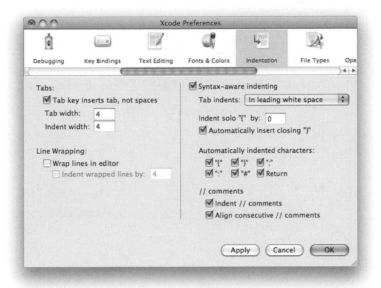

Figure 2.20   Syntax-Aware Indentation Preference

Edit the Implementation File

Now look at Foo.m. It contains the implementations of the methods. In C++ or Java, you might implement a method something like this:

```
public void increment(Object sender) {
    count++;
    textField.setIntValue(count);
}
```

In English, you would say, "**increment** is a public instance method that takes one argument that is an object. The method doesn't return anything. The method increments the count instance variable and then sends the message **setIntValue()** to the textField object with count as an argument."

In Objective-C, the analogous method would look like this:

```
- (void)increment:(id)sender
{
    count++;
    [textField setIntValue:count];
}
```

Objective-C is a very simple language. It has no visibility specifiers: All methods are public, and all instance variables are protected. (In fact, there are visibility specifiers for instance variables, but they are rarely used. The default is protected, and that works nicely.)

In Chapter 3, we will explore Objective-C in all its beauty. For now, simply copy the methods:

```
#import "Foo.h"

@implementation Foo

- (IBAction)generate:(id)sender
{
    // Generate a number between 1 and 100 inclusive
    int generated;
    generated = (random() % 100) + 1;

    NSLog(@"generated = %d", generated);

    // Ask the text field to change what it is displaying
    [textField setIntValue:generated];
}

- (IBAction)seed:(id)sender
{
    // Seed the random number generator with the time
    srandom(time(NULL));
    [textField setStringValue:@"Generator seeded"];
}

@end
```

(Remember that IBAction is the same as void. Neither method returns anything.)

Because Objective-C is C with a few extensions, you can call functions, such as **random()** and **srandom()**, from the standard C and Unix libraries.

Before you build and run the application, you might want to edit your Xcode preferences some more. First, there is a log, usually called *the console*, where your errors will appear when you run your code. You will want that log cleared after each run. Second, you will flip from a .h file to the corresponding .m file a thousand times daily. The key equivalent is Command-Option-UpArrow. You will want the two files to appear in the same window (Figure 2.21).

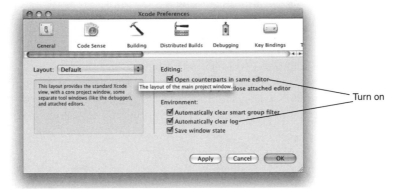

Figure 2.21   Counterparts in Same Editor + Log Clearing

Build and Run

Your application is now finished. Click Build and Go. (If your app is already running, the toolbar item will be disabled; quit your app before trying to run it again.)

If your code has an error, the compiler's message indicating a problem will appear at the view in the upper-right corner. If you click the message, the erroneous line of code will be selected in the view on the lower right. In Figure 2.22, the programmer has forgotten a semicolon.

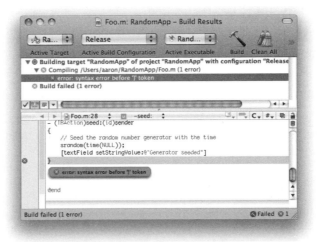

Figure 2.22   Compiling

Launch your application. Click the buttons and see the generated random numbers. Congratulations—you have a working Cocoa application.

Did you see the log statement on the console? When things go badly, the Cocoa classes will log to the console, so you will want to keep an eye on the console while testing your application. There is a menu item for this in the Run menu, but it is probably best to always show the console. In Preferences, set Xcode to show the console whenever an application is run, as shown in Figure 2.23.

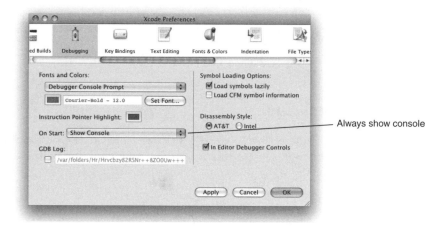

Figure 2.23   Show Console Preference

awakeFromNib

Note that your application is flawed: When the application starts, the word Label appears in the text field instead of anything interesting. Let's fix that problem. You will make the text field display the time and date that the application started.

The nib file is a collection of objects that have been archived. When the program is launched, the objects are brought back to life before the application handles any events from the user. This mechanism is a bit unusual: Most GUI builders generate source code that lays out the user interface. Instead, Interface Builder allows the developer to edit the state of the objects in the interface and to save that state to a file.

After being brought to life but before any events are handled, all objects are automatically sent the message **awakeFromNib**. You will add an **awakeFromNib** method that will initialize the text field's value.

Add the **awakeFromNib** method to Foo.m. For now, simply type it in. You will understand it later on. Briefly, you are creating an instance of **NSCalendarDate** that represents the current time. Then you are telling the text field to set its value to the new calendar date object:

```
- (void)awakeFromNib
{
    NSCalendarDate *now;
    now = [NSCalendarDate calendarDate];
    [textField setObjectValue:now];
}
```

The order in which the methods appear in the file is not important. Just make sure that you add them after @implementation and before @end.

You will never have to call **awakeFromNib**; it gets called automatically. Simply build and run your application again. You should now see the date and time when the app runs (Figure 2.24).

Figure 2.24 Completed Application

In Cocoa, a lot of things (e.g., **awakeFromNib**) get called automatically. Some of the confusion that you may experience as you read this book will come from trying to figure out which methods you have to call and which ones will get called for you automatically. I'll try to make the distinction clear.

Documentation

Before this chapter wraps up, you should know where to find the documentation, as it may prove handy if you get stuck while doing an exercise later in the book. The easiest way to get to the documentation is by choosing Documentation from Xcode's Help menu (Figure 2.25).

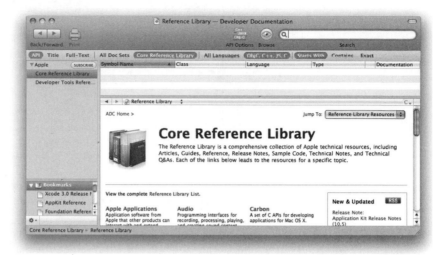

Figure 2.25   The Documentation

If you Option-Double-Click on a method, class, or function name, Xcode will automatically look up that term in the documentation.

What Have You Done?

You have now gone through the steps involved in creating a simple Cocoa application.

- Create a new project.
- Lay out an interface.
- Create custom classes.
- Connect the interface to your custom class or classes.
- Add code to the custom classes.
- Compile.
- Test.

Let's briefly discuss the chronology of an application: When the process is started, it runs the **NSApplicationMain** function, which creates an instance of **NSApplication**. The application object reads the main nib file and unarchives the objects inside. The objects are all sent the message **awakeFromNib**. Then the application object checks for events. The timeline for these events appears in Figure 2.26.

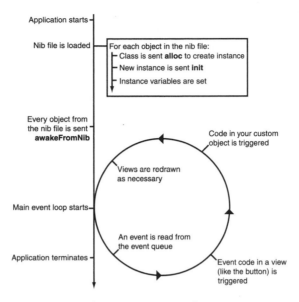

Figure 2.26 A Timeline

When it receives an event from the keyboard and mouse, the window server puts the event data into the event queue for the appropriate application, as shown in Figure 2.27. The application object reads the event data from its queue and

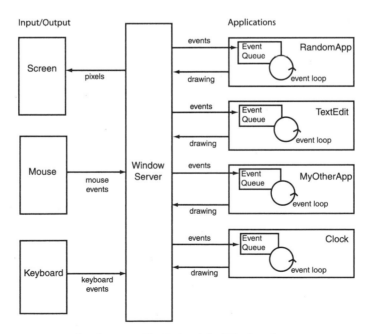

Figure 2.27 The Role of the Window Server

forwards it to a user interface object (like a button), and your code gets triggered. If your code changes the data in a view, the view is redisplayed. Then the application object checks its event queue for another event. This process of checking for events and reacting to them constitutes the *main event loop*.

When the user chooses Quit from the menu, NSApp is sent the **terminate:** message. This ends the process, and all your objects are destroyed.

Puzzled? Excited? Move on to the next chapter so we can fill in some blanks.

Chapter 3
OBJECTIVE-C

Once upon a time, a man named Brad Cox decided that it was time for the world to move toward a more modular programming style. C was a popular and powerful language. Smalltalk was an elegant untyped object-oriented language. Starting with C, Brad Cox added Smalltalk-like classes and message-sending mechanisms. The result, *Objective-C*, is a very simple extension of the C language. In fact, Objective-C was originally simply a C preprocessor and a library.

Objective-C is not a proprietary language. Rather, it is an open standard that has been included in the Free Software Foundation's GNU C compiler (gcc) for many years. Cocoa was developed using Objective-C, and most Cocoa programming is done in Objective-C.

Teaching C and basic object-oriented concepts could consume an entire book. Instead of writing that book, this chapter assumes that you already know a little C and something about objects and introduces you to the basics of Objective-C. If you fit the profile, you will find learning Objective-C to be easy. If you do not, Apple's *The Objective-C Language* is a more gentle introduction.

Creating and Using Instances

Chapter 1 mentioned that classes are used to create objects, that the objects have methods, and that you can send messages to the objects to trigger these methods. In this section, you will learn how to create an object, send messages to it, and destroy it when you no longer need it.

As an example, we will use the class **NSMutableArray**. You can create a new instance of **NSMutableArray** by sending the message **alloc** to the **NSMutableArray** class, like this:

```
[NSMutableArray alloc];
```

This method returns a pointer to the space that was allocated for the object. You could hold onto that pointer in a variable, like this:

```
NSMutableArray *foo;
foo = [NSMutableArray alloc];
```

While working with Objective-C, it is important to remember that foo is only a pointer. In this case, it points to an object.

Before using the object that foo points to, you need to make sure that it is fully initialized. The **init** method will handle this task, so you might write code like this:

```
NSMutableArray *foo;
foo = [NSMutableArray alloc];
[foo init];
```

Take a long look at the last line; it sends the message **init** to the object that foo points to. We would say, "foo is the receiver of the message **init**." Note that a message send consists of a receiver (the object foo points to) and a message (**init**) wrapped in brackets. Note that you can also send messages to *classes*, as demonstrated by sending the message **alloc** to the class **NSMutableArray**.

The method **init** returns the newly initialized object. As a consequence, you will always nest the message sends like this:

```
NSMutableArray *foo;
foo = [[NSMutableArray alloc] init];
```

What about destroying the object when you no longer need it? Chapter 4 talks about this (and all things **NSAutoreleasePool**-related).

Some methods take arguments. If it takes an argument, the method name (called a *selector*) will end with a colon. For example, to add objects to the end of the array, you use the **addObject:** method (assume that bar is a pointer to another object):

```
[foo addObject:bar];
```

If you have multiple arguments, the selector will have multiple parts. For example, to add an object at a particular index, you could use the following:

```
[foo insertObject:bar atIndex:5];
```

Note that **insertObject:atIndex:** is one selector, not two. It will trigger one method with two arguments. This outcome seems strange to most C and Java programmers but should be familiar to Smalltalk programmers. The syntax also makes your code easier to read. For example, it is not uncommon to see a C++ method call like this:

```
if (x.intersectsArc(35.0, 19.0, 23.0, 90.0, 120.0))
```

It is much easier to guess the meaning of the following code:

```
if ([x intersectsArcWithRadius:35.0
                centeredAtX:19.0
                         Y:23.0
                 fromAngle:90.0
                   toAngle:120.0])
```

If it seems odd right now, just use it for a while. Most programmers grow to really appreciate the Objective-C messaging syntax.

You are now at a point where you can read simple Objective-C code, so it is time to write a program that will create an instance of **NSMutableArray** and fill it with ten instances of **NSNumber**.

Using Existing Classes

If it isn't running, start Xcode. Close any projects that you were working on. Under the File menu, choose New Project…. When the panel pops up, choose to create a Foundation Tool (Figure 3.1).

Figure 3.1   Choose Project Type

A *Foundation Tool* has no graphical user interface and typically runs on the command line or in the background as a daemon. Unlike in an application project, you will always alter the **main** function of a Foundation Tool.

Name the project lottery (Figure 3.2). Unlike the names of applications, most tool names are lowercase.

Figure 3.2   Name Project

When the new project appears, select lottery.m under Source. Edit lottery.m to look like this:

```
#import <Foundation/Foundation.h>

int main (int argc, const char * argv[])
{
    NSAutoreleasePool *pool = [[NSAutoreleasePool alloc] init];

    NSMutableArray *array;
    array = [[NSMutableArray alloc] init];
    int i;
    for (i = 0; i < 10; i++) {
        NSNumber *newNumber = [[NSNumber alloc] initWithInt:(i * 3)];
        [array addObject:newNumber];
    }

    for ( i = 0; i < 10; i++) {
        NSNumber *numberToPrint = [array objectAtIndex:i];
        NSLog(@"The number at index %d is %@",  i, numberToPrint);
    }
```

```
        [pool drain];
        return 0;
}
```

Here is the play-by-play for the code:

```
#import <Foundation/Foundation.h>
```

You are including the headers for all the classes in the Foundation framework. The headers are precompiled, so this approach is not as computationally intensive as it sounds.

```
int main (int argc, const char *argv[])
```

The **main** function is declared just as it would be in any Unix C program.

```
        NSAutoreleasePool *pool = [[NSAutoreleasePool alloc] init];
```

This code declares a variable and points it to a new instance of **NSAutoreleasePool**. We will discuss the importance of autorelease pools in the next chapter.

```
        NSMutableArray *array;
```

One variable is declared here: array is a pointer to an instance of **NSMutableArray**. Note that no array exists yet. You have simply declared a pointer that will refer to the array once it is created.

```
        array = [[NSMutableArray alloc] init];
```

Here you are creating the instance of **NSMutableArray** and making the array variable point to it.

```
        for (i = 0; i < 10; i++) {
            NSNumber *newNumber = [[NSNumber alloc] initWithInt:(i*3)];
            [array addObject:newNumber];
        }
```

Inside the for loop, you have created a local variable called newNumber and set it to point to a new instance of **NSNumber**. Then you have added that object to the array.

The array does not make copies of the **NSNumber** objects. Instead, it simply keeps a list of pointers to the **NSNumber** objects. Objective-C programmers make very few copies of objects, because it is seldom necessary.

```
        for ( i = 0; i < 10; i++) {
            NSNumber *numberToPrint = [array objectAtIndex:i];
            NSLog(@"The number at index %d is %@", i, numberToPrint);
        }
```

Here you are printing the contents of the array to the console. **NSLog** is a function much like the C function **printf()**; it takes a format string and a comma-separated list of variables to be substituted into the format string. When displaying the string, **NSLog** prefixes the generated string with the name of the application and a timestamp.

In **printf**, for example, you would use %x to display an integer in hexadecimal form. With **NSLog**, we have all the tokens from **printf** and the token %@ to display an object. The object gets sent the message **description**, and the string it returns replaces %@ in the string. We will discuss the **description** method in detail soon.

All the tokens recognized by **NSLog()** are listed in Table 3.1.

Table 3.1   Possible Tokens in Objective-C Format Strings

Symbol	Displays
%@	id
%d, %D, %i	long
%u, %U	unsigned long
%hi	short
%hu	unsigned short
%qi	long long
%qu	unsigned long long
%x, %X	unsigned long printed as hexadecimal
%o, %O	unsigned long printed as octal
%f, %e, %E, %g, %G	double
%c	unsigned char as ASCII character
%C	unichar as Unicode character
%s	char * (a null-terminated C string of ASCII characters)
%S	unichar * (a null-terminated C string of Unicode characters)
%p	void * (an address printed in hexadecimal with a leading 0x)
%%	A % character

Note: If the @ symbol before the quotes in @"The number at index %d is %@" looks a little strange, remember that Objective-C is the C language with a couple of extensions. One of the extensions is that strings are instances of the class **NSString**. In C, strings are simply pointers to a buffer of characters that ends in the null character. Both C strings and instances of **NSString** can be used in the same file. To differentiate between constant C strings and constant **NSString**s, you must put @ before the opening quote of a constant **NSString**:

```
// C string
char *foo;
```

```
// NSString
NSString *bar;
foo = "this is a C string";
bar = @"this is an NSString";
```

You will use mostly **NSString** in Cocoa programming. Wherever a string is needed, the classes in the frameworks expect an **NSString**. However, if you already have a bunch of C functions that expect C strings, you will find yourself using char * frequently.

You can convert between C strings and **NSString**s:

```
const char *foo = "Blah blah";
NSString *bar;
// Create an NSString from a C string
bar = [NSString stringWithUTF8String:foo];

// Create a C string from an NSString
foo = [bar UTF8String];
```

Because **NSString** can hold Unicode strings, you will need to deal with the multibyte characters correctly in your C strings, and this can be quite difficult and time consuming. (Besides the multibyte problem, you will have to wrestle with the fact that some languages read from right to left.) Whenever possible, you should use **NSString** instead of C strings.

Continuing with the code in **main()**, you have the following:

```
    [pool drain];
    return 0;
}
```

Once again, we will discuss autorelease pools in the next chapter.

In the toolbar, you will see a pop-up for the Active Build Configuration. There are two choices: Debug and Release. While working on your application, you will always want to be in Debug. Before you ship your application, you will do a Release build. How are they different? A Release build is universal and has had its debugging symbols stripped. Thus, the Release build takes about twice as long to compile and has none of the stuff that the debugger needs to do its job.

Click Build and Go (Figure 3.3).

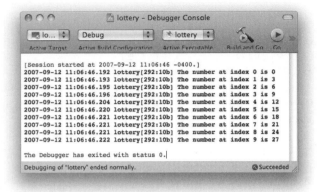

Figure 3.3   Completed Execution

(If your console doesn't appear, use the Run -> Console menu item.)

Sending Messages to nil

In most object-oriented languages, your program will crash if you send a message to nil. In applications written in those languages, you will see many checks for nil before sending a message. In Java, for example, you frequently see the following:

```
if (foo != null) {
    foo.doThatThingYouDo();
}
```

In Objective-C, it is okay to send a message to nil. The message is simply discarded, which eliminates the need for these sorts of checks. For example, this code will build and run without an error:

```
id foo;
foo = nil;
int bar = [foo count];
```

This approach is different from how most languages work, but you will get used to it.

You may find yourself asking over and over, "Argg! Why isn't this method getting called?" Chances are, the pointer you are using, assuming it is not nil, is actually nil.

In the preceding example, what is bar set to? Zero. If bar were a pointer, it would be set to nil (zero for pointers). For other types, the value is less predictable.

NSObject, NSArray, NSMutableArray, and NSString

You have now used these standard Cocoa objects: **NSObject**, **NSMutableArray**, and **NSString**. (All classes that come with Cocoa have names with the **NS** prefix. Classes that you will create will *not* start with **NS**.) These classes are all part of the Foundation framework. Figure 3.4 shows an inheritance diagram for these classes.

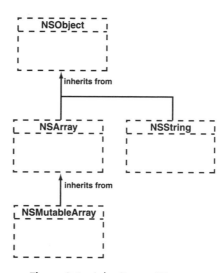

Figure 3.4   Inheritance Diagram

Let's go through a few of the commonly used methods on these classes. For a complete listing, you can access the online documentation from Xcode's Help menu.

NSObject

NSObject is the root of the entire Objective-C class hierarchy. Some commonly used methods on **NSObject** are described next.

    - (id)**init**

Initializes the receiver after memory for it has been allocated. An **init** message is generally coupled with an **alloc** message in the same line of code:

```
TheClass *newObject = [[TheClass alloc] init];
```

    - (NSString *)**description**

Returns an **NSString** that describes the receiver. The debugger's print object command ("po") invokes this method. A good **description** method will often make debugging easier. Also, if you use %@ in a format string, the object that should be substituted in is sent the message **description**. The value returned by the **description** method is put into the log string. For example, in your main function, the line

```
NSLog(@"The number at index %d is %@", i, numberToPrint);
```

is equivalent to

```
NSLog(@"The number at index %d is %@", i,
                        [numberToPrint description]);
```

- (BOOL)**isEqual:**(id)anObject

Returns YES if the receiver and anObject are equal and NO otherwise. You might use it like this:

```
if ([myObject isEqual:anotherObject]) {
    NSLog(@"They are equal.");
}
```

But what does *equal* really mean? In **NSObject**, this method is defined to return YES if and only if the receiver and anObject are the same object— that is, if both are pointers to the same memory location.

Clearly, this is not always the *equal* that you would hope for, so this method is overridden by many classes to implement a more appropriate idea of equality. For example, **NSString** overrides the method to compare the characters in the receiver and anObject. If they have the same characters in the same order, the two strings are considered equal.

Thus, if x and y are **NSString**s, there is a big difference between these two expressions:

```
x == y
```

and

```
[x isEqual:y]
```

The first expression compares the two pointers. The second expression compares the characters in the strings. Note, however, that if x and y are instances of a class that has not overridden **NSObject**'s **isEqual:** method, the two expressions are equivalent.

NSArray

An **NSArray** is a list of pointers to other objects. It is indexed by integers: Thus, if there are *n* objects in the array, the objects are indexed by the integers 0 through *n* – 1. You cannot put a nil in an **NSArray**. (This means that there are no "holes" in an **NSArray**, which may confuse programmers who are used to Java's Object[].) **NSArray** inherits from **NSObject**.

An **NSArray** is created with all the objects that will ever be in it. You can neither add nor remove objects from an instance of **NSArray**. We say that **NSArray** is *immutable*. (Its mutable subclass, **NSMutableArray**, is discussed next.) Immutability is nice in some cases. Because it is immutable, a horde of objects can share one **NSArray** without worrying that one object in the horde might change it. **NSString** and **NSNumber** also are immutable. Instead of changing a string or a number, you will simply create another one with the new value. (In the case of **NSString**, there is also the class **NSMutableString**, which allows its instances to be altered.)

Here are some commonly used methods implemented by **NSArray**:

- (unsigned)**count**

Returns the number of objects currently in the array.

- (id)**objectAtIndex:**(unsigned)i

Returns the object located at index i. If i is beyond the end of the array, you will get an error at runtime.

- (id)**lastObject**

Returns the object in the array with the highest index value. If the array is empty, nil is returned.

- (BOOL)**containsObject:**(id)anObject

Returns YES if anObject is present in the array. This method determines whether an object is present in the array by sending an **isEqual:** message to each of the array's objects and passing anObject as the parameter.

- (unsigned)**indexOfObject:**(id)anObject

Searches the receiver for anObject and returns the lowest index whose corresponding array value is equal to anObject. Objects are considered equal if **isEqual:** returns YES. If none of the objects in the array are equal to anObject, **indexOfObject:** returns NSNotFound.

NSMutableArray

NSMutableArray inherits from **NSArray** but extends it with the ability to add and remove objects. To create a mutable array from an immutable one, use **NSArray**'s **mutableCopy** method.

Here are some commonly used methods implemented by **NSMutableArray**:

```
- (void)addObject:(id)anObject
```

Inserts anObject at the end of the receiver. You are not allowed to add nil to the array.

```
- (void)addObjectsFromArray:(NSArray *)otherArray
```

Adds the objects contained in otherArray to the end of the receiver's array of objects.

```
- (void)insertObject:(id)anObject atIndex:(unsigned)index
```

Inserts anObject into the receiver at index. If index is already occupied, the objects at index and beyond are shifted up one slot to make room. Since index cannot be greater than the number of elements in the array, you will get an error if anObject is nil or if index is greater than the number of elements in the array.

```
- (void)removeAllObjects
```

Empties the receiver of all its elements.

```
- (void)removeObject:(id)anObject
```

Removes all occurrences of anObject in the array. Matches are determined on the basis of anObject's response to the **isEqual:** message.

```
- (void)removeObjectAtIndex:(unsigned)index
```

Removes the object at index and moves all elements beyond index down one slot to fill the gap. You will get an error if index is beyond the end of the array.

As mentioned earlier, you cannot add nil to an array. Sometimes you will want to put an object into an array to represent nothingness. The **NSNull** class exists for exactly this purpose. There is exactly one instance of **NSNull**, so if you want to put a placeholder for nothing into an array, use **NSNull** like this:

```
[myArray addObject:[NSNull null]];
```

NSString

An **NSString** is a buffer of Unicode characters. In Cocoa, all manipulations involving character strings are done with **NSString**. As a convenience, the Objective-C language also supports the @"..." construct to create a string object constant from a 7-bit ASCII encoding:

```
NSString *temp = @"this is a constant string";
```

NSString inherits from **NSObject**. Here are some commonly used methods implemented by **NSString**:

- (id)**initWithFormat:**(NSString *)format, ...

Works like **sprintf**. Here, format is a string containing tokens, such as %d. The additional arguments are substituted for the tokens:

```
int x = 5;
char *y = "abc";
id z = @"123";
NSString *aString = [[NSString alloc] initWithFormat:
            @"The int %d, the C String %s, and the NSString %@",
            x, y, z];
```

- (unsigned int)**length**

Returns the number of characters in the receiver.

- (NSString *)**stringByAppendingString:**(NSString *)aString

Returns a string object made by appending aString to the receiver. The following code snippet, for example, would produce the string "Error: unable to read file."

```
NSString *errorTag = @"Error: ";
NSString *errorString = @"unable to read file.";
NSString *errorMessage;
errorMessage = [errorTag stringByAppendingString:errorString];
```

"Inherits from" versus "Uses" or "Knows About"

Beginning Cocoa programmers are often eager to create subclasses of **NSString** and **NSMutableArray**. Don't. Stylish Objective-C programmers almost never do. Instead, they use **NSString** and **NSMutableArray** as parts of larger objects, a technique known as *composition*. For example, a **BankAccount** class *could* be a subclass of **NSMutableArray**. After all, isn't a bank account simply a collection of transactions? The beginner would follow this path. In contrast, the old hand would create a class **BankAccount** that inherited from **NSObject** and has an instance variable called transactions that would point to an **NSMutableArray**.

It is important to keep track of the difference between *uses* and *is a subclass of*. The beginner would say, "**BankAccount** inherits from **NSMutableArray**." The old hand would say, "**BankAccount** uses **NSMutableArray**." In the common idioms of Objective-C, *uses* is much more common than *is a subclass of*.

You will find it much easier to use a class than to subclass one. Subclassing involves more code and requires a deeper understanding of the superclass. By using composition instead of inheritance, Cocoa developers can take advantage of very powerful classes without really understanding how they work.

In a strongly typed language, such as C++, inheritance is crucial. In an untyped language, such as Objective-C, inheritance is merely a hack that saves the developer some typing. There are only two inheritance diagrams in this entire book. All the other diagrams are object diagrams that indicate which objects know about which other objects. This is much more important information to a Cocoa programmer.

Creating Your Own Classes

Where I live, the state government has decided that the uneducated have entirely too much money: You can play the lottery every week here. Let's imagine that a lottery entry has two numbers between 1 and 100, inclusive. You will write a program that will make up lottery entries for the next ten weeks. Each **LotteryEntry** object will have a date and two random integers (Figure 3.5). Besides learning how to create classes, you will build a tool that will certainly make you fabulously wealthy.

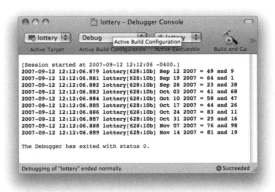

Figure 3.5 Completed Program

Creating the LotteryEntry Class

First, you will create files for the **LotteryEntry** class. In the File menu, choose New file.... Select Objective-C class as the type.

Name the file LotteryEntry.m (Figure 3.6).

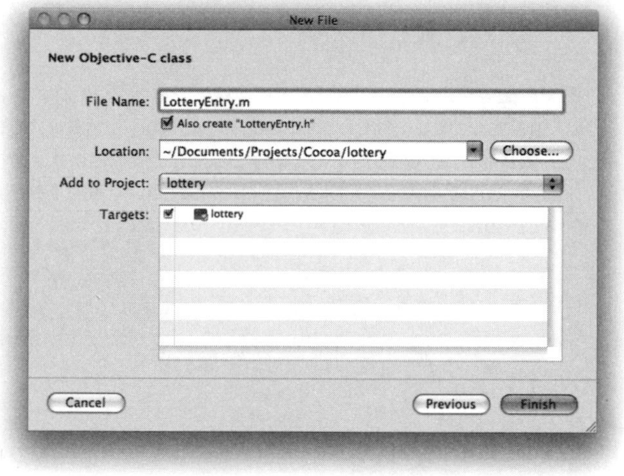

Figure 3.6   Name File

Note that you are also causing LotteryEntry.h to be created.

LotteryEntry.h

Edit the LotteryEntry.h file to look like this:

```
#import <Foundation/Foundation.h>

@interface LotteryEntry : NSObject {
    NSCalendarDate *entryDate;
    int firstNumber;
    int secondNumber;
}
- (void)prepareRandomNumbers;
- (void)setEntryDate:(NSCalendarDate *)date;
- (NSCalendarDate *)entryDate;
- (int)firstNumber;
- (int)secondNumber;
@end
```

You have created a header file for a new class called **LotteryEntry** that inherits from **NSObject**. The header file has three instance variables: entryDate, firstNumber, and secondNumber.

- entryDate is an **NSCalendarDate**.

- firstNumber and secondNumber are both ints.

You have declared five methods in the new class:

- **prepareRandomNumbers** will set firstNumber and secondNumber to random values between 1 and 100. This method takes no arguments and returns nothing.

- **entryDate** and **setEntryDate:** will allow other objects to read and set the variable entryDate. The method **entryDate** will return the value stored in the entryDate variable. The method **setEntryDate:** will allow the value of the entryDate variable to be set. Methods that allow variables to be read and set are called *accessor methods*.

- You have also declared accessor methods for reading firstNumber and secondNumber. (You have not declared accessors for setting these variables; you are going to set them directly in **prepareRandomNumbers**.)

LotteryEntry.m

Edit LotteryEntry.m to look like this:

```
#import "LotteryEntry.h"

@implementation LotteryEntry

- (void)prepareRandomNumbers
{
    firstNumber = random() % 100 + 1;
    secondNumber = random() % 100 + 1;
}

- (void)setEntryDate:(NSCalendarDate *)date
{
    entryDate = date;
}

- (NSCalendarDate *)entryDate
{
    return entryDate;
}

- (int)firstNumber
{
    return firstNumber;
}

- (int)secondNumber
{
    return secondNumber;
}
@end
```

Here is the play-by-play for each method:

> **prepareRandomNumbers** uses the standard **random** function to generate a pseudorandom number. You use the mod operator (%) and add 1 to get the number in the range 1–100.
>
> **setEntryDate:** sets the pointer entryDate to a new value.
>
> **entryDate**, **firstNumber**, and **secondNumber** return the values of variables.

Changing lottery.m

Now let's look at lottery.m. Many of the lines have stayed the same, but several have changed. The most important change is that we are using **LotteryEntry** objects instead of **NSNumber** objects.

Here is the heavily commented code. (You don't have to type in the comments.)

```
#import <Foundation/Foundation.h>
#import "LotteryEntry.h"

int main (int argc, const char *argv[]) {

    NSAutoreleasePool *pool = [[NSAutoreleasePool alloc] init];

    // Create the date object
    NSCalendarDate *now = [[NSCalendarDate alloc] init];

    // Seed the random number generator
    srandom(time(NULL));
    NSMutableArray *array;
    array = [[NSMutableArray alloc] init];

    int i;
    for (i = 0; i < 10; i++){

        // Create a date/time object that is 'i' weeks from now
        NSCalendarDate *iWeeksFromNow;
        iWeeksFromNow = [now dateByAddingYears:0
                                       months:0
                                         days:(i * 7)
                                        hours:0
                                      minutes:0
                                      seconds:0];

        // Create a new instance of LotteryEntry
        LotteryEntry *newEntry = [[LotteryEntry alloc] init];
        [newEntry prepareRandomNumbers];
        [newEntry setEntryDate:iWeeksFromNow];
```

```
        // Add the LotteryEntry object to the array
        [array addObject:newEntry];

    }

    for (LotteryEntry *entryToPrint in array) {
        // Display its contents
        NSLog(@"%@", entryToPrint);
    }
    [pool drain];
    return 0;
}
```

Note the second for loop. Here you are using Objective-C's mechanism for enumerating over the members of a collection.

This program will create an array of LotteryEntry objects, as shown in Figure 3.7.

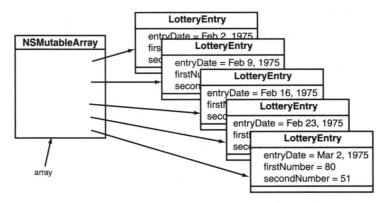

Figure 3.7   Object Diagram

Implementing a description Method

Build and run your application. You should see something like Figure 3.8.

Hmm. Not quite what we hoped for. After all, the program is supposed to reveal the dates and the numbers you should play on those dates, and you can't see either. (You are seeing the default **description** method as defined in **NSObject**.) Next, you will make the **LotteryEntry** objects display themselves in a more meaningful manner.

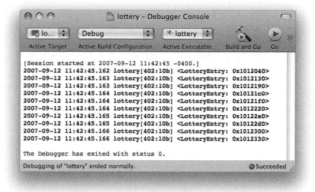

Figure 3.8   Completed Execution

Add a **description** method to LotteryEntry.m:

```
- (NSString *)description
{
    NSString *result;
    result = [[NSString alloc] initWithFormat:@"%@ = %d and %d",
              [entryDate descriptionWithCalendarFormat:@"%b %d %Y"],
              firstNumber, secondNumber];
    return result;
}
```

Build and run the application. Now you should see the dates and numbers (Figure 3.9).

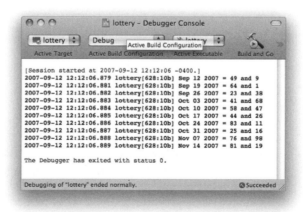

Figure 3.9   Execution with description

NSCalendarDate

Before moving on to any new ideas, let's examine **NSCalendarDate** in some depth. Instances of **NSCalendarDate** have a date and time, a time zone, and a format string. **NSCalendarDate** inherits from **NSDate**.

Instances of **NSCalendarDate** are basically immutable: You can't change the day or time of a calendar date once it is created, although you can change its format string and its time zone. Because it is basically immutable, many objects often share a single calendar date object. There is seldom any need to create a copy of an **NSCalendarDate** object.

Here are some of the commonly used methods implemented by **NSCalendarDate**:

+ (id)**calendarDate**

This method creates and returns a calendar date initialized to the current date and time in the default format for the locale. The time zone will be the time zone to which the machine is set.

This is a *class method*. In the interface file, implementation file, and documentation, class methods are recognizable because they start with + instead of -.

A class method is triggered by sending a message to the class instead of an instance. This one, for example, could be used as follows:

```
NSCalendarDate *now;
now = [NSCalendarDate calendarDate];
```

```
+ (id)dateWithYear:(int)year
            month:(unsigned)month
              day:(unsigned)day
             hour:(unsigned)hour
           minute:(unsigned)minute
           second:(unsigned)second
         timeZone:(NSTimeZone *)aTimeZone
```

This class method returns an autoreleased object. Specifically, this class method creates and returns a calendar date initialized with the specified values. The year value must include the century (for example, 2001 instead of 1). The other values are the standard ones: 1 through 12 for months, 1 through 31 for days, 0 through 23 for hours, and 0 through 59 for both minutes and seconds. The following code fragment shows a calendar date created with a date on 3 August 2000, 4 P.M., Pacific Standard Time (**timeZoneWithName:** returns the **NSTimeZone** object that represents the time zone with the specified name):

```
NSTimeZone *pacific = [NSTimeZone timeZoneWithName:@"PST"]

NSCalendarDate *hotTime = [NSCalendarDate dateWithYear:2000
                                              month:8
                                                day:3
                                               hour:16
                                             minute:0
                                             second:0
                                           timeZone:pacific];
```

```
- (NSCalendarDate *)dateByAddingYears:(int)year
                              months:(int)month
                                days:(int)day
                               hours:(int)hour
                             minutes:(int)minute
                             seconds:(int)second
```

This method returns a calendar date with the year, month, day, hour, minute, and second offsets specified as arguments. A positive offset is the future, and a negative offset represents the past. You used this method in lottery.m. Here, we are creating a day six months after hotTime:

```
NSCalendarDate *coldTime = [hotTime dateByAddingYears:0
                                             months:6
                                               days:0
                                              hours:0
                                            minutes:0
                                            seconds:0];
```

```
- (int)dayOfCommonEra
```

This method returns the number of days since the beginning of 1 A.D.

```
- (int)dayOfMonth
```

This method returns a number that indicates the day of the month (1 through 31) of the receiver.

```
- (int)dayOfWeek
```

This method returns a number that indicates the day of the week (0 through 6) of the receiver, where 0 indicates Sunday.

```
- (int)dayOfYear
```

This method returns a number that indicates the day of the year (1 through 366) of the receiver.

```
- (int)hourOfDay
```

This method returns the hour value (0 through 23) of the receiver.

- (int)**minuteOfHour**

This method returns the minutes value (0 through 59) of the receiver.

- (int)**monthOfYear**

This method returns a number that indicates the month of the year (1 through 12) of the receiver.

- (void)**setCalendarFormat:**(NSString *)format

This method sets the default calendar format for the receiver. A calendar format is a string formatted with date-conversion specifiers, as given in Table 3.2.

Table 3.2   Possible Tokens in the Calendar Format String

Symbol	Meaning
%y	Year without century (00–99)
%Y	Year with century ("1990")
%b	Abbreviated month name ("Jan")
%B	Full month name ("January")
%m	Month as a decimal number (01–12)
%a	Abbreviated weekday name ("Fri")
%A	Full weekday name ("Friday")
%w	Weekday as a decimal number (0–6), where Sunday is 0
%d	Day of the month as a decimal number (01–31)
%e	Same as %d but does not print the leading 0
%j	Day of the year as a decimal number (001–366)
%H	Hour based on a 24-hour clock as a decimal number (00–23)
%I	Hour based on a 12-hour clock as a decimal number (01–12)
%p	A.M./P.M. designation for the locale
%M	Minute as a decimal number (00–59)
%S	Second as a decimal number (00–59)
%F	Milliseconds as a decimal number (000–999)
%x	Date using the date representation for the locale
%X	Time using the time representation for the locale
%c	Shorthand for %X %x, the locale format for date and time
%Z	Time zone name
%z	Time zone offset in hours and minutes from GMT (HHMM)
%%	A % character

- (NSDate *)**laterDate:**(NSDate *)anotherDate

This method is inherited from **NSDate**, compares the receiver to anotherDate, and returns the later of the two.

- (NSTimeInterval)**timeIntervalSinceDate:**(NSDate *)anotherDate

This method returns the interval in seconds between the receiver and anotherDate. If the receiver is earlier than anotherDate, the return value is negative. **NSTimeInterval** is the same as double.

Writing Initializers

Note the following lines in your **main** function:

```
newEntry = [[LotteryEntry alloc] init];
[newEntry prepareRandomNumbers];
```

You are creating a new instance and then immediately calling **prepareRandom-Numbers** to initialize firstNumber and secondNumber. This is something that should be handled by the initializer, so you are going to override the **init** method in your **LotteryEntry** class.

In the LotteryEntry.m file, change the method **prepareRandomNumbers** into an **init** method:

```
- (id)init
{
    [super init];
    firstNumber = random() % 100 + 1;
    secondNumber = random() % 100 + 1;
    return self;
}
```

The **init** method calls the superclass's initializer at the beginning, initializes its own variables, and then returns self, a pointer to the object itself—the object that is running this method. (If you are a Java or a C++ programmer, self is the same as the this pointer.)

Now delete the following line in lottery.m:

```
[newEntry prepareRandomNumbers];
```

In LotteryEntry.h, delete the following declaration:

```
- (void)prepareRandomNumbers;
```

Build and run your program to reassure yourself that it still works.

A few of the initializers in Cocoa will return `nil` if initialization was impossible. A programmer who is worried that the superclass's initializer may be one of these cases will create an initializer that is something like this:

```
- (id)init
{
    if (![super init])
        return nil;

    firstNumber = random() % 100 + 1];
    secondNumber = random() % 100 + 1];
    return self;
}
```

This version will always work and is considered the most correct form; however, none of the classes that you will subclass in this book require these checks. For simplicity, this book will sometimes leave out the check.

Initializers with Arguments

Look at the same place in `lottery.m`. It should now look like this:

```
LotteryEntry *newEntry = [[LotteryEntry alloc] init];
[newEntry setEntryDate:iWeeksFromNow];
```

It might be nicer if you could supply the date as an argument to the initializer. Change those lines to look like this:

```
LotterEntry *newEntry = [[LotteryEntry alloc]
                                initWithEntryDate:iWeeksFromNow];
```

Next, declare the method in `LotteryEntry.h`:

```
- (id)initWithEntryDate:(NSCalendarDate *)theDate;
```

Now, change (and rename) the **init** method in `LotteryEntry.m`:

```
- (id)initWithEntryDate:(NSCalendarDate *)theDate
{
    if (![super init])
        return nil;

    entryDate = theDate;
    firstNumber = random() % 100 + 1;
    secondNumber = random() % 100 + 1;
    return self;
}
```

Build and run your program. It should work correctly.

However, your class **LotteryEntry** has a problem. You are going to e-mail the class to your friend Rex. Rex plans to use the class **LotteryEntry** in his program but might not realize that you have written **initWithEntryDate:**. If he made this mistake, he might write the following lines of code:

```
NSCalendarDate *today = [NSCalendarDate calendarDate];
LotteryEntry *bigWin = [[LotteryEntry alloc] init];
[bigWin setEntryDate:today];
```

This code will not create an error. Instead, it will simply go up the inheritance tree until it finds **NSObject**'s **init** method. The problem is that firstNumber and secondNumber will not get initialized properly—both will be zero.

To protect Rex from his own ignorance, you will override **init** to call your initializer with a default date:

```
- (id)init
{
    return [self initWithEntryDate:[NSCalendarDate calendarDate]];
}
```

Add this method to your LotteryEntry.m file.

Note that **initWithEntryDate:** still does all the work. Because a class can have multiple initializers, we call the one that does the work the *designated initializer*. If a class has several initializers, the designated initializer typically takes the most arguments. You should clearly document which of your initializers is the designated initializer. Note that the designated initializer for **NSObject** is **init**.

Conventions for Creating Initializers

Following are rules that Cocoa programmers try to follow regarding initializers.

- You do not have to create any initializer in your class if the superclass's initializers are sufficient.

- If you decide to create an initializer, you must override the superclass's designated initializer.

- If you create multiple initializers, only one does the work—the designated initializer. All other initializers call the designated initializer.

- The designated initializer of your class will call its superclass's designated initializer.

The day will come when you will create a class that must, must, must have an argument supplied. Override the superclass's designated initializer to throw an exception:

```
- (id)init
{
    [self dealloc];
    @throw [NSException exceptionWithName:@"BNRBadInitCall"
                reason:@"Initialize lawsuit with initWithDefendant:"
            userInfo:nil];
    return nil;
}
```

The Debugger

The Free Software Foundation developed the compiler (gcc) and the debugger (gdb) that come with Apple's developer tools. Apple has made significant improvements to both over the years. This section discusses the processes of setting breakpoints, invoking the debugger, and browsing the values of variables.

While browsing code, you may have noticed a gray margin to the left of your code. If you click in that margin, a breakpoint will be added at the corresponding line. Add a breakpoint in lottery.m at the following line (Figure 3.10):

```
[array addObject:newEntry];
```

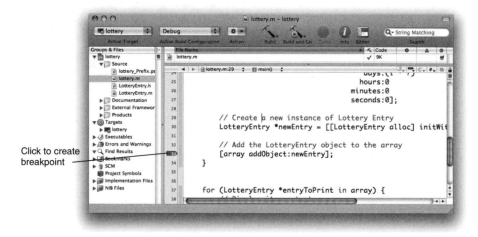

Figure 3.10 Creating a Breakpoint

When you build and run the program, Xcode will start the program in the debugger if you have any breakpoints. To test this, build and run it now. The debugger will take a few seconds to get started and then will run your program until it hits the breakpoint (Figure 3.11).

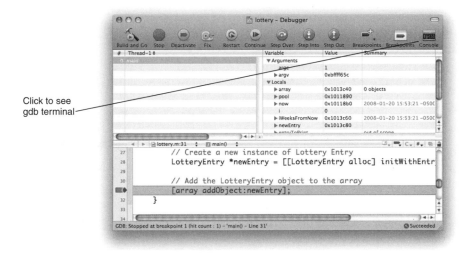

Click to see
gdb terminal

Figure 3.11   Stopped at Breakpoint

In the list on the left, you can see the frames on the stack. Because our breakpoint is in **main()**, the stack is not very deep. In the outline view on the right, you can see the variables and their values. Note that the variable i is currently 0.

The buttons above the stack information are for pausing, continuing, and stepping over, into, and out of functions. Click the Continue button to execute another iteration of the loop. Click the Step Over button to walk through the code line by line.

The gdb debugger, being a Unix thing, was designed to be run from a terminal. To see the terminal-like view of the gdb process, click the tab labeled Console.

In the console, you have full access to all gdb's capabilities. One very handy feature is "print-object" ("po"). If a variable is a pointer to an object, it is sent the message **description** when you "po" it, and the result is printed in the console. Try printing the newEntry variable.

```
po newEntry
```

You should see the result of your **description** method (Figure 3.12).

Exceptions are raised when something goes very wrong. To make the debugger stop whenever an exception is thrown, you will want to add a *symbolic* breakpoint. Any breakpoint for which you don't have a line number is a symbolic breakpoint.

Figure 3.12   Using the gdb Console

In this case, you want a breakpoint on the function **objc_exception_throw**. To see the breakpoint panel in Xcode, choose the Run->Show->Breakpoints menu item. Disable (uncheck) the existing breakpoint. Double-click as indicated, and type objc_exception_throw, as shown in Figure 3.13.

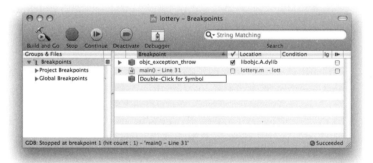

Figure 3.13   Adding a Symbolic Breakpoint

You can test this automatic breakpoint by asking for an index that is not in an array. Immediately after the array is created, ask it what its first object is:

```
array = [[NSMutableArray alloc] init];
NSLog(@"first item = %@", [array objectAtIndex:0]);
```

Rebuild and restart the program. It should stop when the exception is raised.

One of the challenging things about debugging Cocoa programs is that they will often limp along in a broken state for quite a while. Using the macro **NSAssert()**, you can get the program to throw an exception as soon as the train leaves the track. For example, in **initWithEntryDate:**, you might want an exception thrown if the argument is nil. Add a call to **NSAssert()**:

```
- (id)initWithEntryDate:(NSCalendarDate *)theDate
{
    if (![super init])
        return nil;

    NSAssert(theDate != nil, @"Argument must be non-nil");
    entryDate = theDate;
    firstNumber = random() % 100 + 1;
    secondNumber = random() % 100 + 1;
    return self;
}
```

Build it and run it. Your code, being correct, will not throw an exception. So change the assertion to something incorrect:

```
NSAssert(theDate == nil, @"Argument must be non-nil");
```

Now build and run your application. Note that a message, including the name of the class and method, is logged and an exception thrown. Wise use of **NSAssert()** can help you hunt down bugs much more quickly.

You probably do not need your assert calls checked in your completed product. On most projects, there are two build configurations: Debug and Release. In the Debug version, you will want all your asserts checked. In the Release configuration, you will not. I will typically block assertion checking in the Release configuration. To do this, bring up the build info by double-clicking the lottery target. Go to the Build tab and select the Release configuration. Under GCC Preprocessing, add NS_BLOCK_ASSERTIONS to the Preprocessor Macros (Figure 3.14).

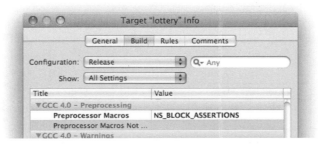

Figure 3.14 Disabling Assertion Checking

Now, if you build and run the Release configuration, you'll see that your assertion is not getting checked. (Before going on, fix your assertion: It should ensure that dates are *not* nil.)

NSAssert() works only inside Objective-C methods. If you need to check an assertion in a C function, use **NSCAssert()**.

That's enough to get you started with the debugger. For more in-depth information, refer to the documentation from the Free Software Foundation (www.gnu.org/).

What Have You Done?

You have written a simple program in Objective-C, including a **main()** function that created several objects. Some of these objects were instances of **LotteryEntry**, a class that you created. The program logged some information to the console.

At this point, you have a fairly complete understanding of Objective-C. Objective-C is not a complex language. The rest of the book is concerned with the frameworks that make up Cocoa. From now on, you will be creating event-driven applications, not command line tools.

For the More Curious: How Does Messaging Work?

As mentioned earlier, an object is like a C struct. **NSObject** declares an instance variable called isa. Because **NSObject** is the root of the entire class-inheritance tree, every object has an isa pointer to the class structure that created the object (Figure 3.15). The class structure includes the names and types of the instance

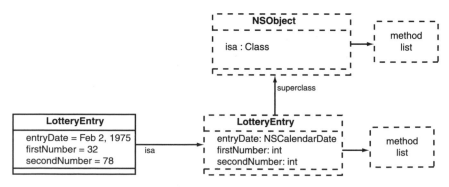

Figure 3.15   Each Object Has a Pointer to Its Class

variables for the class, as well as the implementation of the class's methods. The class structure has a pointer to the class structure for its superclass.

The methods are indexed by the selector. The selector is of type SEL. Although SEL is defined to be char *, it is most useful to think of it as an int. Each method name is mapped to a unique int. For example, the method name **addObject:** might map to the number 12. When you look up methods, you will use the selector, not the string @"addObject:".

As part of the Objective-C data structures, a table maps the names of methods to their selectors. Figure 3.16 shows an example.

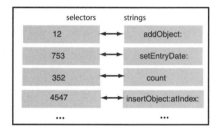

Figure 3.16   The Selector Table

At compile time, the compiler looks up the selectors wherever it sees a message send. Thus,

```
[myObject addObject:yourObject];
```

becomes (assuming that the selector for **addObject:** is 12)

```
objc_msgSend(myObject, 12, yourObject);
```

Here, **objc_msgSend()** looks at myObject's isa pointer to get to its class structure and looks for the method associated with 12. If it does not find the method, it follows the pointer to the superclass. If the superclass does not have a method for 12, it continues searching up the tree. If it reaches the top of the tree without finding a method, the function throws an exception.

Clearly, this is a very dynamic way of handling messages. These class structures can be changed at runtime. In particular, using the **NSBundle** class makes it relatively easy to add classes and methods to your program while it is running. This very powerful technique has been used to create applications that can be extended by other developers.

Challenge

Change the format string on the calendar date objects in your **LotteryEntry** class.

Chapter 4
MEMORY MANAGEMENT

Let's say that there are two instances of **Person** and that each has a favoriteColor, a pointer to a color object. If two people have the same favoriteColor, the objects will have pointers to the same color object. As the people age, their favorite color might change. Eventually, the color object might be no one's favorite (Figure 4.1).

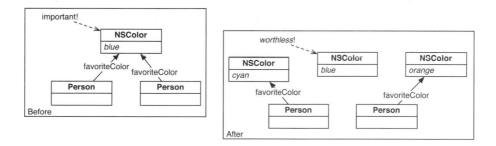

Figure 4.1 The Problem

We do not want this orphaned color to be taking up room in our program's memory. We want the memory deallocated, so that we can put new objects in that memory, but we must be sure that the color is not deallocated while any objects are pointing to it.

This is a relatively tricky problem. Apple has come up with two solutions:

1. The old solution uses *retain counts:* Every object has a retain count, which should represent the number of other objects that have pointers to it. If the color is the favorite of two people, the retain count of that color should be 2. When it goes to zero, the object is deallocated.

2. The new solution, introduced in 10.5, is a *garbage collector,* which babysits the entire object graph, looking for objects that can't be reached from

the variables that are in scope. The unreachable objects are automatically deallocated.

What are the trade-offs? Retain counts are a bit cumbersome: You need to explicitly retain objects that you want to keep around and to explicity release them when you are no longer interested in them. The retain-count mechanism also creates a dastardly problem: object A retains object B, and B retains A. They are an island of garbage that will never go away, because they are retaining each other. This is known as a retain cycle. Figure 4.2 is an example of a common retain cycle.

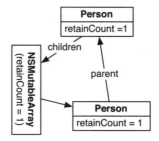

Figure 4.2   An Island of Garbage

Why not always use the garbage collector? If you use the garbage collector, your application will not run on any version of Mac OS before 10.5. Also, the garbage collector requires some CPU time to scan through the objects, looking for garbage. This can sometimes result in poorer performance. In an application that does a lot of audio or video processing, the garbage collector can cause hiccups in the processing while it is doing a scan.

Turning the Garbage Collector On and Off

In the Groups and Files outline view of Xcode, you will see a group called Targets. Every project has at least one target. The target represents one build process and typically results in one product. So, for example, you might have a project with two targets: One builds an application, and the other builds the Spotlight importer for that application's data file.

Look at the lottery project. Double-click the lottery target to open the Inspector. Look at the Build panel. This is where you can set all the variables that control how the program is built.

In the search field, type in Garbage. Many lines will disappear, and you will see Objective-C Garbage Collection. Here, you can choose whether you want the garbage collector enabled. If you choose Unsupported, the garbage collector will not be enabled (Figure 4.3).

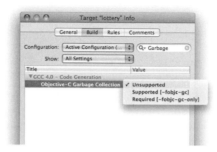

Figure 4.3   Enabling/Disabling the Garbage Collector

The other two choices will enable the garbage collector. You must recompile before the change takes effect. (The difference between Supported and Required is interesting only if you are creating a framework or plug-in that will be used in another application.)

The code in this book is *dual-mode* code. Dual-mode code is leak-free whether or not you are using the garbage collector. When you sit down to write an application, you can choose whether you want to use the garbage collector. You do not have to write dual-mode code all the time.

In the future, you may decide, "This retain-count stuff is for the birds. I'm going to use the garbage collector for everything." I wouldn't blame you. For now, however, learn about the retain-count mechanism. When you study old code or anything that uses lower-level frameworks (such as CoreFoundation), you will want to understand how it works.

(If the retain-count mechanism really disturbs you, read the next section on the garbage collector and skip the remainder of this chapter. While reading the rest of the book, simply ignore any call to **retain**, **release**, or **autorelease**. These methods do nothing if the garbage collector is enabled. Also ignore any implementation of **dealloc**. It will never get called if the garbage collector is enabled.)

Living with the Garbage Collector

Your application will have an instance of **NSGarbageCollector** if and only if it is using the garbage collector. Add a line near the end of lottery.m:

```
[pool drain];
NSLog(@"GC = %@", [NSGarbageCollector defaultCollector]);
return 0;
```

Build and run the tool. Are you using the garbage collector?

If you are using the garbage collector, it is important that you not keep references to objects that you don't care about. In the **main** function of lottery, you should set the now and array pointers to nil when you lose interest in them. Add those lines now:

```
    }
    // Done with 'now'
    now = nil;

    for (LotteryEntry *entryToPrint in array) {
        NSLog(@"%@", entryToPrint);
    }
    // Done with 'array'
    array = nil;
    [pool drain];
    NSLog(@"GC = %@", [NSGarbageCollector defaultCollector]);
    return 0;
}
```

Now the garbage collector will know that it can deallocate the **NSCalendarDate** that now pointed to and the **NSMutableArray** that array pointed to. (In reality, the program almost certainly exits before the garbage collector gets around to deallocating those objects.)

Overall, the garbage collector makes things much easier for the programmer. We have covered all you really need to know. The rest of the chapter is dedicated to retain counts.

Living with Retain Counts

Let's assume for the rest of this chapter that you need to support users of 10.4. Thus, you are going to forego the convenience of the garbage collector and use the retain-count mechanism.

Every object has a retain count. The retain count is an integer. When an object is created by the **alloc** method, the retain count is set to 1. When the retain count becomes zero, the object is deallocated. You increment the retain count by sending the message **retain** to the object. You decrement the retain count by sending the message **release** to the object.

An object's retain count should represent how many other objects have references to it. A retain count of zero indicates that no one cares about it any more. It is deallocated so that the memory it was occupying can be reused.

A commonly used analogy is that of the dog and the leash. Each person who wants to ensure that the dog will stay around retains the dog by attaching a leash to its collar. Many people can retain the dog, and as long as at least one person is retaining the dog, the dog will not go free. When zero people are retaining the dog, it will be deallocated. The retain count of an object, then, is the number of "leashes" on that object (Figure 4.4).

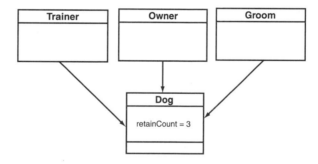

Figure 4.4   Objects Retain Each Other

The retain count gives you a lot of control over how and when objects are deallocated, but it requires that you meticulously retain and release objects. If you release an object too much, it will be deallocated prematurely, and your program will crash. If you retain an object too much, it will never get deallocated, and you will waste memory.

Now you are going to fix the code that we've written thus far to handle retains and releases properly. Back in the lottery project, turn the garbage collector off. You should release the calendar date and the array when you are done with them:

```
    }
    // Done with 'now'
    [now release];
    now = nil;
```

```
    for (LotteryEntry *entryToPrint in array) {
        NSLog(@"%@", entryToPrint);
    }
    // Done with 'array'
    [array release];
    array = nil;
    [pool drain];
    NSLog(@"GC = %@", [NSGarbageCollector defaultCollector]);
    return 0;
}
```

Now the array will be properly deallocated before the process ends.

An array does not make a copy of an object when it is added. Instead, the array stores a pointer to the object and sends it the message **retain**. When the array is deallocated, the objects in the array are sent the message **release**. (Also, if an object is removed from an array, it is sent **release**.)

What about the **LotteryEntry** objects? Let's quickly go over the life of the **LotteryEntry** object in your application.

- When the entry object is created, it has a retain count of 1.

- When the entry object is added to the array, its retain count is incremented to 2.

- When the array is deallocated, it releases the entry. This decrements the retain count to 1.

The **LotteryEntry** object is not being deallocated. In this example, the process ends an instant later, and the operating system reclaims all the memory. Thus, the lack of deallocation is not a big deal. However, in a program that ran a long time, such a memory leak would be a bad thing. To practice being a tidy Objective-C programmer, fix the code.

After inserting the number into the array, release it. The revised loop should look like this:

```
    LotteryEntry *newEntry;
    newEntry = [[LotteryEntry alloc] initWithEntryDate:iWeeksFromNow];
    [array addObject:newEntry];
    [newEntry release];
}
```

Implementing dealloc

When an object with a retain count of 1 is sent **release**, the **dealloc** method will be called. Your **dealloc** method must release any objects that you were retaining and then call the superclasses **dealloc** method. Add a **dealloc** method to LotteryEntry.m:

```
- (void)dealloc
{
    NSLog(@"deallocing %@", self);
    [entryDate release];
    [super dealloc];
}
```

In the **initWithEntryDate:** method, we did not retain the entryDate. Add the necessary retain:

```
- (id)initWithEntryDate:(NSCalendarDate *)theDate
{
    if (![super init])
        return nil;

    entryDate = [theDate retain];
    firstNumber = random() % 100 + 1;
    secondNumber = random() % 100 + 1;
    return self;
}
```

Turn off the garbage collector. Build and run your app. It should work fine, and you should see that the entries are being properly deallocated (Figure 4.5).

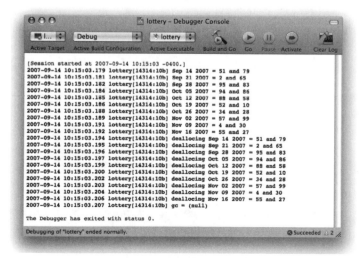

Figure 4.5   Running Without the Garbage Collector

There is, however, still a memory leak.

Creating Autoreleased Objects

You created a description method that looks like this:

```
- (NSString *)description
{
    NSString *result;
    result = [[NSString alloc] initWithFormat:@"%@ = %d and %d",
            [entryDate descriptionWithCalendarFormat:@"%b %d %Y"],
            firstNumber, secondNumber];
    return result;
}
```

This code would work perfectly well but would result in an annoying memory leak. The **alloc** operation always yields an object with a retain count of 1; thus, the string being returned has a retain count of 1. Any object asking for the string would retain it. The string would then have a retain count of 2. When no longer interested in the string, the object would release it. The retain count would become 1. As you see, the string would never be deallocated.

Our next attempt might look something like this:

```
- (NSString *)description
{
    NSString *result;
    result = [[NSString alloc] initWithFormat:@"%@ = %d and %d",
            [entryDate descriptionWithCalendarFormat:@"%b %d %Y"],
            firstNumber, secondNumber];
    [result release];
    return result;
}
```

This code would not work at all. When sent the message **release**, the string's retain count would go to zero, and the string would be deallocated. The object asking for the string would get a pointer to a freed object.

The problem, then, is that you need to return a string, but you do not want to retain it. This is a common problem throughout the frameworks, which leads us to how the **NSAutoreleasePool** is used in a non-GC application.

Objects are added to the current autorelease pool when they are sent the message **autorelease**. When the autorelease pool is drained, it sends the message **release** to all objects in the pool.

In other words, when an object is autoreleased, it is marked to be sent **release** sometime in the future. In particular, in a Cocoa application, an autorelease pool is created before every event is handled and is drained after the event has been handled. Thus, unless the objects in the autorelease pools are being retained, they will be destroyed as soon as the event has been handled.

A correct solution, then, is

```
- (NSString *)description
{
    NSString *result;
    result = [[NSString alloc] initWithFormat:@"%@ = %d and %d",
            [entryDate descriptionWithCalendarFormat:@"%b %d %Y"],
            firstNumber, secondNumber];
    [result autorelease];
    return result;
}
```

Rules Concerning Release

- Objects created by **alloc**, **new**, **copy**, or **mutableCopy** have a retain count of 1 and are not in the autorelease pool.

- If you get an object by *any* other method, assume that it has a retain count of 1 and is in the autorelease pool. If you do not wish it to be deallocated with the current autorelease pool, you must retain it.

Because you will frequently need objects that you are not retaining, many classes have class methods that return autoreleased objects. **NSString**, for example, has **stringWithFormat:**. The simplest correct solution then would be

```
- (NSString *)description
{
    return [NSString stringWithFormat:@"%@ = %d and %d",
            [entryDate descriptionWithCalendarFormat:@"%b %d %Y"],
            firstNumber, secondNumber];
}
```

Temporary Objects

Note that the autoreleased object won't be released until the event loop ends. This behavior makes it perfect for providing an intermediate result. For example, if you had an array of **NSString** objects, you could create a string with all the elements in uppercase and concatenated together, like this:

```
- (NSString *)concatenatedAndAllCaps
{
    int i;
```

```
    NSString *sum = @"";
    NSString *upper;

    for (i=0; i < [myArray count]; i++) {
      upper = [[myArray objectAtIndex:i] uppercaseString];
      sum = [NSString stringWithFormat:@"%@%@", sum, upper];
    }
    return sum;
}
```

With this method, if you have 13 strings in the array, 26 autoreleased strings will be created: 13 by **uppercaseString** and 13 by **stringWithFormat:**; the initial constant string is a special case and doesn't count. One of the resulting strings is returned and may be retained by the object that asked for it. The other 25 strings are deallocated automatically at the end of the event loop. (Note that you would probably get better performance in this example by appending the uppercased string to an **NSMutableString** instead of creating a new string and adding it to the autorelease pool each time through the loop.)

Accessor Methods

An object has instance variables. Other objects cannot access these variables directly. To enable other objects to read and set an instance variable, an object will usually have a pair of accessor methods.

For example, if a class **Rex** has an instance variable named fido, the class will probably have at least two other methods: **fido** and **setFido:**. The **fido** method enables other objects to read the fido variable; the **setFido:** method enables other objects to set the fido variable.

If you have a nonpointer type, the accessor methods are quite simple. For example, if your class has an instance variable called foo of type int, you would create the following accessor methods:

```
- (int)foo
{
    return foo;
}

- (void)setFoo:(int)x
{
    foo = x;
}
```

These methods will allow other objects to get and set the value of foo.

Matters become more complicated if foo is a pointer to an object. In the "setter" method, you need to make sure that the new value is retained and the old value released, as shown in Figure 4.6. If you assume that foo is a pointer to an **NSCalendarDate**, there are three common idioms in setter methods. All three work correctly, and you can probably find some experienced Cocoa programmers who will argue the superiority of any one of them. I'll list the trade-offs after each one.

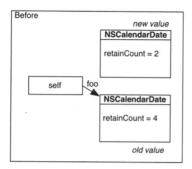

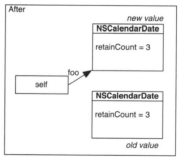

Figure 4.6   Before and After setFoo:

The first idiom is: Retain, then Release:

```
- (void)setFoo:(NSCalendarDate *)x
{
    [x retain];
    [foo release];
    foo = x;
}
```

Here, it is important to retain before releasing. Suppose that you reverse the order. If x and foo are both pointers to the same object that happens to have a retain count of 1, the release would cause the object to be deallocated before it was retained. *Trade-off:* If they are the same value, this method performs an unnecessary retain and release.

The second idiom is: Check Before Change:

```
- (void)setFoo:(NSCalendarDate *)x
{
    if (foo != x) {
      [foo release];
      foo = [x retain];
    }
}
```

Here, you are not setting the variable unless a different value is passed in. *Trade-off:* An extra if statement is necessary.

The final idiom is: Autorelease Old Value:

```
- (void)setFoo:(NSCalendarDate *)x
{
    [foo autorelease];
    foo = [x retain];
}
```

Here, you autorelease the old value. *Trade-off:* An error in retain counts will result in a crash one event loop after the error. This behavior makes the bug harder to track down. In the first two idioms, your crash will happen closer to your error. Also, **autorelease** carries some performance overhead.

You have read the trade-offs, and you can make your own decision on which to use. In this book, I will use Retain, then Release.

The "getter" method for an object is the same as that for a nonpointer type:

```
- (NSCalendarDate *)foo
{
    return foo;
}
```

Most Java programmers would name this method **getFoo**. Don't. Objective-C programmers call this method **foo**. In the common idioms of Objective-C, a method prefixed with **get** takes an address where data can be copied. For example, if you have an **NSColor** object and you want its red, green, blue, and alpha components, you would call **getRed:green:blue:alpha:** as follows:

```
float r, g, b, a;
```

```
[myFavoriteColor getRed:&r green:&g blue:&b alpha:&a];
```

(For readers who might be a bit rusty with their C, & returns the address where the variable holds its data.)

If you used your accessor methods to read the variables, your **description** method would look like this:

```
- (NSString *)description
{
    return [NSString stringWithFormat:@"%@ = %d and %d",
        [self entryDate], [self firstNumber], [self secondNumber]];
}
```

OO purists would argue that this is the most-correct implementation of the **description** method.

Change **setEntryDate:** in LotteryEntry.m to correctly retain the new value and release the old:

```
- (void)setEntryDate:(NSCalendarDate *)date
{
    [date retain];
    [entryDate release];
    entryDate = date;
}
```

What Have You Done?

You have now written a simple program in Objective-C, including a **main()** function that created several objects. Some of these objects were instances of **LotteryEntry**, a class that you created. The program logged some information to the console.

At this point, you have a fairly complete understanding of Objective-C. Objective-C is not a complex language. The rest of the book is concerned with the frameworks that make up Cocoa. From now on, you will be creating event-driven applications, not command line tools.

Chapter 5
TARGET/ACTION

Once upon a time, there was a company called Taligent, which was created by IBM and Apple to develop a set of tools and libraries like Cocoa. About the time Taligent reached the peak of its mindshare, I met one of its engineers at a trade show. I asked him to create a simple application for me: A window would appear with a button, and when the button was clicked, the words "Hello, World!" would appear in a text field. The engineer created a project and started subclassing madly: subclassing the window and the button and the event handler. Then he started generating code: dozens of lines to get the button and the text field onto the window. After 45 minutes, I had to leave. The app still did not work. That day, I knew that the company was doomed. A couple of years later, Taligent quietly closed its doors forever.

Most C++ and Java tools work on the same principles as the Taligent tools. The developer subclasses many of the standard classes and generates many lines of code to get controls to appear on windows. Most of these tools do in fact work.

While writing an application that uses the AppKit framework, you will seldom subclass the classes that represent windows, buttons, or events. Instead, you will create objects that will work with the existing classes. Also, you will not create code to get controls on windows. Instead, the nib file will contain all this information. The resulting application will have significantly fewer lines of code. At first, this outcome may be alarming. In the long run, most programmers find it delightfully elegant.

To understand the AppKit framework, a good place to start is with the class **NSControl**. **NSButton**, **NSSlider**, **NSTextView**, and **NSColorWell** are all subclasses of **NSControl**. A control has a *target* and an *action*. The target is simply a pointer to another object. The action is a message (a selector) to send to the target. Recall that you set the target and action for two buttons in Chapter 2: You set your **Foo** object to be the target of both buttons, and you set the action on one to **seed:** (Figure 5.1) and the action on the other to **generate:**.

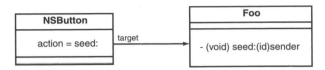

Figure 5.1   A Button Has a Target and an Action

When the user interacts with the control, it sends the `action` message to its `target`. For example, when the button is clicked, the button sends the `target` its `action` message (Figure 5.2).

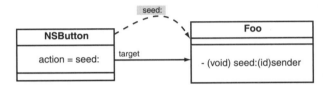

Figure 5.2   The Button Sends a Message

The action methods take one argument: the sender. This enables the receiver to know which control sent the message. Often, you will call back to the sender to get more information. For example, a check box will send its action message when it is turned on and when it is turned off. After getting the action message, the receiver might call back to the button to find out whether it is currently on or off:

```
- (IBAction)toggleFoo:(id)sender
{
    BOOL isOn = [sender state];
    ...
}
```

To better understand **NSControl**, you should become acquainted with its ancestors: **NSControl** inherits from **NSView**, which inherits from **NSResponder**, which inherits from **NSObject**. Each member of the family tree adds some capabilities (Figure 5.3).

At the top of the class hierachy is **NSObject**. All the classes inherit from **NSObject**, and this is where they get the basic methods: **retain**, **release**, **dealloc**, and **init**. **NSResponder** is a subclass of **NSObject**. Responders have the ability to handle events with such methods as **mouseDown:** and **keyDown:**. **NSView** is a subclass of **NSResponder**. **NSView** has a place on a window, where it draws itself. You can create subclasses of **NSView** to display graphs and allow the user to drag and drop data. **NSControl** inherits from **NSView** and adds the target and the action.

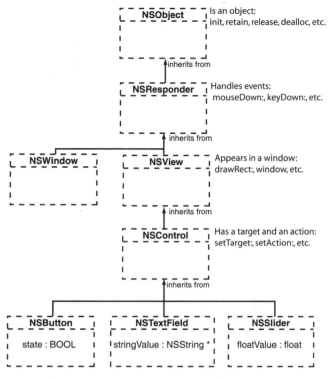

Figure 5.3   Inheritance Diagram for NSControl

Some Commonly Used Subclasses of NSControl

Before using some controls, let's take a brief look at the three most commonly used controls: **NSButton**, **NSSlider**, and **NSTextField**.

NSButton

Instances of **NSButton** can have several different appearances: oval, square, check box. They can also have different behavior when clicked: toggle (like a check box) or momentarily on (like most other buttons). Buttons can have icons and sounds associated with them. Figure 5.4 shows the Attributes Inspector for an **NSButton** in Interface Builder.

Here are three methods that you will frequently send to buttons:

    - (void)**setEnabled:**(BOOL)yn

The user can click on an enabled button. Disabled buttons are grayed out.

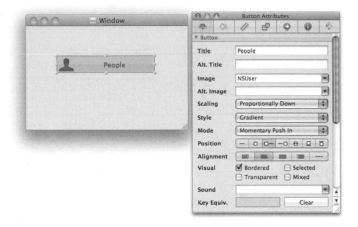

Figure 5.4   Button Inspector

- (int)**state**

This method returns NSOnState (which is 1) if the button is on; NSOffState (which is 0), if the button is off. The method allows you to see whether a check box is checked or unchecked.

- (void)**setState:**(int)aState

This method turns the button on or off and allows you to check or uncheck a check box programmatically. Set the state to NSOnState to check the check box and to NSOffState to uncheck it.

NSSlider

Instances of **NSSlider** can be vertical or horizontal. They can send the action to the target continuously while being changed, or they can wait to send the action until the user releases the mouse button. A slider can have markers and can prevent users from choosing values between the markers (Figure 5.5). Circular sliders are also possible.

Here are two methods of **NSSlider** that you will use frequently:

- (void)**setFloatValue:**(float)x

Moves the slider to x

- (float)**floatValue**

Returns the current value of the slider

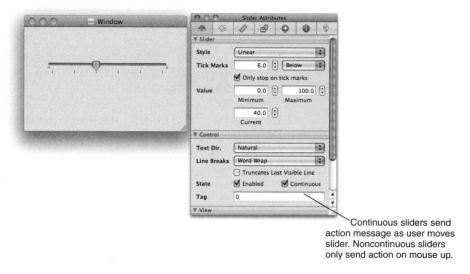

Continuous sliders send
action message as user moves
slider. Noncontinuous sliders
only send action on mouse up.

Figure 5.5   Slider Inspector

NSTextField

An instance of **NSTextField** can allow a user to type a single line of text. Text
fields may or may not be editable. Uneditable text fields are commonly used as
labels on a window. Compared to buttons and sliders, text fields are relatively
complex. We will plumb the depths of the mysteries surrounding text fields in
later chapters. Figure 5.6 shows the Attributes Inspector panel for an **NSTextField**
in Interface Builder.

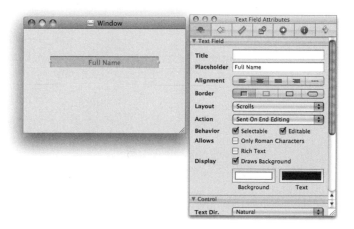

Figure 5.6   Text Field Inspector

Text fields have a placeholder string. When the text field is empty, the placeholder string is displayed in gray.

NSSecureTextField is a subclass of **NSTextField** and is used for such things as passwords. As the user types, bullets appear instead of the typed characters. You cannot copy or cut from an **NSSecureTextField**.

Here are a few of the most commonly used **NSTextField** methods:

- (NSString *)**stringValue**

- (void)**setStringValue:**(NSString *)aString

These methods allow you to get and set the string data being displayed in the text field.

- (NSObject *)**objectValue**

- (void)**setObjectValue:**(NSObject *)obj

These methods allow you to get and set the data being displayed in the text field as an arbitrary object type.

This behavior is helpful if you are using a formatter. **NSFormatter**s are responsible for converting a string into another type, and vice versa. If no formatter is present, these methods use the **description** method.

For example, you might use a text field to allow the user to type in a date. As the programmer, you don't want the string that the user typed in; you want an instance of **NSCalendarDate**. By attaching an **NSDateFormatter**, you ensure that the text field's **objectValue** method will return an **NSCalendarDate**. Also, when you call **setObjectValue:** with an **NSCalendarDate**, the **NSDateFormatter** will format it as a string for the user. (You will create a custom formatter class in Chapter 23.)

Figure 5.7 shows some other controls you might want to play with. Drag them out, inspect them, and see how they act when you compile and run the app.

Figure 5.7   Some Other Controls

Start the SpeakLine Example

As a simple example of using controls, you will build an application that enables users to type in a line of text and hear it spoken by the Mac OS X speech synthesizer. The app will look like Figure 5.8 when you are done with this chapter.

Figure 5.8   Completed Application

Figure 5.9 presents a diagram of the objects that you will create and their pointers to one another. Note that all the classes that start with **NS** are part of the Cocoa frameworks and thus already exist. Your code will be in the **AppController** class.

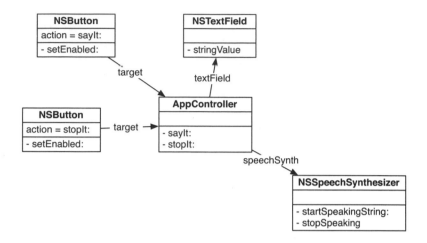

Figure 5.9   Object Diagram

In Xcode, create a new project of type Cocoa Application. Name the project SpeakLine. A new project will appear.

Lay Out the Nib File

Double-click on MainMenu.nib to open it in Interface Builder. From the Library window, drag out a text field and two buttons. Double-click on the text field to change the text to read "Peter Piper picked a peck of pickled peppers" (or some other text that will amuse you when it is spoken by the machine). Change the labels on the buttons to read Speak and Stop. The result should look like Figure 5.8.

In Xcode, create a new class and name it **AppController**, **AppController** will be the target of the two buttons. Each control will trigger a different action method. Add these to AppController.h:

```
#import <Cocoa/Cocoa.h>

@interface AppController : NSObject
{
    IBOutlet NSTextField *textField;
}
- (IBAction)sayIt:(id)sender;
- (IBAction)stopIt:(id)sender;
@end
```

To create one instance of **AppController** in the nib file, drag a blue **NSObject** cube into the doc window. In the Identity Inspector, set its class to **AppController** (Figure 5.10).

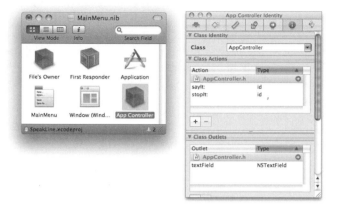

Figure 5.10   Setting the Identity

Making Connections in Interface Builder

Making a connection is analogous to introducing people. You say, "Mrs. Robinson, this is Dr. Pepper." If it is important that Dr. Pepper also know Mrs. Robinson, you would continue, "Dr. Pepper, this is Mrs. Robinson." With objects in Interface Builder, you will drag *from* the object that needs to know *to* the object that it needs to know about. You might also drag the other way to create a connection in the opposite direction, if necessary.

For example, when a user clicks the Stop button, the button needs to send a message to your **AppController**, so the button needs to know about the **AppController**. For this reason, you will Control-drag from the button to the **AppController**. When the pop-up appears, you will indicate that the action will be **stopIt:**, as shown in Figure 5.11.

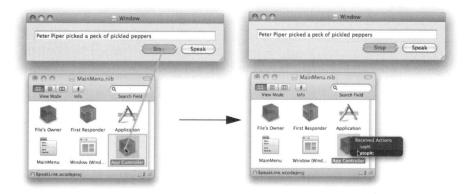

Figure 5.11   Set action for Stop Button

Also, Control-drag from the Speak button to the **AppController** and set its action to be **sayIt:**.

In order to synthesize the speech for the line of text, the **AppController** will need to ask the text field for the line of text. Thus, the **AppController** needs to have a pointer to the text field. Control-click on the **AppController**. When the list of outlets appears, drag from the textField outlet to the text field, as shown in Figure 5.12.

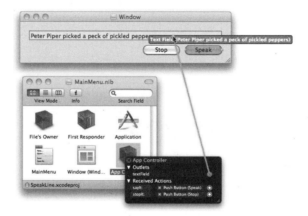

Figure 5.12   Connect AppController to the Text Field

At this point, you have set all but one of the connections shown in the object diagram in Figure 5.9. The missing connection, speechSynth, will be done programmatically—not in Interface Builder.

NSWindow's initialFirstResponder Outlet

When your application runs and the new window appears, users should not have to click on a text field before they type. You can tell the window which view should be receiving keyboard events when the window appears. Control-click on the window icon to get its connection panel. Drag from initialFirstResponder to the text field.

Implementing the AppController Class

Now you need to write some code, so return to Xcode and select the AppController.h file. Add an instance variable named speechSynth of type **NSSpeechSynthesizer**:

```
#import <Cocoa/Cocoa.h>

@interface AppController : NSObject
{
    IBOutlet NSTextField *textField;
    NSSpeechSynthesizer *speechSynth;
}
- (IBAction)sayIt:(id)sender;
- (IBAction)stopIt:(id)sender;

@end
```

Open the AppController.m file. This is where you will make the methods do
something:

```
#import "AppController.h"

@implementation AppController

- (id)init
{
    [super init];

    // Logs can help the beginner understand what
    // is happening and hunt down bugs.
    NSLog(@"init");

    // Create a new instance of NSSpeechSynthesizer
    // with the default voice.
    speechSynth = [[NSSpeechSynthesizer alloc] initWithVoice:nil];
    return self;
}

- (IBAction)sayIt:(id)sender
{
    NSString *string = [textField stringValue];

    // Is the string zero-length?
    if ([string length] == 0) {
        NSLog(@"string from %@ is of zero-length", textField);
        return;
    }
    [speechSynth startSpeakingString:string];
    NSLog(@"Have started to say: %@", string);
}

- (IBAction)stopIt:(id)sender
{
    NSLog(@"stopping");
    [speechSynth stopSpeaking];
}
@end
```

Your application is done. Build it and run it. You should be able to start the recitation of the text in the text field and stop it in midsentence.

Final note: A menu item (an instance of **NSMenuItem**) also has a target and an action. Everything we've talked about in this chapter also applies to menu items.

For the More Curious: Setting the Target Programmatically

Note that the action of a control is a selector. **NSControl** includes the following method:

```
- (void)setAction:(SEL)aSelector
```

But how would you get a selector? The Objective-C compiler directive @selector will tell the compiler to look up the selector for you. For example, to set the action of a button to the method **drawMickey:**, you could do the following:

```
SEL mySelector;
mySelector = @selector(drawMickey:);
[myButton setAction:mySelector];
```

At compile time, @selector(drawMickey:) will be replaced by the selector for **drawMickey:**.

If you needed to find a selector for an **NSString** at runtime, you could use the function **NSSelectorFromString()**:

```
SEL mySelector;
mySelector = NSSelectorFromString(@"drawMickey:");
[myButton setTarget:someObjectWithADrawMickeyMethod];
[myButton setAction:mySelector];
```

Challenge

This exercise is an important challenge that you should do before moving on. Although it is easy to follow my instructions, you will eventually want to create your own applications. Here is where you can start to develop some independence. Feel free to refer back to the earlier examples for guidance.

Create an application that can have only one window open, so it is not a document-based application. Figure 5.13 shows the window before any input has been added. Figure 5.14 shows the window that the application will present to the user.

Figure 5.13   Before Input

When the user types in a string and clicks the button, the message text will display the input string and the number of characters it has (Figure 5.14).

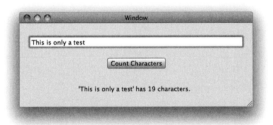

Figure 5.14   After Input

It is important to know how to use the Cocoa classes in your application. For this exercise, you should recognize that the **NSTextField** class has the following methods:

```
- (NSString *)stringValue;
- (void)setStringValue:(NSString *)aString;
```

You will also find it useful to know about the following methods of the class **NSString**:

```
- (int)length;
+ (NSString *)stringWithFormat:(NSString *),...;
```

You will create a controller object with two outlets and one action. (This is hard, and you are not stupid. Good luck!)

Debugging Hints

Now that you are writing code, not simply copying it from the book, you are ready for some debugging hints.

Always watch the console. If a Cocoa object throws an exception, it will be logged to the console, and the event loop will be restarted. If you aren't watching the console, you won't know about the error at all.

Always use the Debug *build configuration during development.* The Release configuration has had its debugging symbols stripped. The debugger will act a bit strangely when it is dealing with a program with no debugging symbols.

Here are some common problems and common fixes:

- *Nothing happens.* You probably forgot to make a connection in Interface Builder. Thus, the pointer is nil. Remember that messages sent to nil do nothing.

- *Made connection, still nothing happens.* You probably misspelled the name of a method. Objective-C is case-sensitive, so setFoo: is completely different from setfoo:. Try putting in a log statement or putting a breakpoint on the method to see whether it is getting called.

- *Application crashes.* Sending a message to an object that has been deallocated will crash your program. (This is difficult to do if you are using the garbage collector.) Hunting these crashers can be difficult— after all, the problem object has already been deallocated. One way to hunt them down is to ask the frameworks to turn your objects into *zombies* instead of deallocating them. When you send a message to a zombie, it throws a descriptive exception that says something like "You tried to send the message -count to a freed instance of the class **Fido**." This will stop the debugger on that line.

  To turn on zombies, double-click on the executable in Xcode. In the Info panel, add two environment variables: set NSZombiesEnabled to YES, and set CFZombieLevel to 16, as shown in Figure 5.15.

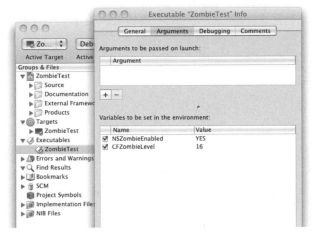

Figure 5.15   Turning on Zombies

- *No objects are being freed, it still crashes.* Check the type of your arguments. For example, this is a great way to crash your app:

```
int x = 5;
NSLog(@"x is %@", x);
```

- *Interface Builder won't let me make a connection.* A .h file is messed up. A missing semicolon? A variable declared to be **NSTabView** instead of **NSTableView**? Look carefully.

Chapter 6
HELPER OBJECTS

Once upon a time (before *Baywatch*), there was a man with no name. Knight Industries decided that if this man were given guns and wheels and booster rockets, he would be the perfect crime-fighting tool. First, they thought, "Let's subclass him and override everything we need to add the guns and wheels and booster rockets." The problem was that to subclass Michael Knight, you would need to know an awful lot about his guts so that you could wire them to guns and booster rockets. So instead, they created a helper object, the Knight Industries 2000, or "KITT the super car."

Note how this is different from the RoboCop approach. RoboCop was a man subclassed and extended. The whole RoboCop project involved dozens of surgeons who extended the man's brain into a fighting machine. This is the approach taken with many object-oriented frameworks.

While approaching the perimeter of an arms dealer's compound, Michael Knight would speak to KITT over his watch-radio. "KITT," he would say, "I need to get to the other side of that wall." KITT would then blast a big hole in the wall with a small rocket. After destroying the wall, Kitt would return control to Michael, who would stroll through the rubble.

Many objects in the Cocoa framework are extended in much the same way. That is, there is an existing object that needs to be extended for your purpose. Instead of subclassing the table view, you simply supply it with a helper object. For example, when a table view is about to display itself, it will turn to the helper object to ask "How many rows of data am I displaying?" "What should be displayed in the first column, second row?"

Thus, to extend an existing Cocoa class, you will frequently write a helper object. This chapter focuses on creating helper objects and connecting them to the standard Cocoa objects.

Delegates

In the SpeakLine application from Chapter 5, the use of your interface would be more obvious if the Stop button remained disabled unless the speech synthesizer were speaking and the Speak button were enabled only when the speech synthesizer was silent. Thus, the **AppController** should enable the button when it starts the speech synthesizer and then disable the button when the speech synthesizer stops.

Many classes in the Cocoa framework have an instance variable called delegate. You can set this variable to point to a helper object. In the documentation for the class, the delegate methods are clearly described. For example, the **NSSpeechSynthesizer** class has the following delegate methods:

```
- (void)speechSynthesizer:(NSSpeechSynthesizer *)sender
        didFinishSpeaking:(BOOL)finishedSpeaking;

- (void)speechSynthesizer:(NSSpeechSynthesizer *)sender
             willSpeakWord:(NSRange)characterRange
                  ofString:(NSString *)string;

- (void)speechSynthesizer:(NSSpeechSynthesizer *)sender
          willSpeakPhoneme:(short)phonemeOpcode;
```

The Apple programmer who wrote **NSSpeechSynthesizer** put these hooks in. He is Michael Knight. You are KITT.

Of the three messages that the speech synthesizer sends to its delegate, you care about only the first one: **speechSynthesizer:didFinishSpeaking:**.

In your application, you will make the **AppController** the delegate of the speech synthesizer and implement **speechSynthesizer:didFinishSpeaking:**. The method will be called automatically when the utterance is complete. The new object diagram is shown in Figure 6.1.

Note that you do not have to implement any of the other delegate methods. The implemented methods will be called; the unimplemented ones will be ignored. Also note that the first argument is always the object that is sending the message—in this case, the speech synthesizer.

In AppController.m, set the delegate outlet of the speech synthesizer:

```
- (id)init
{
    [super init];
    NSLog(@"init");
    speechSynth = [[NSSpeechSynthesizer alloc] initWithVoice:nil];
    [speechSynth setDelegate:self];
    return self;
}
```

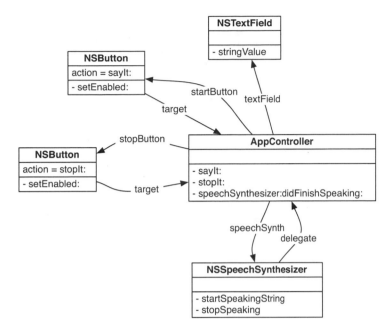

Figure 6.1   New SpeakLine Object Diagram

Next, add the delegate method. For now, simply log a message:

```
- (void)speechSynthesizer:(NSSpeechSynthesizer *)sender
        didFinishSpeaking:(BOOL)complete
{
    NSLog(@"complete = %d", complete);
}
```

Build and run the application. Note that the delegate method is called if you click the Stop button or if the utterance plays all the way to the end; complete is YES only if the utterance plays to the end.

To enable and disable the Stop and Start buttons, you will need outlets for them. Add instance variables to AppController.h:

```
IBOutlet NSButton *stopButton;
IBOutlet NSButton *startButton;
```

Save the file.

Return to the Interface Builder and control-click on the **AppController**. Drag from the stopButton outlet to the Stop button, as shown in Figure 6.2. Also drag from the startButton outlet to the Speak button.

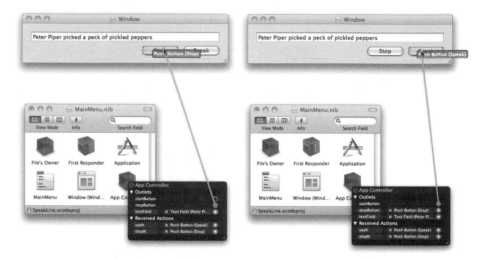

Figure 6.2 Set stopButton startButton Outlets

The Stop button should be disabled when it first appears on screen, so select the button and disable it in the Attributes Inspector, as shown in Figure 6.3. Save the nib file.

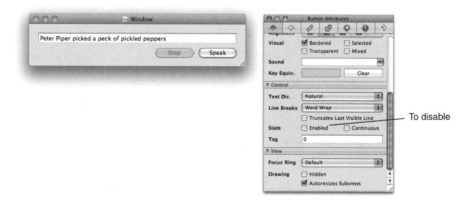

Figure 6.3 Disable Stop Button

In Xcode, edit the AppController.m file to properly enable and disable the button. In **sayIt:**, enable the button:

```
- (IBAction)sayIt:(id)sender
{
    NSString *string = [textField stringValue];
```

```
    if ([string length] == 0) {
        return;
    }

    [speechSynth startSpeakingString:string];
    NSLog(@"Have started to say: %@", string);
    [stopButton setEnabled:YES];
    [startButton setEnabled:NO];
}
```

In **speechSynthesizer:didFinishSpeaking:**, reset the buttons to their initial states:

```
- (void)speechSynthesizer:(NSSpeechSynthesizer *)sender
        didFinishSpeaking:(BOOL)complete
{
    NSLog(@"complete = %d", complete);
    [stopButton setEnabled:NO];
    [startButton setEnabled:YES];
}
```

Build and run the application. You should see that the Stop button is enabled only when the synthesizer is generating speech. The Speak button should be enabled only when the synthesizer is silent.

The NSTableView and Its dataSource

Next, you will add a table view that will enable the user to change the voice, as shown in Figure 6.4.

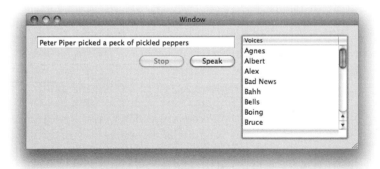

Figure 6.4 Completed Application

A table view is used for displaying columns of data. An **NSTableView** has a helper object called a dataSource, as shown in Figure 6.5. The table view expects its data source to have some methods. We say: "The data source must conform to the NSTableDataSource informal protocol." This is a fancy way of saying that it must implement these two methods:

```
- (int)numberOfRowsInTableView:(NSTableView *)aTableView;
```

The dataSource will reply with the number of rows that will be displayed.

```
- (id)tableView:(NSTableView *)aTableView
    objectValueForTableColumn:(NSTableColumn *)aTableColumn
                        row:(int)rowIndex;
```

The dataSource will reply with the object that should be displayed in the row rowIndex of the column aTableColumn.

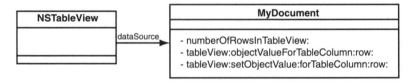

Figure 6.5   NSTableView's dataSource

If you have editable cells in your table view, you will need to implement one more method:

```
- (void)tableView:(NSTableView *)aTableView
  setObjectValue:(id)anObject
  forTableColumn:(NSTableColumn *)aTableColumn
            row:(int)rowIndex;
```

The dataSource takes the input that the user put into row rowIndex of aTableColumn. You do not have to implement this method if your table view is not editable.

Note that you are taking a very passive position in getting data to appear. Your data source will wait until the table view asks for the data. When they first work with **NSTableView** (or **NSBrowser** or **NSOutlineView**, which work in a very similar manner), most programmers want to boss the table view around and tell it, "You will display 7 in the third row in the fifth column." It doesn't work that way. When it is ready to display the third row and the fifth column, the table view will ask its data source for the object to display. Your class is its servant.

You will get the table view to fetch updated information by using **reloadData**. The table view will then reload all the cells that the user can see.

Now you are going to make your instance of **AppController** become the data source of the table view. This involves two steps: implementing the two methods listed earlier and setting the table view's dataSource outlet to the instance of **AppController**. Figure 6.6 is a diagram of where you are going.

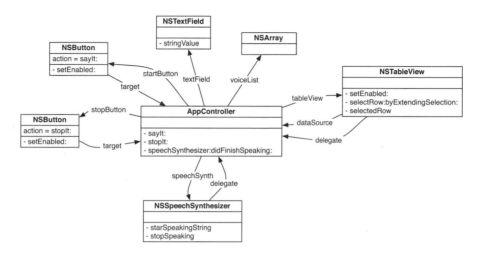

Figure 6.6   Object Diagram

First, add the declaration of two instance variables to AppController.h:

```
#import <Cocoa/Cocoa.h>

@interface AppController : NSObject
{
    IBOutlet NSTextField *textField;
    IBOutlet NSButton *startButton;
    IBOutlet NSButton *stopButton;
    IBOutlet NSTableView *tableView;
    NSArray *voiceList;
    NSSpeechSynthesizer *speechSynth;
}
```

Save the file. In AppController.m, change the **init** method to initialize voiceList:

```
- (id)init
{
    [super init];
    speechSynth = [[NSSpeechSynthesizer alloc] initWithVoice:nil];
    [speechSynth setDelegate:self];
    voiceList = [[NSSpeechSynthesizer availableVoices] retain];
    return self;
}
```

Lay Out the User Interface

Open `MainMenu.nib`. You will edit the window to look like Figure 6.7.

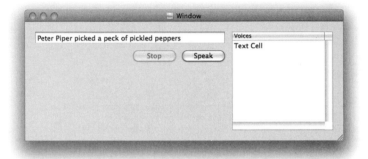

Figure 6.7   Completed Interface

Drag an **NSTableView** onto the window (Figure 6.8).

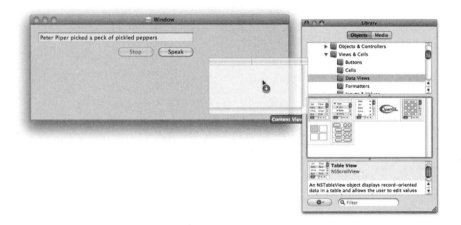

Figure 6.8   Drop a Table View on the Window

Select the table view so that you can look at its attributes in the Inspector (Figure 6.9). This may be a bit challenging. The table view is inside the scroll view, and the table view column is inside the table view. Experiment. You will know that you have selected the table view when the title of the Inspector window is Table

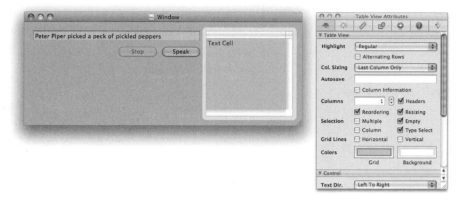

Figure 6.9   Inspect the Table View

View Attributes. In the Inspector, make the table view have only one column. Also, disable column selection.

Double-click the header of the column to change the title to Voices.

Make Connections

First, you will set the dataSource outlet of the **NSTableView** to be your instance of **AppController**. Select the **NSTableView**. Control-click in the table view to bring up the connections panel. Drag from the dataSource outlet to the **AppController**.

If you do not see dataSource in the Inspector, you have selected **NSScrollView**, not **NSTableView** inside it. The scroll view is the object that takes care of scrolling and the scroll bars. You will learn more about scroll views in Chapter 17. For now, simply click in the interior of the table view until the title of the connection panel says **NSTableView** (Figure 6.10).

Also, set the **AppController** to be the delegate of the table view.

Next, you will connect your **AppController** object's tableView outlet to the table view. Control-click on the **AppController**. Connect the tableView outlet to the table view (Figure 6.11).

Save the nib file and close it.

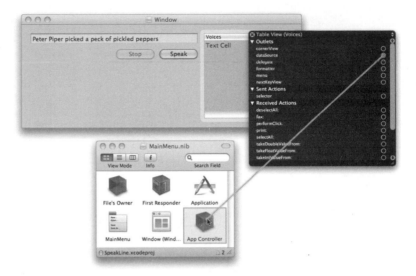

Figure 6.10 Set the tableView's dataSource Outlet

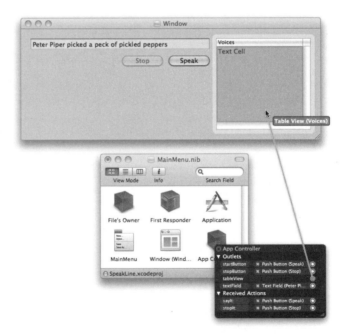

Figure 6.11 Set the AppController's Object's tableView Outlet

Edit AppController.m

Implement the data source methods in AppController.m:

```
- (int)numberOfRowsInTableView:(NSTableView *)tv
{
    return [voiceList count];
}

- (id)tableView:(NSTableView *)tv
        objectValueForTableColumn:(NSTableColumn *)tableColumn
                            row:(int)row
{
    NSString *v = [voiceList objectAtIndex:row];
    return v;
}
```

The identifer for a voice is a long string, such as com.apple.speech.synthe-sis.voice.Fred. If you want only the name Fred, replace the last method with this one:

```
- (id)tableView:(NSTableView *)tv
    objectValueForTableColumn:(NSTableColumn *)tableColumn
                        row:(int)row
{
    NSString *v = [voiceList objectAtIndex:row];
    NSDictionary *dict = [NSSpeechSynthesizer attributesForVoice:v];
    return [dict objectForKey:NSVoiceName];
}
```

(The screen shots in this chapter assume that you've done the pretty version.)

Next, build and run the application. Note that now, you get a list of the possible voices, but selecting a voice doesn't do anything yet.

Besides having a dataSource outlet, a table view has a delegate outlet. The delegate is informed whenever the selection changes. In AppController.m, implement **tableViewSelectionDidChange:**. (The class **NSNotification** will be introduced later in this book. For now, simply note that you are passed a notification object as an argument to this delegate method.)

```
- (void)tableViewSelectionDidChange:(NSNotification *)notification
{
    int row = [tableView selectedRow];
    if (row == -1) {
        return;
    }
```

```
    NSString *selectedVoice = [voiceList objectAtIndex:row];
    [speechSynth setVoice:selectedVoice];
    NSLog(@"new voice = %@", selectedVoice);
}
```

The speech synthesizer will not allow you to change the voice while it is speaking, so you should prevent the user from changing the selected row. The table view should be enabled and disabled with startButton:

```
- (IBAction)sayIt:(id)sender
{
    NSString *string = [textField stringValue];
    if ([string length] == 0) {
        return;
    }

    [speechSynth startSpeakingString:string];
    NSLog(@"Have started to say: %@", string);
    [stopButton setEnabled:YES];
    [startButton setEnabled:NO];
    [tableView setEnabled:NO];
}
- (void)speechSynthesizer:(NSSpeechSynthesizer *)sender
        didFinishSpeaking:(BOOL)complete
{
    NSLog(@"complete = %d", complete);
    [stopButton setEnabled:NO];
    [startButton setEnabled:YES];
    [tableView setEnabled:YES];
}
```

Your users will want to see that the default voice is selected in the table view when the application starts. In **awakeFromNib**, select the appropriate row and scroll to it if necessary:

```
- (void)awakeFromNib
{
    // When the table view appears on screen, the default voice
    // should be selected
    NSString *defaultVoice = [NSSpeechSynthesizer defaultVoice];
    int defaultRow = [voiceList indexOfObject:defaultVoice];
    [tableView selectRow:defaultRow byExtendingSelection:NO];
    [tableView scrollRowToVisible:defaultRow];
}
```

Build and run the application. If the speech synthesizer is speaking, you should get a system beep when you try to change the voice. If it is not speaking, you should be able to change the voice.

Common Errors in Implementing a Delegate

People make two very common errors when implementing a delegate:

- *Misspelling the name of the method.* The method will not be called, and you will not get any error or warning from the compiler. The best way to avoid this problem is to copy and paste the declaration of the method from the documentation or the header file.

- *Forgetting to set the delegate outlet.* You will not get any error or warning from the compiler if you make this error.

Object Delegates

Delegation is a design pattern that you will see used many places in Cocoa. Here are some of the AppKit framework classes that have `delegate` outlets:

`NSAlert`
`NSAnimation`
`NSApplication`
`NSBrowser`
`NSDatePicker`
`NSDrawer`
`NSFontManager`
`NSImage`
`NSLayoutManager`
`NSMatrix`
`NSMenu`
`NSPathControl`
`NSRuleEditor`
`NSSavePanel`
`NSSound`
`NSSpeechRecognizer`
`NSSpeechSynthesizer`
`NSSplitView`
`NSTabView`
`NSTableView`
`NSText`
`NSTextField`
`NSTextStorage`
`NSTextView`
`NSTokenField`
`NSToolbar`
`NSWindow`

For the More Curious: How Delegates Work

The delegate doesn't have to implement all the methods, but if the object does implement a delegate method, it will get called. In many languages, this sort of thing would be impossible. How is it achieved in Objective-C?

NSObject has the the following method:

```
- (BOOL)respondsToSelector:(SEL)aSelector
```

Because every object inherits (directly or indirectly) from **NSObject**, every object has this method. It returns YES if the object has a method called aSelector. Note that aSelector is a SEL, not an **NSString**.

Imagine for a moment that you are the engineer who has to write **NSTableView**. You are writing the code that will change the selection from one row to another. You think to yourself, "I should check with the delegate." To do so, you add a snippet of code that looks like this:

```
// About to change to row "rowIndex"

// Set the default behavior
BOOL ok = YES;

// Check whether the delegate implements the method
if ([delegate respondsToSelector:
                          @selector(tableView:shouldSelectRow:)])
{
    // Execute the method
    ok = [delegate tableView:self shouldSelectRow:rowIndex];
}

// Use the return value
if (ok)
{
    ...actually change the selection...
}
```

Note that the delegate is sent the message only if it has implemented the method. If the delegate doesn't implement the message, the default behavior happens. (In reality, the result from **respondsToSelector:** is usually cached by the object with the delegate outlet. This makes performance considerably faster than would be implied by the preceding code.)

After writing this method, you would carefully make note of its existence in the documentation for your class.

If you wanted to see the checks for the existence of the delegate methods, you could override **respondsToSelector:** in your delegate object:

```
- (BOOL)respondsToSelector:(SEL)aSelector
{
    NSString *methodName = NSStringFromSelector(aSelector);
    NSLog(@"respondsToSelector:%@", methodName);
    return [super respondsToSelector:aSelector];
}
```

You might want to try adding this method to AppController.m now.

Challenge: Make a Delegate

Create a new application with one window. Make an object that is a Delegate of the window. As the user resizes the window, make sure that it always remains twice as tall as it is wide.

Here is the signature of the Delegate method you will implement:

```
- (NSSize)windowWillResize:(NSWindow *)sender
                    toSize:(NSSize)frameSize;
```

The first argument is the window being resized. The second argument is a C struct that contains the size that the user has asked for:

```
typedef struct _NSSize {
    float width;
    float height;
} NSSize;
```

Here is how you create an NSSize that is 200 points wide and 100 points tall:

```
NSSize mySize;
mySize.width = 200.0;
mySize.height = 100.0;
NSLog(@"mySize is %f wide and %f tall", mySize.width, mySize.height);
```

You can set the intial size of the window in the Size Inspector in Interface Builder.

Challenge: Make a Data Source

Make a to-do list application. The user will type tasks into the text field. When the user clicks the Add button, you will add the string to a mutable array, and the new task will appear at the end of the list (Figure 6.12).

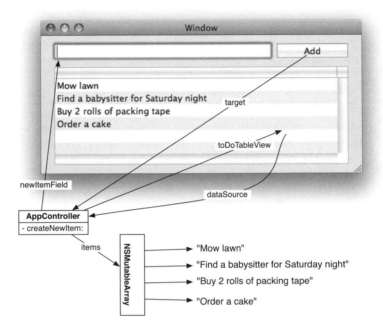

Figure 6.12   Diagram of Challenge

You get extra points for making the table view editable. (*Hint:* **NSMutableArray** has a method **-replaceObjectAtIndex:withObject:**.)

Chapter 7

KEY-VALUE CODING; KEY-VALUE OBSERVING

Key-value coding (KVC) is a mechanism that allows you to set and get the value of a variable by its name. The name is simply a string, but we refer to that name as a *key*. So, for example, imagine that you have a class called **Student** that has an instance variable called firstName of type NSString:

```
@interface Student : NSObject
{
    NSString *firstName;
}
...
@ends
```

If you had an instance of **Student**, you could set its firstName like this:

```
Student *s = [[Student alloc] init];
[s setValue:@"Larry" forKey:@"firstName"];
```

You could read the value of its firstName like this:

```
NSString *x = [s valueForKey:@"firstName"];
```

The methods **setValue:forKey:** and **valueForKey:** are defined in **NSObject**. Even though this doesn't look like rocket science, the ability to read and set a variable by its name is really powerful. The rest of this chapter will be a simple example that should illustrate some of that power.

Key-Value Coding

In Xcode, create a new project of type Cocoa Application. Name the project KVCFun. In the project, create a new file of type Objective-C Class. Name the class **AppController**.

At this point in our exploration of key-value coding, you simply need an instance of **AppController** to be created with the MainMenu.nib file read in. Drag out a custom object and set its class to be **AppController** (Figure 7.1).

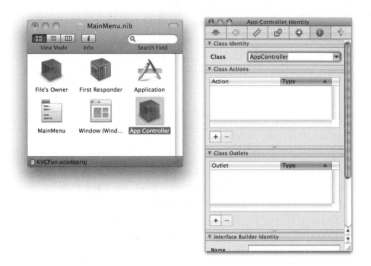

Figure 7.1   Create AppController

Save the nib file.

Back in Xcode, open AppController.h, and add an instance variable called fido of type int:

```
@interface AppController : NSObject
{
    int fido;
}
@end
```

In AppController.m, you are going to create an **init** method that sets and reads fido by using key-value coding. This is a bit silly because it is going to be a long-winded way to get a simple result. This is designed to be illustrative rather than practical.

What makes the method so long-winded is that the key-value coding methods work with objects, so instead of passing an int, you will need to create an **NSNumber**. Add this method to AppController.m:

```
- (id)init
{
    [super init];
```

```
    [self setValue:[NSNumber numberWithInt:5]
            forKey:@"fido"];
    NSNumber *n = [self valueForKey:@"fido"];
    NSLog(@"fido = %@", n);
    return self;
}
```

The key-value coding mechanism will automatically convert the **NSNumber** to an int before using it to set the value of fido. Build and run the application, but don't expect much. When the blank window appears, "fido = 5" will be logged to the console.

If you have accessor methods for getting and setting fido, they will be used. You must, however, give them the correct names. The getter must be called **fido**, and the setter must be called **setFido:**. Note that this is more than simply a convention; if you give your accessors nonstandard names, they will not get called by the key-value coding methods. Add **fido** and **setFido:** to AppController.m:

```
- (int)fido
{
    NSLog(@"-fido is returning %d", fido);
    return fido;
}

- (void)setFido:(int)x
{
    NSLog(@"-setFido: is called with %d", x);
    fido = x;
}
```

Declare these methods in AppController.h:

```
- (int)fido;
- (void)setFido:(int)x;
```

Build and run the application. Note that your accessor methods are being called.

Bindings

Many graphical objects in Cocoa have *bindings*. When you bind a key, such as fido, to an attribute of the graphical object (like its value or its font color), the view will automatically keep those in sync. You are going to add a slider, bind its value to fido, and see how it uses key-value coding to them in sync.

Open `MainMenu.nib`. Drop a slider on the window. In the Attributes Inspector, make the slider Continuous (Figure 7.2).

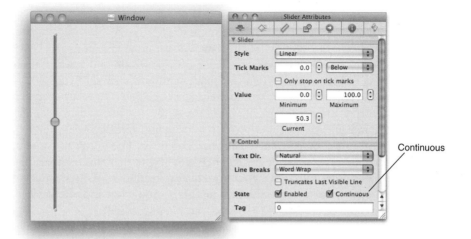

Continuous

Figure 7.2   Make Slider Continuous

In the Bindings Inspector, bind the value of the slider to the fido key of the instance of **AppController** (Figure 7.3).

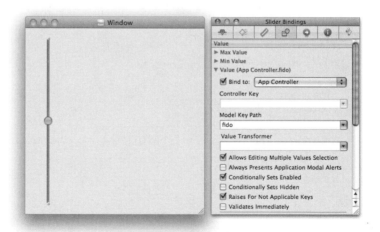

Figure 7.3   Bind Value of Slider to fido

Build and run the application. Note that the slider uses **valueForKey:** to get its initial value, which triggers your **fido** method. As you move the slider, it calls **setValue:forKey:** to update the fido variable, which triggers your **setFido:** method.

Key-Value Observing

What happens if fido is changed by something other than the slider? How would the slider know that it has a new value?

When the slider is created, it tells the **AppController** that it is observing its fido key. Whenever the value of fido is changed by the accessor methods or by key-value coding, the **AppController** sends a message to the slider, notifying it that fido has changed.

Open MainMenu.nib again. Add a Label text field to the window, and bind its value to **AppController**'s fido key (Figure 7.4).

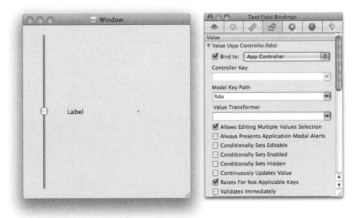

Figure 7.4   Bind Value of Text Field to fido

Build and run the app. Note that when you move the slider, **setFido:** is called. This notifies the text field that fido has changed. The text field uses **valueForKey:** to get the new value of fido. Thus, you see the **fido** method getting called.

Making Keys Observable

In the previous section, I mentioned that when you use accessors or key-value coding to change the value for a key, the observers are automatically notified of the change. What happens if you change the variable directly?

Open `AppController.h` and declare a new action method:

```
- (IBAction)incrementFido:(id)sender;
```

In `AppController.m`, implement the method:

```
- (IBAction)incrementFido:(id)sender
{
    fido++;
    NSLog(@"fido is now %d", fido);
}
```

Open `MainMenu.nib`. Add a button to the window, label the button Increment Fido, and Control-drag from the button to the instance **AppController**. The button should trigger the **incrementFido:** action (Figure 7.5).

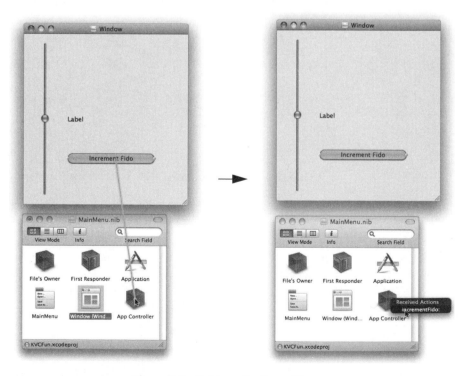

Figure 7.5   Set target/action of Button

You would hope that when the button is clicked, the slider would move and the text field would update itself. Sadly, neither happens. Try building and running the application.

If you are going to change the variable directly, you will need to explicitly trigger the notification of the observers. Change the **incrementFido:** method:

```
- (IBAction)incrementFido:(id)sender
{
    [self willChangeValueForKey:@"fido"];
    fido++;
    NSLog(@"fido is now %d", fido);
    [self didChangeValueForKey:@"fido"];
}
```

Build and run the application now; the Increment Fido button should work correctly.

Two other solutions would work. First, you could use key-value coding:

```
- (IBAction)incrementFido:(id)sender
{
    NSNumber *n = [self valueForKey:@"fido"];
    NSNumber *npp = [NSNumber numberWithInt:[n intValue] + 1];
    [self setValue:npp forKey:@"fido"];
}
```

Or, you could use the accessor method to change fido:

```
- (IBAction)incrementFido:(id)sender
{
    [self setFido:[self fido] + 1];
}
```

Type this version in. Then build and run it.

Figure 7.6 is an object diagram of what you have done. Note the use of half-arrows to represent bindings.

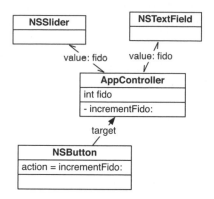

Figure 7.6   Object Diagram

Properties and Their Attributes

As you can guess, we spend a lot of time calling accessor methods. In Objective-C 2.0, Apple gives programmers the option of calling accessors by using dot notation. If you have a pointer rover to an object with a getter method **rex**, you can call it like this:

```
NSLog(@"Rover's rex is %@", rover.rex);
```

To call **setRex:**, you could do this:

```
rover.rex = [NSDate date];
```

Overall, I think that this is a rather silly addition to the language since we already had a syntax for sending messages. So I won't be using it in this book.

What about writing the accessor methods? If your object has 12 instance variables, do you need to write 12 setters and 12 getters?

@property and @synthesize

With Objective-C 2.0, Apple introduced a very elegant way to eliminate a lot of this code. In the AppController.h file, replace the declaration of the **fido** and **setFido:** methods with the declaration of a *property*:

```
@interface AppController : NSObject {
    int fido;
}
```

```
@property(readwrite, assign) int fido;
@end
```

This one line is equivalent to declaring **setFido:** and **fido** methods.

In AppController.m, you can use @synthesize to implement the accessor methods. Delete your **fido** and **setFido:** methods, and replace them with this line:

```
@synthesize fido;
```

Note that everything still works. (Naturally, you won't see the log statements anymore.)

Attributes of a Property

In general, the declaration of a property looks like this:

```
@property (attributes) type name;
```

The attributes can include readwrite (the default) or readonly. A property marked readonly gets no setter method.

To describe how the setter method should work, the attributes can also include one of the following: assign, retain, copy. Let's look at each in turn:

- assign (the default) makes a simple assignment happen. assign does not retain the new value. If you are dealing with an object type and you are not using the garbage collector, you probably don't want assign.

- retain releases the old value and retains the new value. This attribute is used only for Objective-C object types. If you are using the garbage collector, assign and retain are equivalent.

- copy makes a copy of the new value and assigns the variable to the copy. This attribute is often used for properties that are strings.

Finally, the attributes can also include nonatomic. If your application is multithreaded, it is sometimes important that your setter methods be *atomic*. That is, the execution of the setter method from one thread will not conflict with the execution of the same setter method on another thread. By default, the @synthesize call will generate accessors with this property. On an application that is not using the garbage collector, this involves using a lock to ensure that only one thread at a time is executing the setter. Creating and using the locks introduces some overhead. If you know that the accessors for a property don't need to be atomic, you can eliminate the overhead by adding nonatomic to the attributes.

For the More Curious: Key Paths

Objects are often arranged in a network. For example, a person might have a spouse who has a scooter that has a model name (Figure 7.7).

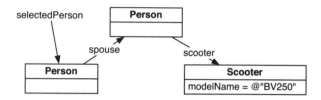

Figure 7.7   Objects Are a Directed Graph

To get the model name of the selected person's spouse's scooter, you can use a key path:

```
NSString *mn;
mn = [selectedPerson valueForKeyPath:@"spouse.scooter.modelName"];
```

We'd say that spouse and scooter are relationships of the **Person** class and that modelName is an attribute of the **Scooter** class.

There are also operators that you can include in key paths. For example, if you have an array of **Person** objects, you could get their average expectedRaise by using key paths:

```
NSNumber *theAverage;
theAverage = [employees valueForKeyPath:@"@avg.expectedRaise"];
```

Here are some commonly used operators:

```
@avg
@count
@max
@min
@sum
```

Now that you know about key paths, you can create bindings programmatically. If you had a text field in which you wanted to show the average expected raise of the arranged objects of an array controller, you could create a binding, like this:

```
[textField bind:@"value"
      toObject:employeeController
   withKeyPath:@"arrangedObjects.@avg.expectedRaise"
       options:nil];
```

Of course, it is usually easier to create a binding in Interface Builder.

Use the **unbind:** method to remove the binding:

```
[textField unbind:@"value"];
```

For the More Curious: Key-Value Observing

How did the text field become an observer of the `fido` key in the
AppController object? When it wakes up from being in the nib, the text field
adds itself as an observer. If you wanted to become an observer of this key, your
line of code might look something like this:

```
[theAppController addObserver:self
                forKeyPath:@"fido"
                    options:NSKeyValueObservingOld
                    context:somePointer];
```

This method is defined in **NSObject**. It is how you say, "Hey! Send me a message
whenever `fido` changes." The options and context determine what extra data is
sent along with that message when `fido` changes. The method that is triggered
looks like this:

```
- (void)observeValueForKeyPath:(NSString *)keyPath
                ofObject:(id)object
                  change:(NSDictionary *)change
                context:(void *)context
{
...
}
```

The keyPath, in this case, would be @"fido", and the `object` would be the
AppController. The `context` would be the pointer `somePointer` supplied as
the context when you became an observer. The dictionary `change` is a collection
of key-value pairs that can hold the old value of `fido` and/or the new value.

Chapter 8
NSARRAYCONTROLLER

In the object-oriented programming community, a very common design pattern is *Model-View-Controller*. In this design pattern, each class you write should fall into exactly one of the following groups:

- *Model:* Model classes describe your data. For example, if you write banking systems, you would probably create a model class called **SavingsAccount** that would have a list of transactions and a current balance. The best model classes include nothing about the user interface and can be used in several applications.

- *View:* A view class is part of the GUI. For example, **NSSlider** is a view class. The best view classes are general-purpose classes and can be used in several applications.

- *Controller:* Application-specific controller classes are responsible for controlling the flow of the application. The user needs to see the data, so a controller object reads the model from a file or a database and then displays the model by using view classes. When the user makes changes, the view objects inform the controller, which subsequently updates the model objects. The controller also saves the data to the filesystem or database.

Until Mac OS X 10.3, Cocoa programmers wrote in their controller objects a lot of code that simply moved data from the model objects into the view objects and back again. To make common sorts of controller classes easier to write, Apple introduced **NSController** and bindings.

NSController is an abstract class (Figure 8.1). **NSObjectController**, a subclass of **NSController**, displays the information *content* for an object. **NSArrayController** is a controller that has an array of data objects as its content. In this exercise, we will use an **NSArrayController**.

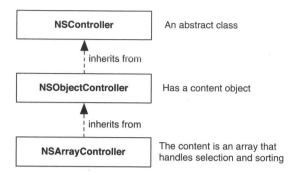

Figure 8.1   Controller Classes

Starting the RaiseMan Application

Over the next few chapters, you will create a full-featured application for keeping track of employees and the raise that each person will receive this year. As this book progresses, you will add file saving, undo, user preferences, and printing capabilities. After this chapter, the application will look like Figure 8.2.

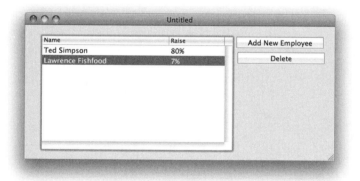

Figure 8.2   Completed Application

(Yes, experienced Cocoa programmers, you could create an application like this using CoreData, but I want you to see how it is done manually. Then, CoreData will not seem so magical.)

In Xcode

Create a new project in Xcode. Choose the Cocoa Document-based Application for the type, and name the application RaiseMan.

What is a *document-based* application? It is an application in which several documents can be open simultaneously. TextEdit, for example, is a document-based application. System Preferences, on the other hand, is not a document-based application. You will learn more about document architecture in the next chapter.

The object diagram for this application is shown in Figure 8.3. The table columns are connected to the **NSArrayController** by bindings rather than by outlets.

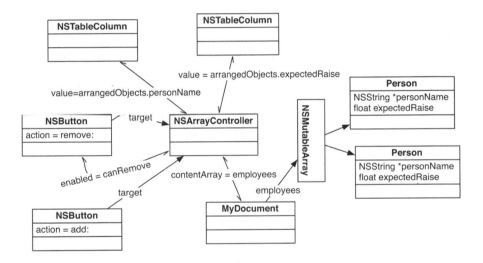

Figure 8.3 Object Diagram

Note that the class **MyDocument** has already been created for you. **MyDocument** is a subclass of **NSDocument**. The document object is responsible for reading and writing files. In this exercise, we will use an **NSArrayController** and bindings to construct our simple interface, so we won't be adding any code to **MyDocument** just yet.

To create a new **Person** class, choose the File -> New File... menu item. When presented with the possibilities, choose Objective-C Class. Name the new file Person.m, and make sure that it is going to create a Person.h file, as shown in Figure 8.4.

Figure 8.4 Creating a Person Class

Edit the Person.h file to declare two properties:

```
#import <Foundation/Foundation.h>

@interface Person : NSObject {
    NSString *personName;
    float expectedRaise;
}
@property (readwrite, copy) NSString *personName;
@property (readwrite) float expectedRaise;
@end
```

Now edit Person.m to implement these methods and to override **init** and **dealloc**:

```
#import "Person.h"

@implementation Person

- (id)init
{
    [super init];
    expectedRaise = 5.0;
    personName = @"New Person";
    return self;
}

- (void)dealloc
{
    [personName release];
    [super dealloc];
}
```

```
@synthesize personName;
@synthesize expectedRaise;
@end
```

Note that **Person** is a model class—it has no information about the user interface. As such, the class doesn't need to know about all the Cocoa frameworks. Thus, instead of importing Cocoa/Cocoa.h, we are importing Foundation/Foundation.h. Either would work, but importing the smaller framework is more stylish. It indicates, for example, that this class could be reused in a command-line tool.

Declare the employees array, which will contain instances of the **Person** class, in MyDocument.h:

```
@interface MyDocument : NSDocument
{
    NSMutableArray *employees;
}
- (void)setEmployees:(NSMutableArray *)a;
```

Now in MyDocument.m, create the **setEmployees:** method. In **dealloc**, use it to release the array:

```
- (id)init
{
    [super init];
    employees = [[NSMutableArray alloc] init];
    return self;
}

- (void)dealloc
{
    [self setEmployees:nil];
    [super dealloc];
}

- (void)setEmployees:(NSMutableArray *)a
{
    // This is an unusual setter method.  We are going to add a lot
    // of smarts to it in the next chapter.
    if (a == employees)
        return;

    [a retain];
    [employees release];
    employees = a;
}
```

In Interface Builder

In Xcode, double-click MyDocument.nib to open it in Interface Builder.

Delete the text field Your document contents here. Drop a table view and two buttons on the window. Relabel and arrange them as shown in Figure 8.5.

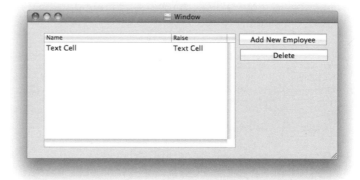

Figure 8.5   Document Window

From Cocoa->Objects & Controllers -> Controllers, drag out an **NSArrayController**, and drop it in the doc window.

In the Inspector, set its Object Class Name to **Person**. Add the keys for personName and expectedRaise, as shown in Figure 8.6.

Bind the Content Array of the array controller to the employees array of File's Owner, which is the instance of **MyDocument** (Figure 8.7).

The first column of the table view will display each employee's name. Click and double-click the column to select it. (At no time in this book will you ever bind to the scroll view, table view, or the cell; doing so is a common mistake, so keep an eye on the title of the Inspector window.) In the Bindings Inspector, set the value to display the personName of the arrangedObjects of the **NSArrayController**, as shown in Figure 8.8 (page 130).

The second column of the table view displays each employee's expected raise. Drop a number formatter (from Library->Cocoa->Views & Cells->Formatters) on the column's cell. In the Inspector, set the formatter to display the number as a percentage, as shown in Figure 8.9 (page 130).

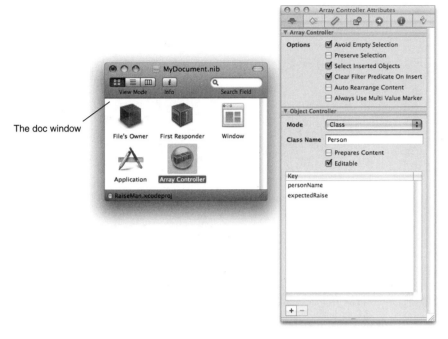

Figure 8.6   Controller Classes

Figure 8.7   Bind Content Array

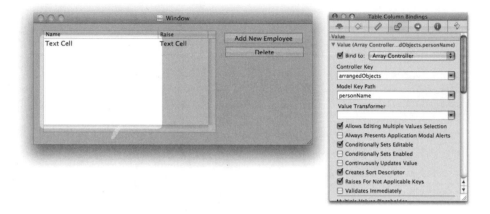

Figure 8.8   Binding the personName Column

Figure 8.9   Adding a Number Formatter

Reselect the second column. In the Bindings Inspector, set value to display the expectedRaise of the arrangedObjects of the **NSArrayController**, as shown in Figure 8.10.

Control-drag to make the array controller become the target of the Add New Employee button. Set the action to **add:**.

Control-drag to make the array controller become the target of the Delete button. Set the action to **remove:**. Also, in the Bindings Inspector, bind the button's enabled binding to the canRemove attribute of the **NSArrayController**, as shown in Figure 8.11.

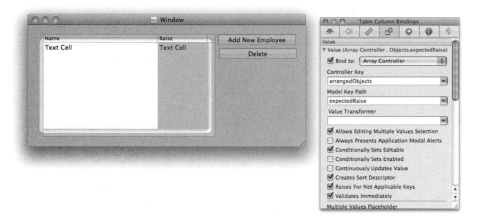

Figure 8.10   Bind Second Column to expectedRaise of arrangedObjects

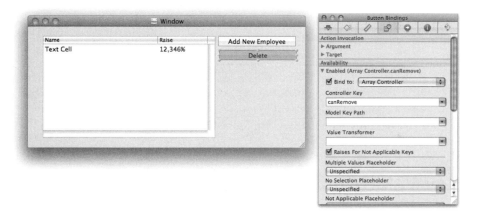

Figure 8.11   Binding the enabled Attribute of the Delete Button

The user will also want to delete the selected employees by pressing the Delete key on his or her keyboard. Select the button; in the Attributes Inspector, set the keyboard equivalent to the Delete key (Figure 8.12).

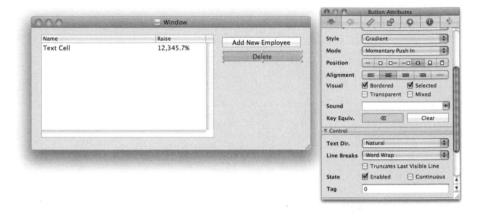

Figure 8.12   Make Delete Key Trigger Delete Button

Build and run your application. You should be able to create and delete **Person** objects. You should also be able to edit the attributes of the **Person** objects by using the table view. Finally, you should be able to open multiple untitled documents. (No, you can't save those documents to a file. Soon, Grasshopper.)

Key-Value Coding and nil

Note that our example contains very little code. You described what should be displayed in each of the columns in Interface Builder, but there is no code that calls the accessor methods of your **Person** class. How does this work? Key-value coding. Key-value coding makes generic, reusable classes, such as **NSArrayController**, possible.

Note that the key-value coding methods will automatically coerce the type for you. For example, when the user types in a new expected raise, the formatter creates an instance of **NSNumber**. The key-value coding method **setValue:forKey:** automatically converts that into a **float** before calling **setExpectedRaise:**. This behavior is extremely convenient.

There is, however, a problem with converting an NSDecimalNumber * into a float: Pointers can be nil, but floats cannot. If **setValue:forKey:** is passed a nil value that needs to be converted into a nonpointer type, it will call its own

```
- (void)setNilValueForKey:(NSString *)s
```

method. This method, as defined in **NSObject**, throws an exception. Thus, if the user left the Expected Raise field empty, your object would throw an exception. Typically, you will override **setNilValueForKey:** so that it sets the instance variable to a default value. In this case, you are going to override this method in your **Person** class and set expectedRaise to 0.0. Add the following method to Person.m:

```
- (void)setNilValueForKey:(NSString *)key
{
    if ([key isEqual:@"expectedRaise"]) {
        [self setExpectedRaise:0.0];
    } else {
        [super setNilValueForKey:key];
    }
}
```

Note that when you apply a formatter (as you have done) it is sometimes unnecessary to override **setNilValueForKey:** because the formatter, depending on how it is configured, may prevent nil values from being entered.

Add Sorting

While the application is running, click the column headers and note that sorting works but does so badly. In particular, it is using the strongly case-sensitive **compare:** method to order the names. For example, "Z" will come before "a". Let's change the method used for sorting.

Open MyDocument.nib. You can set the sorting criteria in the Attributes Inspector for each column. Users will be able to choose on which attribute the data will be sorted, by clicking on the header of the column containing that attribute.

Select the column that displays personName. In the Inspector, set the Sort Key to be personName and the Selector to be **caseInsensitiveCompare:**, as shown in Figure 8.13.

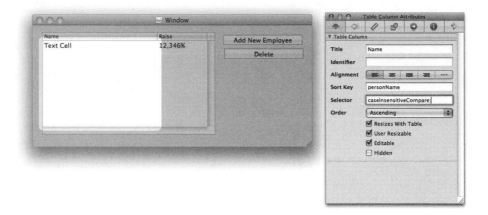

Figure 8.13   Sorting on personName

The **caseInsensitiveCompare:** method is part of **NSString**. For example, you might do this:

```
NSString *x = @"Piaggio";
NSString *y = @"Italjet"
NSComparisonResult result = [x caseInsensitiveCompare:y];

// Would x come first in the dictionary?
if (result == NSOrderedAscending)  {
     ...
}
```

NSComparisonResult is simply an integer. NSOrderedAscending is –1. NSOrderedSame is 0. NSOrderedDescending is 1.

Build and run your application. Click the header of the column to sort the data. Click again to see the data in reverse order.

For the More Curious: Sorting without NSArrayController

In Chapter 6, you created a table view by implementing the dataSource methods explicitly. You might have wondered then how you could implement this sorting behavior in your own application.

The information that you added to the columns of the table is packed into an array of **NSSortDescriptor** objects. A sort descriptor includes the key, a selector, and an indicator of whether data should be sorted into ascending or descending order. If you have an **NSMutableArray** of objects, you can use the following method to sort it:

```
- (void)sortUsingDescriptors:(NSArray *)sortDescriptors
```

An optional table view dataSource method is triggered when the user clicks the header of a column with a sort descriptor:

```
- (void)tableView:(NSTableView *)tableView
  sortDescriptorsDidChange:(NSArray *)oldDescriptors
```

Thus, if you have a mutable array that holds the information for a table view, you can implement the method like this:

```
- (void)tableView:(NSTableView *)tableView
          sortDescriptorsDidChange:(NSArray *)oldDescriptors
{
    NSArray *newDescriptors = [tableView sortDescriptors];
    [myArray sortUsingDescriptors:newDescriptors];
    [tableView reloadData];
}
```

Voila! You have sorting in your application.

Challenge 1

Make the application sort people based on the number of characters in their names. You can complete this challenge using only Interface Builder; the trick is to use a key path. (*Hint:* Strings have a **length** method.)

Challenge 2

In the first edition of this book, readers created the RaiseMan application without using **NSArrayController** or the bindings mechanism. (These features were added in Mac OS X 10.3.) To do so, readers used the ideas from previous chapters. The challenge, then, is to rewrite the RaiseMan application without using **NSArrayController** or the bindings mechanism. Bindings often seem rather magical, and it is good to know how to do things without resorting to magic.

Be sure to start afresh with a new project. In the next chapter, we will build on your existing project.

The **Person** class will stay exactly the same. In MyDocument.nib, you will set the identifier of each column to be the name of the variable you would like displayed. Then, the **MyDocument** class will be the dataSource of the table view and the target of the Create New and Delete buttons. **MyDocument** will have an array of **Person** objects that it displays. To get you started, here is MyDocument.h:

```
#import <Cocoa/Cocoa.h>
@class Person;

@interface MyDocument : NSDocument
{
    NSMutableArray *employees;
    IBOutlet NSTableView *tableView;
}
- (IBAction)createEmployee:(id)sender;
- (IBAction)deleteSelectedEmployees:(id)sender;
@end
```

Here are the interesting parts of MyDocument.m:

```
- (id)init
{
    [super init];
    employees = [[NSMutableArray alloc] init];
    return self;
}
- (void)dealloc
{
    [employees release];
    [super dealloc];
}

#pragma mark Action methods

- (IBAction)deleteSelectedEmployees:(id)sender
{
    // Which row is selected?
    NSIndexSet *rows = [tableView selectedRowIndexes];

    // Is the selection empty?
    if ([rows count] == 0) {
        NSBeep();
        return;
    }
    [employees removeObjectsAtIndexes:rows];
    [tableView reloadData];
}
```

```
- (IBAction)createEmployee:(id)sender
{
    Person *newEmployee = [[Person alloc] init];
    [employees addObject:newEmployee];
    [newEmployee release];
    [tableView reloadData];
}

#pragma mark Table view dataSource methods

- (int)numberOfRowsInTableView:(NSTableView *)aTableView
{
    return [employees count];
}

- (id)tableView:(NSTableView *)aTableView
        objectValueForTableColumn:(NSTableColumn *)aTableColumn
                            row:(int)rowIndex
{
    // What is the identifier for the column?
    NSString *identifier = [aTableColumn identifier];

    // What person?
    Person *person = [employees objectAtIndex:rowIndex];

    // What is the value of the attribute named identifier?
    return [person valueForKey:identifier];
}

- (void)tableView:(NSTableView *)aTableView
    setObjectValue:(id)anObject
    forTableColumn:(NSTableColumn *)aTableColumn
            row:(int)rowIndex
{
    NSString *identifier = [aTableColumn identifier];
    Person *person = [employees objectAtIndex:rowIndex];

    // Set the value for the attribute named identifier
    [person setValue:anObject forKey:identifier];
}
```

Once you have it working, be sure to add sorting!

Chapter 9
NSUndoManager

Using **NSUndoManager**, you can add undo capabilities to your applications in a very elegant manner. As objects are added, edited, and deleted, the undo manager keeps track of all messages that must be sent to undo these changes. As you invoke the undo mechanism, the undo manager keeps track of all messages that must be sent to redo *those* changes. This mechanism works by using two stacks of **NSInvocation** objects.

This is a pretty heavy topic to cover so early in a book. (Sometimes when I think about undo, my head starts to swim a bit.) However, undo interacts with the document architecture. If we tackle this work now, you will see in the next chapter how the document architecture is supposed to work.

NSInvocation

As you might imagine, it is handy to be able to package up a message—including the selector, the receiver, and all arguments—as an object that can be invoked at your leisure. Such an object is an instance of **NSInvocation**.

One exceedingly convenient use for invocations is in message forwarding. When an object is sent a message that it does not understand, the message-sending system, before raising an exception, checks whether the object has implemented

```
- (void)forwardInvocation:(NSInvocation *)x
```

If the object has such a method, the message sent is packed up as an **NSInvocation**, and **forwardInvocation:** is called.

How the NSUndoManager Works

Suppose that the user opens a new RaiseMan document and makes three edits:

- Inserts a new record
- Changes the name from "New Employee" to "Rex Fido"
- Changes the raise from 0 to 20

As each edit is performed, your controller will add an invocation that would undo that edit to the undo stack. For the sake of simplifying the prose, let's say, "The *inverse* of the edit gets added to the undo stack." Figure 9.1 shows what the undo stack would look like after these three edits.

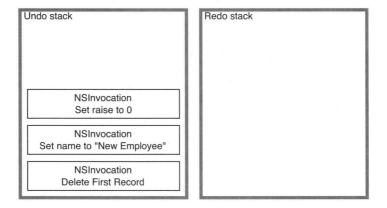

Figure 9.1 The Undo Stack

If the user now chooses the Undo menu item, the first invocation is taken off the stack and invoked. This would change the person's raise back to zero. If the user chooses the Undo menu item again, it would change the person's name back to "New Employee."

Each time an item is popped off the undo stack and invoked, the inverse of the undo operation must be added to the redo stack. Thus, after undoing the two operations just described, the undo and redo stacks should look like Figure 9.2.

The undo manager is actually quite clever: When the user is doing edits, the undo invocations go onto the undo stack. When the user is undoing edits, the undo invocations go onto the redo stack. When the user is redoing edits, the undo invocations go onto the undo stack. These tasks are handled automatically for

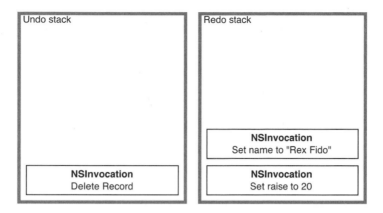

Figure 9.2 The Revised Undo Stack

you; your only job is to give the undo manager the inverse invocations that need to be added.

Now suppose that you are writing a method called **makeItHotter** and that the inverse of this method is called **makeItColder**. Here is how you would enable the undo:

```
- (void)makeItHotter
{
    temperature = temperature + 10;
    [[undoManager prepareWithInvocationTarget:self] makeItColder];
    [self showTheChangesToTheTemperature];
}
```

As you might guess, the **prepareWithInvocationTarget:** method notes the target and returns the undo manager itself. Then, the undo manager cleverly overrides **forwardInvocation:** such that it adds the invocation for **makeItColder:** to the undo stack.

To complete the example, you would implement **makeItColder**:

```
- (void)makeItColder
{
    temperature = temperature - 10;
    [[undoManager prepareWithInvocationTarget:self] makeItHotter];
    [self showTheChangesToTheTemperature];
}
```

Note that we have again registered the inverse with the undo manager. If **makeItColder** is invoked as a result of an undo, this inverse will go onto the redo stack.

The invocations on either stack are grouped. By default, all invocations added to a stack during a single event are grouped together. Thus, if one user action causes changes in several objects, all the changes are undone by a single click of the Undo menu item.

The undo manager can also change the label on the Undo and Redo menu items. For example, Undo Insert is more descriptive than simply Undo. To set the label, use the following code:

```
[undoManager setActionName:@"Insert"];
```

How do you get an undo manager? You can create one explicitly, but note that each instance of **NSDocument** already has its own undo manager.

Adding Undo to RaiseMan

Let's give the user the ability to undo the effects of clicking the Add New Employee and Delete buttons, as well as the ability to undo the changes made to **Person** objects in the table. The necessary code will go into your **MyDocument** class.

When designing a class, I tend to think of my instance variables as having one of four possible purposes:

1. *Simple attributes*. For example, each student has a first name. Simple attributes are typically numbers or instances of **NSString**, **NSDate**, or **NSData**.

2. *To-one relationships*. For example, each student has a school. It is like a simple attribute, but the type is a complex object, not a simple one. To-one relationships are implemented using pointers: An instance of **Student** has a pointer to an instance of **School**.

3. *Ordered to-many relationships*. For example, each playlist has a list of songs. The songs are in a particular order. Relationships of this kind are typically implemented using an **NSMutableArray**.

4. *Unordered to-many relationships*. For example, each department has a bunch of employees. You can display the employees in a particular order (e.g., sorted by last name), but that ordering is not inherent in the relationship. This order is typically implemented using an **NSMutableSet**.

Earlier, we discussed how we could set simple attributes and to-one relationships by using key-value coding. Remember that when setting or getting a value for fido, key-value coding will use the accessors if they exist. Similarly, we can create accessors for ordered and unordered to-many relationships.

Let's say, for example, that an instance of **Playlist** has an **NSMutableArray** of **Song** objects. If you want to manipulate that array by using key-value coding, you will ask the playlist for its **mutableArrayValueForKey:**. You will get back a proxy object. That proxy object knows that it represents the array that holds the songs.

```
id arrayProxy = [playlist mutableArrayValueForKey:@"songs"];
int songCount = [arrayProxy count];
```

In this example, when it is asked for the **count**, the proxy object will ask the **PlayList** object whether it has a **countOfSongs** method. If it does, it will call the method and return the result. If there is no such method, it will get the array of songs and ask that for its **count** (Figure 9.3). Note, then, that naming the method **countOfSongs** is not merely a convention: The key-value coding mechanism goes looking for a method with the right name.

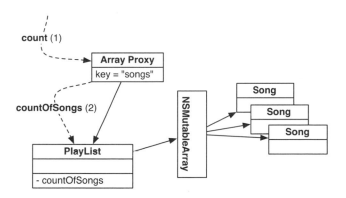

Figure 9.3   Key-Value Coding for Ordered Relationships

There are several cases, so here is a list:

```
id arrayProxy = [playlist mutableArrayValueForKey:@"songs"];

int x = [arrayProxy count]; // is the same as
int x = [playlist countOfSongs]; // if countOfSongs exists

id y = [arrayProxy objectAtIndex:5] // is the same as
id y = [playlist objectInSongsAtIndex:5]; // if the method exists

[arrayProxy insertObject:p atIndex:4] // is the same as
[playlist insertObject:p inSongsAtIndex:4]; // if the method exists
```

```
[arrayProxy removeObjectAtIndex:3] // is the same as
[playlist removeObjectFromSongsAtIndex:3] // if the method exists
```

There is a similar set of calls for unordered to-many relationships (Figure 9.4).

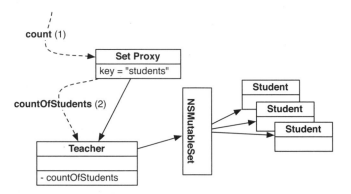

Figure 9.4   Key-Value Coding for Unordered Relationships

```
id setProxy = [teacher mutableSetValueForKey:@"students"];

int x = [setProxy count]; // is the same as
int x = [teacher countOfStudents]; // if countOfStudents exists

[setProxy addObject:newStudent]; // is the same as
[teacher addStudentsObject:newStudent]; // if the method exists

[setProxy removeObject:expelledStudent]; // is the same as
[teacher removeStudentsObject:expelledStudent]; // if the method exists
```

Because we have bound the contentArray of the array controller to the employees array of the **MyDocument** object, the array controller will use key-value coding to add and remove **Person** objects. You will take advantage of this to add undo invocations to the undo stack when people are added and removed. Add these methods to MyDocument.m:

```
- (void)insertObject:(Person *)p inEmployeesAtIndex:(int)index
{
    NSLog(@"adding %@ to %@", p, employees);
    // Add the inverse of this operation to the undo stack
    NSUndoManager *undo = [self undoManager];
    [[undo prepareWithInvocationTarget:self]
                        removeObjectFromEmployeesAtIndex:index];
    if (![undo isUndoing]) {
        [undo setActionName:@"Insert Person"];
    }
```

```
    // Add the Person to the array
    [employees insertObject:p atIndex:index];
}

- (void)removeObjectFromEmployeesAtIndex:(int)index
{
    Person *p = [employees objectAtIndex:index];
    NSLog(@"removing %@ from %@", p, employees);
    // Add the inverse of this operation to the undo stack
    NSUndoManager *undo = [self undoManager];
    [[undo prepareWithInvocationTarget:self] insertObject:p
                                    inEmployeesAtIndex:index];
    if (![undo isUndoing]) {
        [undo setActionName:@"Delete Person"];
    }

    [employees removeObjectAtIndex:index];
}
```

These methods will be called automatically when the **NSArrayController** wishes to insert or remove **Person** objects: for example, when the Create New and Delete buttons send it **insert:** and **remove:** messages.

Declare the methods in MyDocument.h:

```
- (void)removeObjectFromEmployeesAtIndex:(int)index;
- (void)insertObject:(Person *)p inEmployeesAtIndex:(int)index;
```

Because you use the class **Person**, you will need to make the compiler aware of it at the beginning of MyDocument.h:

```
#import <Cocoa/Cocoa.h>
@class Person;
```

Also, you'll need to import Person.h at the top of MyDocument.m:

```
#import "Person.h"
```

At this point, you have made it possible to undo deletions and insertions. Undoing edits will be a little trickier. Before tackling this task, build and run your application. Test the undo capabilities that you have at this point. Note that redo also works.

Key-Value Observing

In Chapter 7, we discussed key-value coding. To review: Key-value coding is a way to read and change a variable's value by using its name. *Key-value observing* allows you to be informed when these sorts of changes occur.

To enable undo capabilities for edits, you will want your document object to be informed of changes to the keys `expectedRaise` and `personName` for all of its **Person** objects. A method in **NSObject** allows you to register to be informed of these changes:

```
- (void)addObserver:(NSObject *)observer
       forKeyPath:(NSString *)keyPath
          options:(NSKeyValueObservingOptions)options
          context:(void *)context;
```

You supply the object that should be informed as `observer` and the key path for which you wish to be informed about changes. The `options` variable defines what you would like to have included when you are informed about the changes. For example, you can be told about the old value (before the change) and the new value (after the change). The `context` variable is a pointer to data that you would like sent with the rest of the information. You can use it for whatever you wish. I typically leave it `NULL`.

When a change occurs, the observer is sent the following message:

```
- (void)observeValueForKeyPath:(NSString *)keyPath
                      ofObject:(id)object
                        change:(NSDictionary *)change
                      context:(void *)context;
```

The observer is told which key path changed in which object. Here, `change` is a dictionary that, depending on the options you asked for when you registered as an observer, may contain the old value and/or the new value. Of course, it is sent the `context` pointer supplied when it was registered as an observer. I typically ignore `context`.

Undo for Edits

The first step is to register your document object to observe changes to its **Person** objects. Add the following methods to `MyDocument.m`:

```
- (void)startObservingPerson:(Person *)person
{
    [person addObserver:self
            forKeyPath:@"personName"
                options:NSKeyValueObservingOptionOld
                context:NULL];

    [person addObserver:self
            forKeyPath:@"expectedRaise"
```

```
                        options:NSKeyValueObservingOptionOld
                        context:NULL];
}

- (void)stopObservingPerson:(Person *)person
{
    [person removeObserver:self forKeyPath:@"personName"];
    [person removeObserver:self forKeyPath:@"expectedRaise"];
}
```

Call these methods every time a **Person** enters or leaves the document:

```
- (void)insertObject:(Person *)p inEmployeesAtIndex:(int)index
{
    // Add the inverse of this operation to the undo stack
    NSUndoManager *undo = [self undoManager];
    [[undo prepareWithInvocationTarget:self]
        removeObjectFromEmployeesAtIndex:index];
    if (![undo isUndoing]) {
        [undo setActionName:@"Insert Person"];
    }

    // Add the Person to the array
    [self startObservingPerson:p];
    [employees insertObject:p atIndex:index];
}

- (void)removeObjectFromEmployeesAtIndex:(int)index
{
    Person *p = [employees objectAtIndex:index];
    // Add the inverse of this operation to the undo stack
    NSUndoManager *undo = [self undoManager];
    [[undo prepareWithInvocationTarget:self] insertObject:p
                                      inEmployeesAtIndex:index];
    if (![undo isUndoing]) {
        [undo setActionName:@"Delete Person"];
    }
    [self stopObservingPerson:p];
    [employees removeObjectAtIndex:index];
}

- (void)setEmployees:(NSMutableArray *)a
{
    if (a == employees)
        return;

    for (Person *person in employees) {
        [self stopObservingPerson:person];
    }

    [a retain];
    [employees release];
    employees = a;
```

```
    for (Person *person in employees) {
        [self startObservingPerson:person];
    }
}
```

Now implement the method that does edits and is its own inverse:

```
- (void)changeKeyPath:(NSString *)keyPath
            ofObject:(id)obj
             toValue:(id)newValue
{
    // setValue:forKeyPath: will cause the key-value observing method
    // to be called, which takes care of the undo stuff
    [obj setValue:newValue forKeyPath:keyPath];
}
```

Implement the method that will be called whenever a **Person** object is edited, either by the user or by the **changeKeyPath:ofObject:toValue:** method. Note that it puts a call to **changeKeyPath:ofObject:toValue:** on the stack with the old value for the changed key.

```
- (void)observeValueForKeyPath:(NSString *)keyPath
                      ofObject:(id)object
                        change:(NSDictionary *)change
                       context:(void *)context
{
    NSUndoManager *undo = [self undoManager];
    id oldValue = [change objectForKey:NSKeyValueChangeOldKey];

    // NSNull objects are used to represent nil in a dictionary
    if (oldValue == [NSNull null]) {
        oldValue = nil;
    }
    NSLog(@"oldValue = %@", oldValue);
    [[undo prepareWithInvocationTarget:self] changeKeyPath:keyPath
                                                  ofObject:object
                                                   toValue:oldValue];
    [undo setActionName:@"Edit"];
}
```

That should do it. Once you build and run your application, undo and redo should work flawlessly.

Note that as you make changes to the document, a dot appears in the red close button in the window's title bar to indicate that changes have been made but have not been saved. In the next chapter, you will learn how to save them to a file.

Begin Editing on Insert

Your app is coming along nicely, but your users will complain, "Why do I have to double-click to start editing after an insert? It is obvious that I am going to immediately change the name of the new person. Can't you start the editing as part of the insert?"

Oddly, this is a little tricky to do. So, I'm going to give you the code snippet you need. First, MyDocument.h is going to need an action and two instance variables:

```
@interface MyDocument : NSDocument
{
    NSMutableArray *employees;
    IBOutlet NSTableView *tableView;
    IBOutlet NSArrayController *employeeController;
}
- (IBAction)createEmployee:(id)sender;
```

Save that file. (You must always save your .h file for its outlets and actions to show up in Interface Builder.) In Interface Builder, Control-drag from the Add New Employee button to the File's Owner (which is the instance of **MyDocument**). Set its action to **createEmployee:** (Figure 9.5).

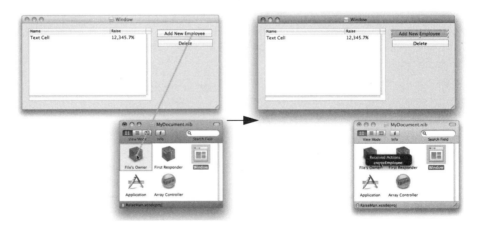

Figure 9.5   Set target/action of Add Button

Control-click on File's Owner, and drag to connect the tableView outlet to the table view and the employeeController outlet to the array controller (Figure 9.6).

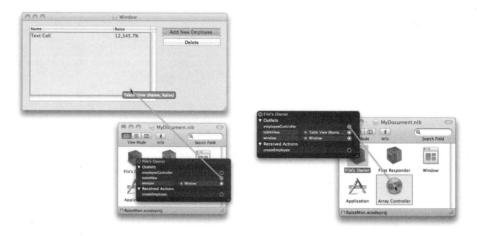

Figure 9.6   Set Outlets

In MyDocument.m, add the **createEmployee:** method:

```
- (IBAction)createEmployee:(id)sender
{
    NSWindow *w = [tableView window];

    // Try to end any editing that is taking place
    BOOL editingEnded = [w makeFirstResponder:w];
    if (!editingEnded) {
        NSLog(@"Unable to end editing");
        return;
    }
    NSUndoManager *undo = [self undoManager];

    // Has an edit occurred already in this event?
    if ([undo groupingLevel]) {
        // Close the last group
        [undo endUndoGrouping];
        // Open a new group
        [undo beginUndoGrouping];
    }
    // Create the object
    Person *p = [employeeController newObject];

    // Add it to the content array of 'employeeController'
    [employeeController addObject:p];
    [p release];
```

```
// Re-sort (in case the user has sorted a column)
[employeeController rearrangeObjects];

// Get the sorted array
NSArray *a = [employeeController arrangedObjects];

// Find the object just added
int row = [a indexOfObjectIdenticalTo:p];
NSLog(@"starting edit of %@ in row %d", p, row);

// Begin the edit in the first column
[tableView editColumn:0
                  row:row
            withEvent:nil
               select:YES];
}
```

I don't really expect you to understand every line of that code now, but browse through the method and try to get the gist. Build and run the application.

For the More Curious: Windows and the Undo Manager

A view can add edits to the undo manager. **NSTextView**, for example, can put onto the undo manager each edit that a person makes to the text. This can be enabled in Interface Builder (Figure 9.7).

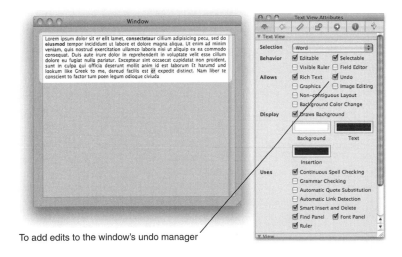

To add edits to the window's undo manager

Figure 9.7 NSTextView Inspector

How does the text view know which undo manager to use? First, it asks its delegate. **NSTextView** delegates can implement this method:

```
- (NSUndoManager *)undoManagerForTextView:(NSTextView *)tv;
```

Next, it asks its window. **NSWindow** has a method for this purpose:

```
- (NSUndoManager *)undoManager;
```

The window's delegate can supply an undo manager for the window by implementing the following method:

```
- (NSUndoManager *)windowWillReturnUndoManager:(NSWindow *)window;
```

The Undo/redo menu items reflect the state of the undo manager for the key window. (The key window is what most users call the *active window*. Cocoa developers call it *key* because it is the one that will get the keyboard events if the user types.)

Chapter 10

ARCHIVING

While an object-oriented program is running, a complex graph of objects is being created. It is often necessary to represent this graph of objects as a stream of bytes, a process called *archiving* (Figure 10.1). This stream of bytes can then be sent across a network connection or written into a file. For example, when you save a nib file, Interface Builder is archiving objects into a file. (Instead of *archiving*, a Java programmer would call this process *serialization*.)

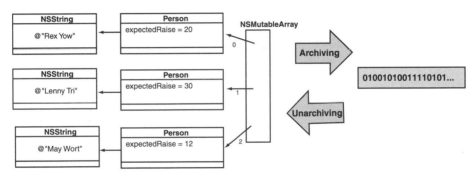

Figure 10.1   Archiving

When you need to recreate the graph of objects from the stream of bytes, you will *unarchive* it. For example, when your application starts up, it unarchives the objects from the nib file created by Interface Builder.

Although objects have both instance variables and methods, only the instance variables and the name of the class go into the archive. In other words, only data, not code, goes into the archive. As a result, if one application archives an object and another application unarchives the same object, both applications must have the code for the class linked in. In the nib file, for example, you have used such classes as **NSWindow** and **NSButton** from the AppKit framework. If you do not link it against the AppKit framework, your application will be unable to create the instances of **NSWindow** and **NSButton** that it finds in the archive.

There was once a shampoo ad that said, "I told two friends, and they told two friends, and they told two friends, and so on, and so on, and so on." The implication was that as long as you told your friends about the shampoo, everyone who matters would eventually wind up using the shampoo. Object archiving works in much the same way. You archive a root object, it archives the objects to which it is attached, they archive the objects to which they are attached, and so on, and so on, and so on. Eventually, every object that matters will be in the archive.

Archiving involves two steps. First, you need to teach your objects how to archive themselves. Second, you need to cause the archiving to occur.

The Objective-C language has a construct called a *protocol*, which is identical to the Java construct called an *interface*. That is, a protocol is a list of method declarations. When you create a class that implements a protocol, it promises to implement all the methods declared in the protocol.

NSCoder and NSCoding

One protocol is **NSCoding**. If your class implements **NSCoding**, it promises to implement the following methods:

- (id)**initWithCoder:**(NSCoder *)coder;

- (void)**encodeWithCoder:**(NSCoder *)coder;

An **NSCoder** is an abstraction of a stream of bytes. You can write your data to a coder or read your data from a coder. The **initWithCoder:** method in your object will read data from the coder and save that data to its instance variables. The **encodeWithCoder:** method in your object will read its instance variables and write those values to the coder. In this chapter, you will implement both methods in your **Person** class.

NSCoder is actually an *abstract class*. You won't ever create instances of an abstract class. Instead, an abstract class has some capabilities that are intended to be inherited by subclasses. You will create instances of the concrete subclasses. Namely, you will use **NSKeyedUnarchiver** to read objects from a stream of data, and you will use **NSKeyedArchiver** to write objects to the stream of data.

Encoding

NSCoder has many methods, but most programmers find themselves using only a few of them repeatedly. Here are the methods most commonly used when you are encoding data onto the coder:

```
- (void)encodeObject:(id)anObject forKey:(NSString *)aKey
```

This method writes anObject to the coder and associates it with the key aKey. This will cause anObject's **encodeWithCoder:** method to be called (and they told two friends, and they told two friends…).

For each of the common C primitive types (e.g., int and float), **NSCoder** has an encode method:

```
- (void)encodeBool:(BOOL)boolv forKey:(NSString *)key
```

```
- (void)encodeDouble:(double)realv forKey:(NSString *)key
```

```
- (void)encodeFloat:(float)realv forKey:(NSString *)key
```

```
- (void)encodeInt:(int)intv forKey:(NSString *)key
```

To add encoding to your **Person** class, add the following method to Person.m:

```
- (void)encodeWithCoder:(NSCoder *)coder
{
    [coder encodeObject:personName forKey:@"personName"];
    [coder encodeFloat:expectedRaise forKey:@"expectedRaise"];
}
```

If you looked at the documentation for **NSString**, you would see that it implements the **NSCoding** protocol. Thus, the personName knows how to encode itself.

All the commonly used AppKit and Foundation classes implement the **NSCoding** protocol, with the notable exception of **NSObject**. Because it inherits from **NSObject**, **Person** doesn't call [super encodeWithCoder:coder]. If **Person**'s superclass *had* implemented the **NSCoding** protocol, the method would have looked like this:

```
- (void)encodeWithCoder:(NSCoder *)coder
{
    [super encodeWithCoder:coder];
    [coder encodeObject:personName forKey:@"personName"];
    [coder encodeFloat:expectedRaise forKey:@"expectedRaise"];
}
```

The call to the superclass's **encodeWithCoder:** method would give the superclass a chance to write its variables onto the coder. Thus, each class in the hierarchy writes only its instance variables—and not its superclass's instance variables—onto the coder.

Decoding

When decoding data from the coder, you will use the analogous decoding methods:

- (id)**decodeObjectForKey:**(NSString *)aKey

- (BOOL)**decodeBoolForKey:**(NSString *)key

- (double)**decodeDoubleForKey:**(NSString *)key

- (float)**decodeFloatForKey:**(NSString *)key

- (int)**decodeIntForKey:**(NSString *)key

If, for some reason, the stream does not include the data for a key, you will get zero for the result. For example, if the object did not write out data for the key foo when the stream was first written, the coder will return 0.0 if it is later asked to decode a float for the key foo. If asked to decode an object for the key foo, the coder will return nil.

To add decoding to your **Person** class, add the following method to your Person.m file:

```
- (id)initWithCoder:(NSCoder *)coder
{
   [super init];
   personName = [[coder decodeObjectForKey:@"personName"] retain];
   expectedRaise = [coder decodeFloatForKey:@"expectedRaise"];
   return self;
}
```

Once again, you did not call the superclass's implementation of **initWithCoder:**, because **NSObject** doesn't have one. If **Person**'s superclass *had* implemented the **NSCoding** protocol, the method would have looked like this:

```
- (id)initWithCoder:(NSCoder *)coder
{
   [super initWithCoder:coder];
   personName = [[coder decodeObjectForKey:@"personName"] retain];
   expectedRaise = [coder decodeFloatForKey:@"expectedRaise"];
   return self;
}
```

You may now be saying, "Chapter 3 said that the designated initializer does all the work and calls the superclass's designated initializer. It said that all other initializers call the designated initializer. But **Person** has an **init** method, which is its designated initializer, and this new initializer doesn't call it." You are right: **initWithCoder:** is an exception to initializer rules.

You have now implemented the methods in the **NSCoding** protocol. To declare your **Person** class as implementing the **NSCoding** protocol, you will edit the Person.h file. Change the declaration of your class to look like this:

```
@interface Person : NSObject <NSCoding> {
```

Now try to compile the project. Fix any errors. If you like, you could run the application at this point. However, although you have taught **Person** objects to encode themselves, you haven't asked them to do so. Thus, you will see no change in the behavior of your application.

The Document Architecture

Applications that deal with multiple documents have a lot in common. All can create new documents, open existing documents, save or print open documents, and remind the user to save edited documents when he or she tries to close a window or quit the application. Apple supplies three classes—**NSDocumentController**, **NSDocument**, and **NSWindowController**—that take care of most of the details for you. Together, these three classes constitute the *document architecture*.

The purpose of the document architecture relates to the Model-View-Controller design pattern discussed in Chapter 8. In RaiseMan, your subclass of **NSDocument**—with the help of **NSArrayController**—acts as the controller, will have a pointer to the model objects, and will be responsible for the following duties:

- Saving the model data to a file
- Loading the model data from a file
- Displaying the model data in the views
- Taking user input from the views and updating the model

Info.plist and NSDocumentController

When it builds an application, Xcode includes a file called Info.plist. (Later in this chapter, you will change Info.plist.) When the application is launched, it reads from Info.plist, which tells it what type of files it works with. If it finds that it is a document-based application, it creates an instance of **NSDocumentController** (Figure 10.2). You will seldom have to deal with the document controller; it lurks in the background and takes care of a bunch of details for you. For example, when you choose the New or Save All menu item, the document controller

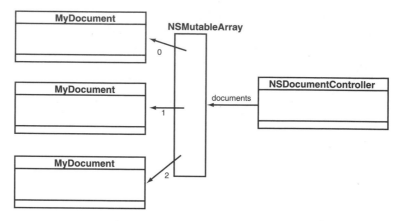

Figure 10.2   Document Controller

handles the request. If you need to send messages to the document controller, you could get to it like this:

```
NSDocumentController *dc;
dc = [NSDocumentController sharedDocumentController];
```

The document controller has an array of document objects—one for each open document.

NSDocument

The document objects are instances of a subclass of **NSDocument**. In your RaiseMan application, for example, the document objects are instances of **MyDocument**. For many applications, you can simply extend **NSDocument** to do what you want; you don't have to worry about **NSDocumentController** or **NSWindowController** at all.

Saving

The menu items Save, Save As..., Save All, and Close are all different, but all deal with the same problem: getting the model into a file or a file wrapper. (A file wrapper is a directory that looks like a file to the user.) To handle these menu items, your **NSDocument** subclass must implement one of three methods:

```
- (NSData *)dataOfType:(NSString *)aType
            error:(NSError *)e
```

Your document object supplies the model to go into the file as an **NSData** object. **NSData** is essentially a buffer of bytes. It is the easiest and most

popular way to implement saving in a document-based application. Return
nil if you are unable to create the data object, and the user will get an alert
sheet indicating that the save attempt failed. Note that you are passed the
type, which allows you to save the document in one of several possible
formats. For example, if you wrote a graphics program, you might allow
the user to save the image as a gif or a jpg file. When you are creating the
data object, aType indicates the format that the user has requested for saving
the document. If you are dealing with only one type of data, you may
simply ignore aType. To signal that you are unable to save the data, return
nil and create an **NSError** object that describes what went wrong.

```
- (NSFileWrapper *)fileWrapperOfType:(NSString *)aType
                               error:(NSError *)e
```

Your document object returns the model as an **NSFileWrapper** object. It
will be written to the filesystem in the location chosen by the user.

```
- (BOOL)writeToURL:(NSURL *)absoluteURL
            ofType:(NSString *)typeName
             error:(NSError **)outError;
```

Your document object is given the URL and the type and is responsible for
storing the data into the URL. (The URL is typically merely a file on the
filesystem.) Return YES if the save is successful and NO if the save fails. If
you return NO, you should create an **NSError** object that describes what
went wrong.

NSError can be a bit confusing. The idea is that if the method is, for some
reason, unable to do it's job, it creates an **NSError** and puts a pointer to
that error in the supplied address. For example, if I wanted to read an
NSData from a file, I would supply an address where the pointer to the
error would be placed:

```
NSError *e;
NSData *d = [NSData dataWithContentsOfFile:@"/tmp/x.txt"
                                  options:0
                                    error:&error];
// Did the read fail?
if (d == nil) {
     NSLog(@"Read failed: %@", [error localizedDescription];
}
```

Thus, **NSData** will either return a data object or create an error object.

In these save and load methods, you will be responsible for creating an
NSError if the methods fail.

Loading

The Open..., Open Recent, and Revert To Saved menu items, although different, all deal with the same basic problem: getting the model from a file or file wrapper. To handle these menu items, your **NSDocument** subclass must implement one of three methods:

```
- (BOOL)readFromData:(NSData *)data
              ofType:(NSString *)typeName
               error:(NSError **)outError
```

Your document is passed an **NSData** object that holds the contents of the file that the user is trying to open. Return YES if you successfully create a model from the data. If you return NO, the user will get an Alert panel that should explain why it was unable to parse the file. The contents of the Alert panel will be determined by the **NSError** object you give it.

```
- (BOOL)readFromFileWrapper:(NSFileWrapper *)fileWrapper
                     ofType:(NSString *)typeName
                      error:(NSError **)outError;
```

Your document reads the data from an **NSFileWrapper** object.

```
- (BOOL)readFromURL:(NSURL *)absoluteURL
             ofType:(NSString *)typeName
              error:(NSError **)outError;
```

Your document object is passed a URL (usually merely a path to a file on the filesystem). The document reads the data from the file.

After implementing one save method and one load method, your document will know how to read from and write to files. When opening a file, the document will read the document file before reading the nib file. As a consequence, you will not be able to send messages to the user interface objects immediately after loading the file (because they won't exist yet). To solve this problem, your document object is sent the following method after the nib file is read:

```
- (void)windowControllerDidLoadNib:(NSWindowController *)x;
```

In your **NSDocument** subclass, you will implement this method to update the user interface objects.

If the user chooses Revert To Saved from the menu, the model is loaded, but **windowControllerDidLoadNib:** is not called. You will, therefore, also have to update the user interface objects in the method that loads the data, just in case it was a revert operation. One common way to deal with this possibility is to check one of the outlets set in the nib file. If it is nil, the nib file has not been loaded, and there is no need to update the user interface.

NSWindowController

The final class that we might discuss in the document architecture would be **NSWindowController**, but you will not initially need to worry about it. Each window that a document opens will typically create an instance of **NSWindowController**. As most applications have only one window per document, the default behavior of the window controller is usually perfect. Nevertheless, you might want to create a custom subclass of **NSWindowController** in the following situations.

- You need to have more than one window on the same document. For example, in a CAD program, you might have a window of text that describes the solid and another window that shows a rendering of the solid.

- You want to put the user interface controller logic and model controller logic into separate classes.

- You want to create a window without a corresponding **NSDocument** object. You will do this in Chapter 12.

Saving and NSKeyedArchiver

Now that you have taught your object to encode and decode itself, you will use it to add saving and loading to your application. When it is time to save your people to a file, your **MyDocument** class will be asked to create an instance of **NSData**. Once your object has created and returned an **NSData** object, it will be automatically written to a file.

To create an **NSData** object, you will use the **NSKeyedArchiver** class. **NSKeyedArchiver** has the following class method:

```
+ (NSData *)archivedDataWithRootObject:(id)rootObject
```

This method archives the objects into the **NSData** object's buffer of bytes.

Once again, we return to the idea of "I told two friends, and they told two friends." When you encode an object, it will encode its objects, and they will encode their objects, and so on, and so on, and so on. What you will encode, then, is the employees array. It will encode the **Person** objects to which it has references. Because you implemented **encodeWithCoder:**, each **Person** object will, in turn, encode the personName string and the expectedRaise float.

To add saving capabilities to your application, edit the method **dataOfType:error:** in MyDocument.m so that it looks like this:

```
- (NSData *)dataOfType:(NSString *)aType
              error:(NSError **)outError
{
    // End editing
    [[tableView window] endEditingFor:nil];

    // Create an NSData object from the employees array
    return [NSKeyedArchiver archivedDataWithRootObject:employees];
}
```

Note that I ignored the error argument. There will be no errors.

Loading and NSKeyedUnarchiver

Now you will add the ability to load files to your application. Once again, **NSDocument** has taken care of most of the details for you.

To do the unarchiving, you will use **NSKeyedUnarchiver**, which has the following handy method:

```
+ (id)unarchiveObjectWithData:(NSData *)data
```

In your **MyDocument** class, edit your **readFromData:ofType:error:** method to look like this:

```
- (BOOL)readFromData:(NSData *)data
            ofType:(NSString *)typeName
             error:(NSError **)outError
{
    NSLog(@"About to read data of type %@", typeName);
    NSMutableArray *newArray = nil;
    @try {
        newArray = [NSKeyedUnarchiver unarchiveObjectWithData:data];
    }
    @catch (NSException *e) {
        if (outError) {
            NSDictionary *d = [NSDictionary
                dictionaryWithObject:@"The data is corrupted."
                              forKey:NSLocalizedFailureReasonErrorKey];
            *outError = [NSError errorWithDomain:NSOSStatusErrorDomain
                                            code:unimpErr
                                        userInfo:d];
        }
        return NO;
    }
```

```
    [self setEmployees:newArray];
    return YES;
}
```

You could update the user interface after the nib file is loaded, but **NSArray-Controller** will handle it for you; the **windowControllerDidLoadNib:** method doesn't need to do anything. Leave it here for now; you will add to it in Chapter 13:

```
- (void)windowControllerDidLoadNib:(NSWindowController *)aController
{
    [super windowControllerDidLoadNib:aController];

}
```

Note that your document is asked which nib file to load when a document is opened or created. This method also needs no changing:

```
- (NSString *)windowNibName
{
    return @"MyDocument";
}
```

The window is automatically marked as edited when you make an edit, because you have properly enabled the undo mechanism. When you register this document's changes with the undo manager for this document, it will automatically mark the document as edited.

At this point, your application can read and write to files. Compile your application and try it out. Everything should work correctly, but all your files will have the extension .????. You need to define an extension for your application in the Info.plist.

Setting the Extension and Icon for the File Type

RaiseMan files will have the extension .rsmn, and .rsmn files will have an icon. First, find an .icns file and copy it into your project. A fine icon is found at /Developer/Examples/AppKit/CompositeLab/BBall.icns. Drag it from the Finder into the Groups and Files view of Xcode. Drop it in the Resources group (Figure 10.3).

Figure 10.3   Drag Icon into Project

Xcode will bring up a sheet. Make sure that you check Copy items into destination group's folder (Figure 10.4). This will copy the icon file into your project directory.

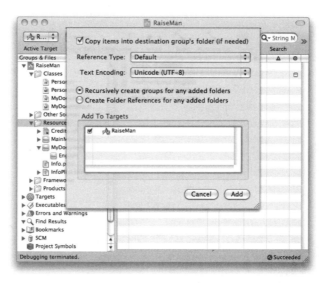

Figure 10.4   Make It a Copy

To set the document-type information, select the RaiseMan target in Xcode, and choose Get Info from the File menu. Under the Properties tab, set the identifier for your application to be com.bignerdranch.RaiseMan. Set the Icon File to be BBall. In the document-types table view, set the name to be RaiseMan Doc. Set the Extensions to be rsmn. Set the icon for the file type to be BBall. See Figure 10.5. The columns in the screenshot have been reordered so that you can see the important information.

Figure 10.5 Specify Icon and Document Types

Build and run your application. You should be able to save data to a file and read it in again. In Finder, the BBall.icns icon will be used as the icon for your .rsmn files.

An application is a directory containing the nib files, images, sounds, and executable code for the application. In Terminal, try the following:

```
> cd /Applications/TextEdit.app/Contents
> ls
```

You will see three interesting things:

1. The Info.plist file, which includes the information about the application, its file types, and associated icons. Finder uses this information.

2. The MacOS/ directory, which contains the executable code.

3. The Resources/ directory, which has the images, sounds, and nib files that the application uses. You will see localized resources for several different languages.

For the More Curious: Preventing Infinite Loops

The astute reader may be wondering: "If object A causes object B to be encoded, and object B causes object C to be encoded, and then object C causes object A to be encoded again, couldn't it just go around and around in an infinite loop?" It would, but **NSKeyedArchiver** was designed with this possibility in mind.

When an object is encoded, a unique token is also put onto the stream. Once archived, the object is added to the table of encoded objects under that token. When told to encode the same object again, **NSKeyedArchiver** simply puts a token in the stream.

When it decodes an object from the stream, **NSKeyedUnarchiver** puts both the object and its token in a table. If it finds a token with no associated data, the unarchiver knows to look up the object in the table instead of creating a new instance.

This idea led to the **NSCoder** method that often confuses developers when they read the documentation:

```
- (void)encodeConditionalObject:(id)anObject forKey:(NSString *)aKey
```

This method is used when object A has a pointer to object B, but object A doesn't really care whether B is archived. However, if *another* object *has* archived B, A would like the token for B put into the stream. If no other object has archived B, it will be treated like `nil`.

For example, if you were writing an **encodeWithCoder:** method for an **Engine** object (Figure 10.6), it might have an instance variable called `car` that is a pointer to the **Car** object that it is part of. If you are simply archiving the **Engine**, you wouldn't want the entire **Car** archived. But if you were archiving the entire **Car**, you would want the `car` pointer set. In this case, you would make the **Engine** object encode the `car` pointer conditionally.

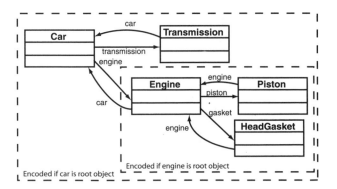

Figure 10.6   Conditional Encoding Example

For the More Curious: Creating a Protocol

Creating your own protocol is very simple. Here is a protocol with two methods. It would typically be in a file called Foo.h.

```
@protocol Foo
- (void)fido:(int)x;
- (float)rex;
@end
```

With Objective-C 2.0, **@optional** was added to the protocol grammar. Now you can indicate which methods in the protocol are required and which are optional:

```
@protocol Foo
- (void)fido:(int)x;
- (float)rex;
@optional
- (int)rover;
- (void)spot:(int)x;
@end
```

In this example, **fido:** and **rex** are required; **rover** and **spot:** are optional.

If you had a class that wanted to implement the **Foo** protocol and the **NSCoding** protocol, the class would look like this:

```
#import "Spunky.h"
#import "Foo.h"

@interface ZsaZsa:Spunky <Foo, NSCoding>
...etc...
@end
```

A class doesn't have to redeclare any method it inherits from its superclass, nor does it have to redeclare any of the methods from the protocols it implements. Thus, in our example, the interface file for the class **ZsaZsa** is not required to list any of the methods in **Spunky** or **Foo** or **NSCoding**.

For the More Curious: Document-Based Applications without Undo

The **NSUndoManager** for your application knows when unsaved edits have occurred. Also, the window is automatically marked as edited. But what if you've written an application and you are not registering your changes with the undo manager?

NSDocument keeps track of how many changes have been made. It has a method for this purpose:

```
- (void)updateChangeCount:(NSDocumentChangeType)change;
```

The NSDocumentChangeType can be one of the following: NSChangeDone, NSChangeUndone, or NSChangeCleared. NSChangeDone increments the change count, NSChangeUndone decrements the change count, and NSChangeCleared sets the change count to 0. The window is marked as dirty unless the change count is 0.

Universal Type Identifiers

One of the enduring problems in working with computers is embodied in the question: "What does this data represent?" On the Mac, this question gets asked in several places: when a file is opened from the Finder, when data is copied off the pasteboard, and when a file is indexed by Spotlight or viewed through Quicklook. Thus far, there have been several anwers: file extensions, creator codes, and MIME types.

Apple has decided that the long-term solution to the problem is universal type identifiers (UTIs). A UTI is a string that identifies the type of a file. UTIs are organized hierarchically.

Inside the Info.plist file for your application, you can define which UTIs your application can read and write—including new, custom UTIs. The Info.plist is an XML file that has a dictionary of key-value pairs. To export new UTIs, you will add a new key: UTExportedTypeDeclarations. For example, if you wanted to create a UTI for your RaiseMan documents, you could add the following to your Info.plist:

```
<key>UTExportedTypeDeclarations</key>
<array>
    <dict>
        <key>UTTypeIdentifier</key>
        <string>com.bignerdranch.raiseman-doc</string>
        <key>UTTypeDescription</key>
        <string>RaiseMan Document</string>
        <key>UTTypeConformsTo</key>
        <array>
            <string>public.data</string>
        </array>
        <key>UTTypeTagSpecification</key>
```

```
    <dict>
            <key>com.apple.ostype</key>
            <string>rsmn</string>
            <key>public.filename-extension</key>
            <array>
                    <string>rsmn</string>
            </array>
    </dict>
  </dict>
</array>
```

Then you can use the UTI in your properties inspector, as shown in Figure 10.7.

Figure 10.7   Setting the UTI

You can find the entire list of system-defined UTIs in Apple's documentation.

Chapter 11
BASIC CORE DATA

At this point, you've implemented an application that keeps track of an array of objects, takes care of undo, and handles saving and loading from a file. As you can imagine, there are an awful lot of applications like the one you just wrote.

Apple decided to make this type of application extremely easy to write:

- **NSArrayController** will hold on to an array of objects.

- Bindings will eliminate much of the glue code that would be necessary to keep the model objects in sync with the views.

- **NSManagedObjectContext** will observe the instance variables of your data objects, take care of undo for you, and take care of loading and saving the data.

So, the punchline is: Using Core Data and bindings, the RaiseMan application that you have written can be created with no code at all. In this section, you are going to write a simple Core Data application (not unlike RaiseMan) that has no code.

NSManagedObjectModel

In order to know how to save and load the data in your objects, the system needs to know something about that data. What are the names of the attributes of your object? What are their types? To supply this information, you will create a model. Xcode has an editor that will make it easy for you to describe your data-bearing objects. At runtime, this file will be read in, and an instance of **NSManagedObjectModel** will be created.

The model uses terminology that is a little different from what we are used to. Instead of *class*, the model uses the term *entity*. Instead of *instance variable*, the model uses the word *property*.

In the model are two kinds of properties: *attributes* and *relationships*. An attribute holds a simple data type, such as a string, a date, or a number. We will talk about relationships in a later chapter.

The RaiseMan application used an **NSDocument** subclass named **MyDocument**. In this application, you will have an **NSPersistentDocument** subclass called **MyDocument**. **NSPersistentDocument** automatically reads in the model and creates an **NSManagedObjectContext**. **NSPersistentDocument** will eliminate the need for many lines of code.

Start Xcode and create a new project of type Core Data Document-based Application. Name the project CarLot. Imagine that you own several used car lots. This application will enable you to keep track of the cars that you wish to sell. When it is done, it will look like Figure 11.1.

Figure 11.1   Completed Application

In the new project, under Models, open MyDocument.xcdatamodel. At the bottom of the Entity table view, click the + button to create a new entity. Name the entity Car.

With the **Car** entity selected, choose Add Attribute in the pop-up at the bottom of the Properties table view. Add six attributes and give them the following names and types:

Name	Type
condition	Int 16
datePurchased	Date
makeModel	String
onSpecial	Boolean
photo	Binary data
price	Decimal

Figure 11.2 shows what it looks like in the modeler.

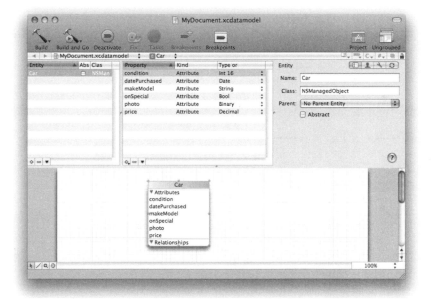

Figure 11.2   Completed Model

Although we could put lots of other things in the model, that is enough for this exercise.

Interface

Open MyDocument.nib. In the window, delete the text field Your document contents here. Drag an array controller into the doc window. The array controller will be using the document object's **NSManagedObjectContext** to fetch and store data. Use the Bindings Inspector to bind the array controller's managedObjectContext to the File's Owner's managedObjectContext (Figure 11.3).

Figure 11.3   Give the Array Controller a Managed Object Context

In the Attributes Inspector, set the array controller to fetch from the **Car** entity
(Figure 11.4). Also, turn on the Prepares Content option, so that the array
controller will fetch immediately after it is created. (The label under the objects
in the doc window can be set to anything you like. Here, I have set the label of
the array controller to Cars. Once you have several array controllers in a nib, the
labels will eliminate a lot of confusion.)

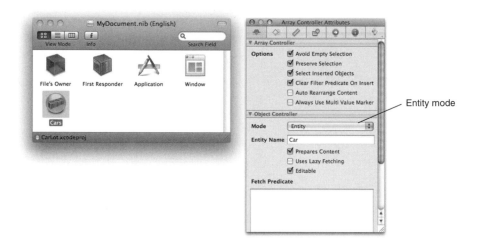

Figure 11.4   Inspect the Attributes of the Cars Array Controller

Create and Configure Views

Drag out a table view (from Cocoa->Views & Cells->Data Views). In the Attributes Inspector, give it three columns. Name the columns Make/Model, Price, and Special. Drop a number formatter (from Cocoa->Views & Cells -> Formatters) on the Price column. Select the formatter (represented by a little circle in the column), and configure it to show currency. Use the 10.4+ formatter, and set the style to Currency. Also, check the boxes Generate Decimal Numbers and Always Shows Decimal (Figure 11.5).

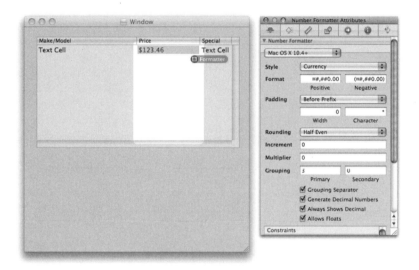

Figure 11.5   Configure Formatter

The third column will be populated by check boxes, so drop a check box cell (from Cocoa->Views & Cells->Cells) on the third column. Select the cell, and clear its title (Figure 11.6).

Below the table view, drop on the window an **NSDatePicker**, two buttons, an **NSImageView** (called Image Well in the Library), and an **NSLevelIndicator**. Put label text fields next to the date picker and the level indicator. The buttons should be labeled New and Delete.

The labels should be Date Purchased: and Condition:. In the Attributes Inspector of the **NSLevelIndicator**, set its min to 0 and its max to 5. Set its style to Rating mode (to get the stars). Also, make the level indicator editable. See Figure 11.7.

Figure 11.6   Drop Check Box Cell

Figure 11.7   Attributes of the NSLevelIndicator

Make the **NSImageView** editable by using the Attributes Inspector.

Select the date picker, the image view, the two labels, and the level indicator. Using the Layout -> Embed Objects In -> Box menu item, wrap them in a box (Figure 11.8).

Figure 11.8   Embed in a Box

Connections and Bindings

Now, you are going to do a bunch of bindings. I will walk you through it step by step; Figure 11.9 is a diagram of the bindings that you are going to create between your views and the array controller.

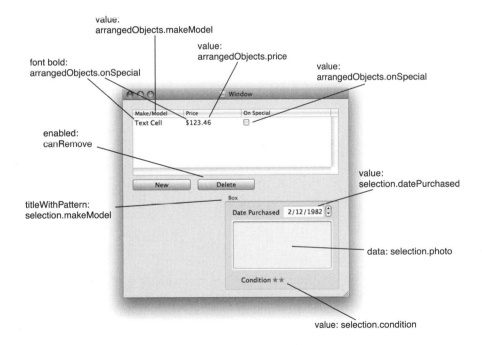

Figure 11.9   Summary of Bindings

A reminder: You will never bind to a scroll view, a table view, or a cell in this book. You will, however, bind to table view columns, which have cells and are inside table views, which are, in turn, inside scroll views.

Bind the `value` of each column (Cars is the **NSArrayController**):

Binding	Bind to	Controller Key	Key Path
value of Col 0	Cars	arrangedObjects	makeModel
value of Col 1	Cars	arrangedObjects	price
value of Col 2	Cars	arrangedObjects	onSpecial

Make the New button trigger the **add:** method of the array controller (Figure 11.10).

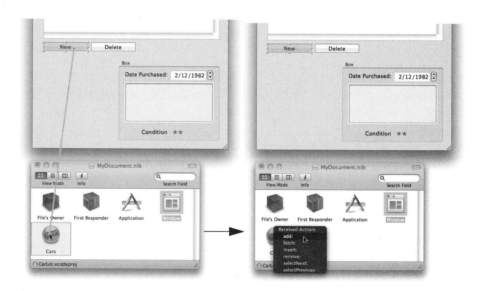

Figure 11.10 Set target/action of New Button

Make the Delete button trigger the **remove:** method of the array controller.

Bind the value of the controls to the selection of the array controller:

Binding	Bind to	Controller Key	Key Path
value of date picker	Cars	selection	datePurchased
enabled of Delete button	Cars	canRemove	
value of level indicator	Cars	selection	condition

Bind the Data (not Value) of the image view to Cars. Choose the controller key
selection and the keypath photo. Also, check the box that says Conditionally Sets
Editable (Figure 11.11)

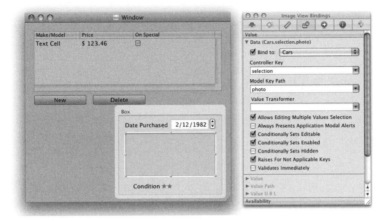

Figure 11.11   image View Binding

Bind the Title With Pattern of the box to Cars. Set the Controller Key to
selection. Set the Model Key Path to makeModel. Set the Display Pattern to
Details for %{title1}@. Set the No Selection Placeholder to <No selection>.
Set the Null Placeholder <no Make/Model>. See Figure 11.12.

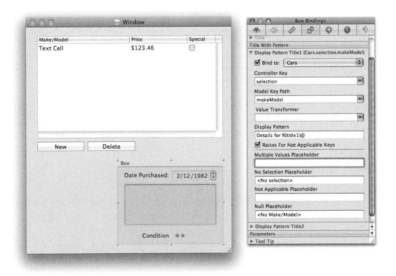

Figure 11.12   Box Binding

Let's also make the text of the first two columns appear in boldface if the car is on special. Bind the Font Bold binding to Cars's arrangedObjects onSpecial (Figure 11.13).

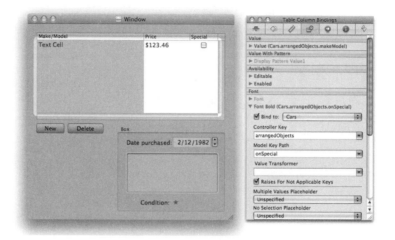

Figure 11.13   Specials Appear in Boldface

You are done. Build and run the application. Saving and loading should work. Undo should work. Magic, eh?

How Core Data Works

Although you have written no code, many objects will be created to make this work. Figure 11.14 is a diagram of some of them.

So, the **NSPersistentDocument** reads in the model you created and uses it to create an instance of **NSManagedObjectModel**. In our case, the managed object model has one **NSEntityDescription**, which describes our **Car** entity. That entity description has several instances of **NSAttributeDescription**.

Once it has the model, the persistent document creates an instance of **NSPersistentStoreCoordinator** and an instance of **NSManagedObjectContext**. The **NSManagedObjectContext** fetches instances of **NSManagedObject** from the object store. While those managed objects are in memory, the managed object context observes them. Whenever the data inside the managed objects is changed, the managed object context registers the undo action with the document's **NSUndoManager**. The managed object context also knows which objects have been changed and need to be saved.

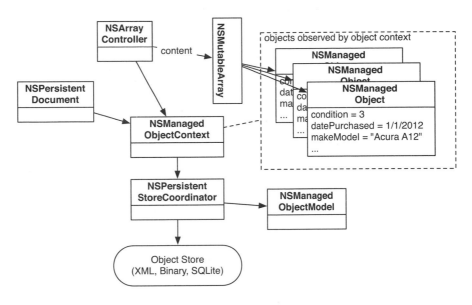

Figure 11.14   Overview of Core Data

So, among the classes in the Core Data framework, you will find yourself interacting with **NSManagedObjectContext** the most. To fetch objects, you will use **NSManagedObjectContext**. To save changes to your object graph, you will use **NSManagedObjectContext**.

Given that we are probably going to add cars to the system when we purchase them, it would be nice if the datePurchased attribute were set to the current date. One good way to do this is to subclass **NSArrayController** and override its **newObject** method.

In Xcode, create a new file of type Objective-C Class. Name the class **CarArrayController**. In CarArrayController.h, make it a subclass of **NSArrayController**:

```
#import <Cocoa/Cocoa.h>
@interface CarArrayController : NSArrayController
{}
@end
```

In CarArrayController.m, override **newObject**.

```
- (id)newObject
{
    id newObj = [super newObject];
    NSDate *now = [NSDate date];
```

```
        [newObj setValue:now forKey:@"datePurchased"];
        return newObj;
}
```

In Interface Builder, select the array controller. In the Identity Inspector, set the class to be **CarArrayController** (Figure 11.15).

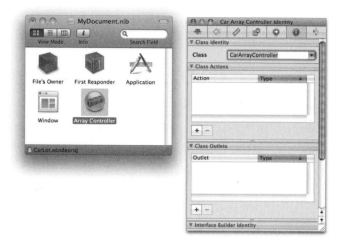

Figure 11.15   Change Class of Array Controller

Build and run your application. When new cars are added, their datePurchased attribute should be initialized to the current date.

Chapter 12

NIB FILES AND NSWINDOWCONTROLLER

In RaiseMan, you are already using two nib files: `MainMenu.nib` and `MyDocument.nib`. `MainMenu.nib` is automatically loaded by **NSApplication** when the application first launches. `MyDocument.nib` is automatically loaded each time an instance of `MyDocument` is created. In this section, you will learn how to load nib files by using **NSWindowController**.

Why would you want to load a nib file? Most commonly, your application will have several windows, such as a Find panel and a Preferences panel, that are used only occasionally. By postponing loading the nib until the window is needed, your application will launch more quickly. Furthermore, if the user never needs the window, your program will use less memory.

NSPanel

In this chapter, you will create a Preferences panel. The panel will be an instance of **NSPanel**, which is a subclass of **NSWindow**. There are not that many differences between a panel and a general window, but because a panel is meant to be auxiliary (as opposed to a document window), it acts a little differently.

- A panel can become the key window but without becoming the main window. For example, when bringing up a print panel, the user can type into it (it is key), but the document the user was looking at remains the main window (that is what will be printed). **NSApplication** has a `mainWindow` outlet and a `keyWindow` outlet. Both outlets point at the same window unless a panel is involved; panels do not typically become the main window.

- If it has a close button, you can close a panel by pressing the Escape key.

- Panels do not appear in the window list in the Window menu. After all, a user looking for a window is probably looking for a document, not a panel.

All windows have a Boolean variable called hidesOnDeactivate. If that variable is set to YES, the window will hide itself when the application is not active. Most document windows have this variable set to NO; most auxilary panels have it set to YES. This mechanism reduces screen clutter. You can set hidesOnDeactivate in the Attributes Inspector in Interface Builder.

Adding a Panel to the Application

The Preferences panel that you are going to add will not do anything except appear for now. In the next chapter, however, you will learn about user defaults and will make the Preferences panel do something.

The Preferences panel will be in its own nib file. You will create an **NSWindowController** subclass called **PreferenceController**. An instance of **PreferenceController** will act as the controller for the Preferences panel. When creating an auxiliary panel, it is important to remember that you may want to reuse it in the next application. Creating a class to act only as a controller and a nib that contains only the panel makes it easier to reuse the panel in another application. Hip programmers would say, "By making the application more modular, we can maximize reuse." The modularity also makes it easier to divide tasks among several programmers. A manager can say, "Rex, you are in charge of the Preferences panel. Only you may edit the nib file and the preference controller class."

The objects on the Preferences panel will be connected to the preference controller. In particular, the preference controller will be the target of a color well and the check box. The Preferences panel will appear when the user clicks on the Preferences... menu item. When running, it will look like Figure 12.1.

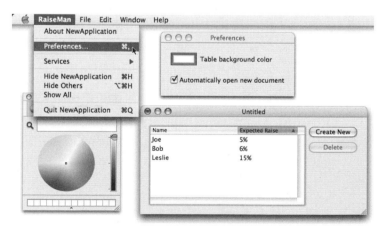

Figure 12.1   Completed Application

Figure 12.2 presents a diagram of the objects that you will create and the nib files in which they will reside.

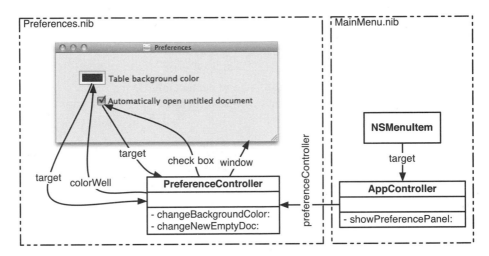

Figure 12.2   Object/Nib Diagram

Open the RaiseMan project and create a new Objective-C class named **AppController**. Edit AppController.h to look like this:

```
#import <Cocoa/Cocoa.h>
@class PreferenceController;

@interface AppController : NSObject {
    PreferenceController *preferenceController;
}
- (IBAction)showPreferencePanel:(id)sender;

@end
```

Note the Objective-C syntax:

```
@class PreferenceController;
```

This tells the compiler that there is a class **PreferenceController**. You can then make the following declaration without importing the header file for **PreferenceController**:

```
PreferenceController *preferenceController;
```

You could replace

```
@class PreferenceController;
```

with

```
#import "PreferenceController.h"
```

This statement would import the header, and the compiler would learn that **PreferenceController** was a class. Because the `import` command requires the compiler to parse more files, `@class` will often result in faster builds.

Note that you must always import the superclass's header file, because the compiler needs to know which instance variables are declared in the superclass. In this case, NSObject.h is imported by <Cocoa/Cocoa.h>.

Setting Up the Menu Item

Open MainMenu.nib. In Interface Builder, drag an **NSObject** from the Library (under Objects & Controllers). In the Identity Inspector, set its class to **AppController** (Figure 12.3).

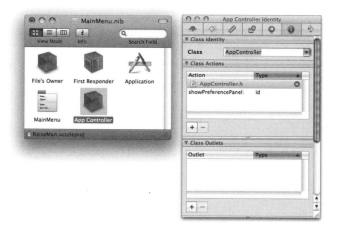

Figure 12.3   Create an Instance of AppController

Control-drag from the Preferences... menu item to the **AppController**. Make it the `target`, and set the `action` to **showPreferencePanel:** (Figure 12.4).

Close the nib file.

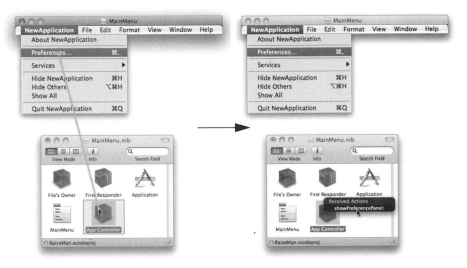

Figure 12.4 Set the target of the Menu Item

AppController.m

Now you need to write the code for **AppController**. Make the contents of
AppController.m look like this:

```
#import "AppController.h"
#import "PreferenceController.h"

@implementation AppController

- (IBAction)showPreferencePanel:(id)sender
{
    // Is preferenceController nil?
    if (!preferenceController) {
        preferenceController = [[PreferenceController alloc] init];
    }
    NSLog(@"showing %@", preferenceController);
    [preferenceController showWindow:self];
}
@end
```

This code creates the instance of **PreferenceController** only once. If it is non-
nil, the preferenceController variable simply sends the message
showWindow: to the existing instance.

Note also that we import PreferenceController.h into the .m file that uses it.

In Xcode, choose New File... from the File menu, and create a new **Objective-C NSWindowController subclass**. Name it **PreferenceController** (Figure 12.5).

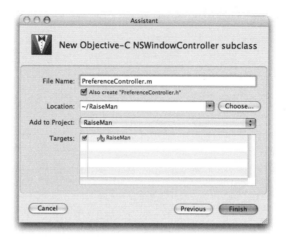

Figure 12.5   Create Files for PreferenceController

Edit PreferenceController.h to look like this:

```
#import <Cocoa/Cocoa.h>

@interface PreferenceController : NSWindowController {
    IBOutlet NSColorWell *colorWell;
    IBOutlet NSButton *checkbox;
}
- (IBAction)changeBackgroundColor:(id)sender;
- (IBAction)changeNewEmptyDoc:(id)sender;
@end
```

Preferences.nib

In Xcode, create a new, empty nib file named Preferences.nib (Figure 12.6).

You will see that there are XIB and NIB files. They serve the same function, but NIB files are a binary format and XIB files are XML. XIB files are compiled into NIB files when you build your app. Why would anyone use XIB files? They work nicely with version-control systems, such as Subversion.

Double-click Preferences.nib to open it in Interface Builder. Bring up the Identity Inspector, select File's Owner, and set its class to **PreferenceController** (Figure 12.7).

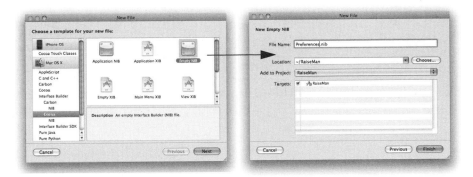

Figure 12.6   Create an Empty Nib

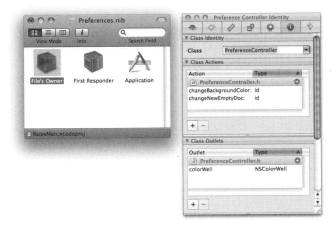

Figure 12.7   Set File's Owner to be a PreferenceController

File's Owner

When a nib file is loaded into an application that has been running for a while, the objects that already exist need to establish some connection to the objects read from the nib file. File's Owner provides this connection. File's Owner is a placeholder in a nib file for an object that will already exist when the nib file is loaded. An object loading a nib file will provide the owner object. The owner is put into the place that File's Owner represents. In your application, the owner will be the **PreferenceController** instance that was created by the **AppController**.

The use of File's Owner is confusing to many people. You will not instantiate **PreferenceController** in the nib file. Instead, you have just informed the nib

file that the owner (which will be provided when the nib file is loaded) is a
`PreferenceController`.

Lay Out the User Interface

Create a new panel by dragging a panel from the Library (under Application->
Windows) and dropping it anywhere on the screen (Figure 12.8).

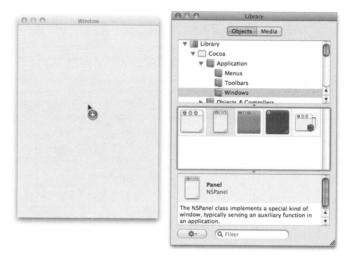

Figure 12.8   Create an Instance of NSPanel

Make the panel smaller, and drop a color well and a check box on it. Label them
as shown in Figure 12.9. (Check boxes have labels, but you will have to drag out
a text field to label the color well.)

Figure 12.9   Completed Interface

Set the target of the color well to be File's Owner (your `PreferenceController`),
and set the action to be **changeBackgroundColor:** (Figure 12.10).

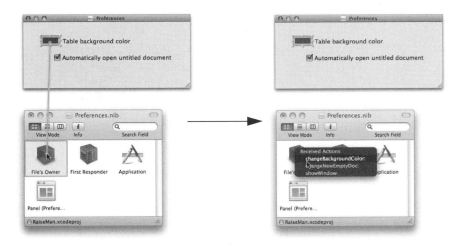

Figure 12.10   Set the target of the Color Well

Also, make your **PreferenceController** be the target of the check box, and set the action to be **changeNewEmptyDoc:**.

Control-click on File's Owner to bring up the connections window. Set the colorWell outlet of File's Owner to the color well object. Set the checkbox outlet of File's Owner to the check box object (Figure 12.11).

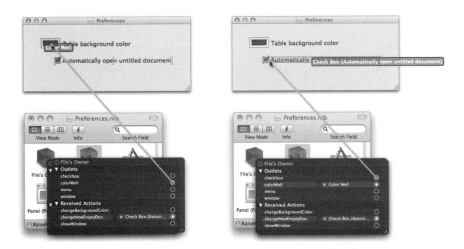

Figure 12.11   Set the colorWell and checkbox Outlets

Control-click File's Owner to get the connection window. Connect the window outlet to the panel (Figure 12.12).

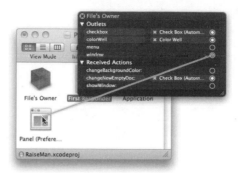

Figure 12.12   Set the window Outlet of File's Owner

Open the **Attributes Inspector** for the panel. Disable resizing. Change the title on the window to **Preferences**. Save the nib file. See Figure 12.13.

Figure 12.13   The New Window's Attributes

PreferenceController.m

In Xcode, edit the `PreferenceController.m` to look like this:

```
#import "PreferenceController.h"

@implementation PreferenceController

- (id)init
{
    if (![super initWithWindowNibName:@"Preferences"])
        return nil;
```

```
    return self;
}

- (void)windowDidLoad
{
    NSLog(@"Nib file is loaded");
}

- (IBAction)changeBackgroundColor:(id)sender
{
    NSColor *color = [colorWell color];
    NSLog(@"Color changed: %@", color);
}

- (IBAction)changeNewEmptyDoc:(id)sender
{
    int state = [checkbox state];
    NSLog(@"Checkbox changed %d", state);
}

@end
```

Note that you set the name of the nib file to be loaded in the **init** method. This nib file will be loaded automatically when it is needed. The instance of **PreferenceController** will be substituted for File's Owner in the nib file.

After the nib file is loaded, the **PreferenceController** will be sent **windowDidLoad**. It offers an opportunity (similar to **awakeFromNib** or **windowControllerDidLoadNib:**) for the controller object to initialize the user interface objects that have been read from the nib file.

When sent **showWindow:** for the first time, the **NSWindowController** automatically loads the nib file and moves the window on screen and to the front. The nib file is loaded only once. When the user closes the preferences panel, it is moved off screen but is not deallocated. The next time the user asks for the preferences panel, it is simply moved on screen.

The **changeBackgroundColor:** and **checkboxChanged:** methods are quite boring right now—they simply print out a message. In the next chapter, you will change them to update the user's defaults database.

Build and run the application. The new panel should appear, and altering the check box or color well should result in a message in the console (Figure 12.14).

The first time a user encounters a color well, it may seem confusing. If you click on the edge of the color well, the edge becomes highlighted, the color panel appears, and the well is in "active" mode.

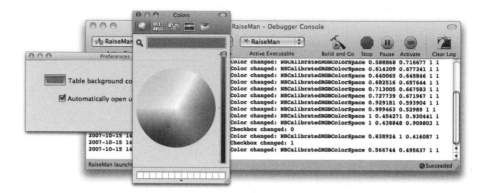

Figure 12.14   Completed Application

For the More Curious: NSBundle

A *bundle* is a directory of resources that may be used by an application. Resources include such things as images, sounds, compiled code, and nib files. (Users often use the word *plug-in* instead of *bundle*.) The class **NSBundle** is a very elegant way of dealing with bundles.

Your application is a bundle. In Finder, an application looks to the user like any other file, but it is in fact a directory filled with nib files, compiled code, and other resources. We call this directory the *main bundle* of the application.

Some resources in a bundle can be localized. For example, you could have two versions of foo.nib: one for English speakers and one for French speakers. The bundle would have two subdirectories: English.lproj and French.lproj. You would put an appropriate version of foo.nib in each. When your application asks the bundle to load foo.nib, the bundle will automatically load the French version of foo.nib if the user set the preferred language to French. We cover localization in Chapter 16.

To get the main bundle of an application, use the following code:

```
NSBundle *myBundle = [NSBundle mainBundle];
```

This is the most commonly used bundle. If you need to access resources in another directory, however, you could ask for the bundle at a certain path:

```
NSBundle *goodBundle;
goodBundle = [NSBundle bundleWithPath:@"~/.myApp/Good.bundle"];
```

Once you have an **NSBundle** object, you can ask it for its resources:

```
// Extension is optional
NSString *path = [goodBundle pathForImageResource:@"Mom"];
NSImage *momPhoto = [[NSImage alloc] initWithContentsOfFile:path];
```

A bundle may have a library of code. If you ask for a class from the bundle, the bundle will link in the library and search for a class by that name:

```
Class newClass = [goodBundle classNamed:@"Rover"];
id newInstance = [[newClass alloc] init];
```

If you do not know the name of any classes in the bundle, you can simply ask for the principal class:

```
Class aClass = [goodBundle principalClass];
id anInstance = [[aClass alloc] init];
```

As you see, **NSBundle** is handy in many ways. In this section, the **NSBundle** was responsible (behind the scenes) for loading the nib file. If you wanted to load a nib file without an **NSWindowController**, you could do it like this:

```
BOOL successful = [NSBundle loadNibNamed:@"About" owner:someObject];
```

Note that you would supply the object that will act as File's Owner.

Challenge

Create a nib file with a custom About panel. Add an outlet to **AppController** to point to the new window. Also add a **showAboutPanel:** method. Load the nib by using **NSBundle**, and make **AppController** File's Owner.

Chapter 13
USER DEFAULTS

Many applications have Preferences panels that allow the user to choose a preferred appearance or behavior. The user's choices go into the user defaults database in the user's home directory. Note that only the choices that vary from the factory defaults are saved in the user defaults database. If you go to ~/Library/Preferences, you can see your user defaults database. The files are in property list format; you can browse through them with Property List Editor.

The **NSUserDefaults** class allows your application to register the factory defaults, save the user's preferences, and read previously saved user preferences.

The color well that you dropped into the Preferences window in Chapter 12 will determine the background color of the table view. When the user changes his or her preference, your application will write the new preference to the user defaults database. When it creates a new document window, your application will read from the user defaults database. As a consequence, only windows created after the change will be affected (Figure 13.1).

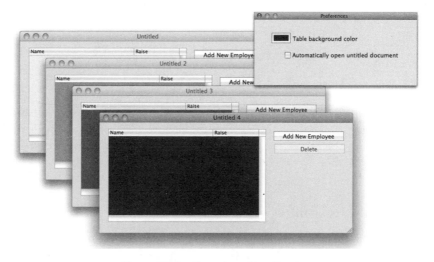

Figure 13.1 Completed Application

Have you noticed that every time you start the application, it brings up an untitled document? The Automatically open new document check box will allow the user to choose whether the untitled document should appear.

NSDictionary and NSMutableDictionary

Before you do anything with user defaults, you need to know about classes **NSDictionary** (Figure 13.2) and **NSMutableDictionary**. A dictionary is a collection of key-value pairs. The keys are strings, and the values are pointers to objects.

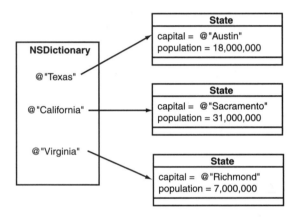

Figure 13.2   An Instance of NSDictionary

A string can be a key only once in a dictionary. When you want to know the value to which a key is bound, you will use the **objectForKey:** method:

```
anObject = [myDictionary objectForKey:@"foo"];
```

If the key is not in the dictionary, this method will return `nil`.

NSMutableDictionary is a subclass of **NSDictionary**. An instance of **NSDictionary** is created with all the keys and values it will ever have. You can query the object, but you cannot change it. **NSMutableDictionary**, on the other hand, allows you to add and remove keys and values.

NSDictionary

A dictionary is implemented as a hash table, so looking up keys is very fast. Here are a few of the most commonly used methods in the class **NSDictionary**:

- (NSArray *)**allKeys**

Returns a new array containing the keys in the dictionary.

- (unsigned)**count**

Returns the number of key-value pairs in the dictionary.

- (id)**objectForKey:**(NSString *)aKey

Returns the value associated with aKey or nil if no value is associated with aKey.

- (NSEnumerator *)**keyEnumerator**

Enumerators are also known as *iterators*, or *enumerations*. You can use them to step through all the members of a collection. The preceding method returns an enumerator that steps through all the keys in the dictionary. Here is how you would use one to list all the key-value pairs in a dictionary:

```
NSEnumerator *e = [myDict keyEnumerator];
for (NSString *s in e) {
    NSLog(@"key is %@, value is %@", s, [myDict objectForKey:s]);
}
```

- (NSEnumerator *)**objectEnumerator**

Returns an enumerator that steps through all the values in the dictionary. (The class **NSArray** also has a method, **objectEnumerator**, that returns an enumerator that steps through the elements in the array.)

NSMutableDictionary

+ (id)**dictionary**

Creates an empty dictionary.

- (void)**removeObjectForKey:**(NSString *)aKey

Removes aKey and its associated value object from the dictionary.

- (void)**setObject:**(id)anObject **forKey:**(NSString *)aKey

Adds an entry to the dictionary, consisting of aKey and its corresponding value object anObject. The value object receives a retain message before being added to the dictionary. If aKey already exists in the receiver, the receiver's previous value object for that key is sent a release message, and anObject takes its place.

NSUserDefaults

Every application comes with a set of defaults from the factory. When a user edits his or her defaults, only the differences between the user's wishes and the factory defaults are stored in the user's defaults database. Thus, every time the application starts up, you need to remind it of the factory defaults. This operation is called *registering defaults*.

After registering, you will use the user defaults object to determine how the user wants the app to behave. This process is called *reading and using the defaults*. The data from the user's defaults database will be read automatically from the filesystem.

You will also create a Preferences panel that will allow the user to set the defaults. The changes to the defaults object will be written automatically to the filesystem. This process is known as *setting the defaults* (Figure 13.3).

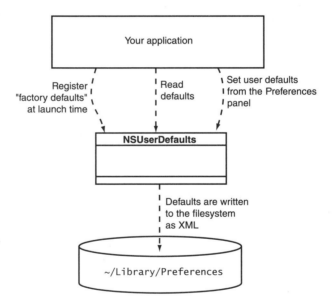

Figure 13.3   NSUserDefaults and the Filesystem

Here are some commonly used methods that are implemented in **NSUserDefaults**:

+ (NSUserDefaults *)**standardUserDefaults**

Returns the shared defaults object.

```
- (void)registerDefaults:(NSDictionary *)dictionary
```
Registers the factory defaults for the application.

```
- (void)setBool:(BOOL)value    forKey:(NSString *)defaultName
- (void)setFloat:(float)value forKey:(NSString *)defaultName
- (void)setInteger:(int)value forKey:(NSString *)defaultName
- (void)setObject:(id)value    forKey:(NSString *)defaultName
```
Methods for changing and saving a user's wishes.

```
- (BOOL)boolForKey:(NSString *)defaultName
- (float)floatForKey:(NSString *)defaultName
- (int)integerForKey:(NSString *)defaultName
- (id)objectForKey:(NSString *)defaultName
```
Methods for reading the defaults. If the user hasn't changed them, the factory defaults are returned.

```
- (void)removeObjectForKey:(NSString *)defaultName
```
Removes the user's preference, so that the application will return to using the factory defaults.

Precedence of Different Types of Defaults

So far, we have talked about two levels of precedence: What the user writes to his or her defaults database overrides the factory defaults. In fact, several more levels of precedence exist. These levels of default settings are known as *domains*. Here are the domains used by an application, from highest to lowest priority:

- *Arguments:* Passed on the command line. Most people start their applications by double-clicking on an icon instead of by working from the command line, so this feature is seldom used in a production app.

- *Application:* What comes from the user's defaults database.

- *Global:* What the user has set for his or her entire system.

- *Language:* What is set based on the user's preferred language.

- *Registered defaults:* The factory defaults for the app.

Setting the Identifier for the Application

What is the property list file in ~/Library/Preferences created for this application called? By default, it uses the identifier of the application that created it. You set this identifier in Chapter 10 to be com.bignerdranch.RaiseMan, so the filename will be com.bignerdranch.RaiseMan.plist.

Creating Keys for the Names of the Defaults

You will be registering, reading, and setting defaults in several classes in your application. To make sure that you always use the same name, you should declare those strings in a single file and then simply #import that file into any file in which you use the names.

There are several ways to do this. For example, you could use the C preprocessor's #define command, but most Cocoa programmers use global variables for this purpose. Add the following lines to your PreferenceController.h file after the #import statement:

```
extern NSString * const BNRTableBgColorKey;
extern NSString * const BNREmptyDocKey;
```

Now define these variables in PreferenceController.m. Put them after the #import lines but before @implementation :

```
NSString * const BNRTableBgColorKey = @"TableBackgroundColor";
NSString * const BNREmptyDocKey = @"EmptyDocumentFlag";
```

Why would you declare global variables that simply contain a constant string? After all, you could simply remember what the string was and type it in whenever you need it. The problem is that you might misspell the string. If the string is surrounded by quotes, the compiler will accept the misspelled string. In contrast, if you misspell the name of a global variable, the compiler will catch your error.

To keep the global variables from conflicting with another company's global variables, you have prefixed them with BNR (for Big Nerd Ranch). Global variables from Cocoa are prefixed with NS. These prefixes are important only when you start using classes and frameworks developed by third parties. (Note that class names are also global. You might prefer to prefix all your class names with BNR to keep them from conflicting with anyone else's classes.)

Registering Defaults

Each class is sent the message **initialize** before any other message. To ensure that your defaults are registered early, you will override **initialize** in AppController.m:

```
+ (void)initialize
{
    // Create a dictionary
    NSMutableDictionary *defaultValues = [NSMutableDictionary dictionary];

    // Archive the color object
    NSData *colorAsData = [NSKeyedArchiver archivedDataWithRootObject:
                                                [NSColor yellowColor]];

    // Put defaults in the dictionary
    [defaultValues setObject:colorAsData forKey:BNRTableBgColorKey];
    [defaultValues setObject:[NSNumber numberWithBool:YES]
                    forKey:BNREmptyDocKey];

    // Register the dictionary of defaults
    [[NSUserDefaults standardUserDefaults]
                                    registerDefaults: defaultValues];
    NSLog(@"registered defaults: %@", defaultValues);
}
```

Because this is a class method, its declaration is prefixed with +.

Note that we had to store the color as a data object. **NSColor** objects do not know how to write themselves out as property list, so we pack them into a data object that does. The *property list* classes—**NSString**, **NSArray**, **NSDictionary**, **NSCalendarDate**, **NSData**, and **NSNumber**—do know how to write themselves out as property lists. A property list comprises any combination of these classes. For example, a dictionary containing arrays of dates is a property list.

Letting the User Edit the Defaults

Next, you will alter the **PreferenceController** class so that the Preferences panel will cause the defaults database to get updated. Declare the following methods in PreferenceController.h:

```
- (NSColor *)tableBgColor;
- (BOOL)emptyDoc;
```

Make your PreferenceController.m file look like this:

```
#import "PreferenceController.h"

NSString * const BNRTableBgColorKey = @"TableBackgroundColor";
NSString * const BNREmptyDocKey = @"EmptyDocumentFlag";

@implementation PreferenceController

- (id)init
{
    if (![super initWithWindowNibName:@"Preferences"])
        return nil;

    return self;
}

- (NSColor *)tableBgColor
{
    NSUserDefaults *defaults = [NSUserDefaults standardUserDefaults];
    NSData *colorAsData = [defaults objectForKey:BNRTableBgColorKey];
    return [NSKeyedUnarchiver unarchiveObjectWithData:colorAsData];
}

- (BOOL)emptyDoc
{
    NSUserDefaults *defaults = [NSUserDefaults standardUserDefaults];
    return [defaults boolForKey:BNREmptyDocKey];
}

- (void)windowDidLoad
{
    [colorWell setColor:[self tableBgColor]];
    [checkbox setState:[self emptyDoc]];
}

- (IBAction)changeBackgroundColor:(id)sender
{
    NSColor *color = [colorWell color];
    NSData *colorAsData =
                [NSKeyedArchiver archivedDataWithRootObject:color];
    NSUserDefaults *defaults = [NSUserDefaults standardUserDefaults];
    [defaults setObject:colorAsData forKey:BNRTableBgColorKey];
}

- (IBAction)changeNewEmptyDoc:(id)sender
{
    int state = [checkbox state];
    NSUserDefaults *defaults = [NSUserDefaults standardUserDefaults];
    [defaults setBool:state forKey:BNREmptyDocKey];
}

@end
```

In the **windowDidLoad** method, you are reading the defaults and making the color well and check box reflect the current settings. In **changeBackgroundColor:** and **changeNewEmptyDoc:**, you are updating the defaults database.

You should now be able to build and run your application. It will read and write to the defaults database, so the Preferences panel will display the last color you chose and indicate whether the check box was on or off. You have not, however, done anything with this information yet, so the untitled document will continue to appear, and the background of the table view will continue to be white.

Using the Defaults

Now you are going to use the defaults. First, you will make your **AppController** become a delegate of the **NSApplication** object and suppress the creation of an untitled document, depending on the user defaults. Then, in **MyDocument**, you will set the background color of the table view from the user defaults.

Suppressing the Creation of Untitled Documents

As before, there are two steps to creating a delegate: implementing the delegate method and setting the **delegate** outlet to point to the object (Figure 13.4).

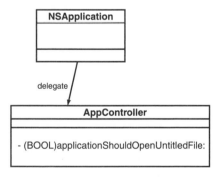

Figure 13.4   The delegate Suppresses Creation of Untitled Documents

Before automatically creating a new untitled document, the **NSApplication** object will send the message **applicationShouldOpenUntitledFile:** to its delegate. In AppController.m, add the following method:

```
- (BOOL)applicationShouldOpenUntitledFile:(NSApplication *)sender
{
    NSLog(@"applicationShouldOpenUntitledFile:");
```

```
    return [[NSUserDefaults standardUserDefaults]
                            boolForKey:BNREmptyDocKey];
}
```

To make your **AppController** the delegate of the **NSApplication** object, open
the MainMenu.nib file, and Control-click File's Owner—which represents the
NSApplication object—to bring up its connection window. Drag from delegate
to your **AppController** (Figure 13.5).

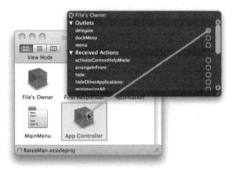

Figure 13.5   Select the delegate Outlet

Setting the Background Color on the Table View

After the nib file for a new document window has been successfully unarchived,
your **MyDocument** object is sent the message **windowControllerDidLoadNib:**. At
that moment, you can update the background color of the table view.

You should already have this method in MyDocument.m; simply edit it to look like
this:

```
- (void)windowControllerDidLoadNib:(NSWindowController *)aController
{
    [super windowControllerDidLoadNib:aController];
    NSUserDefaults *defaults = [NSUserDefaults standardUserDefaults];
    NSData *colorAsData;
    colorAsData = [defaults objectForKey:BNRTableBgColorKey];

    [tableView setBackgroundColor:
            [NSKeyedUnarchiver unarchiveObjectWithData:colorAsData]];
}
```

Also, make sure that you import PreferenceController.h at the beginning of
MyDocument.m so that you can use the global variables that are declared there.

Build and run your application.

For the More Curious: NSUserDefaultsController

Sometimes, you will want to bind to a value from the **NSUserDefaults** object. An **NSUserDefaultsController** class makes this possible. All the nibs in your application will use a single shared instance of **NSUserDefaultsController**.

For example, if you wanted to use bindings, instead of target/action, to deal with the check box on the Preferences panel, you would bind it to the shared **NSUserDefaultsController**'s value.EmptyDocumentFlag (Figure 13.6).

Figure 13.6   Binding to the NSUserDefaultsController

For the More Curious: Reading and Writing Defaults from the Command Line

The user defaults database is found in ~/Library/Preferences/. To edit it from the command line, you use a tool called *defaults*. For example, to see your defaults for Xcode, you can bring up the Terminal and enter the following command:

```
defaults read com.apple.Xcode
```

You should see all your defaults for Xcode. The first few lines of mine look like this:

```
{
    DocViewerHasSetPrefs = YES;
    NSNavBrowserPreferedColumnContentWidth = 155;
    NSNavLastCurrentDirectoryForOpen = "~/RaiseMan";
    NSNavLastRootDirectoryForOpen = "~";
```

```
NSNavPanelExpandedSizeForOpenMode = "{518, 400}";
NSNavPanelFileListModeForOpenMode = 1;
```

You can also write to the defaults database. To set Xcode's default directory in the **NSOpenPanel** to the /Users directory, you could enter this:

```
defaults write com.apple.Xcode NSNavLastRootDirectoryForOpen /Users
```

Try this:

```
defaults read com.bignerdranch.RaiseMan
```

To see your global defaults, enter this:

```
defaults read NSGlobalDomain
```

Challenge

Add to the Preferences panel a button that will remove all the user's defaults. Label the button Reset Preferences. Don't forget to update the Preferences window to reflect the new defaults.

Chapter 14

USING NOTIFICATIONS

A user may have several RaiseMan documents open when he or she decides that it is too hard to read them with a purple background. The user opens the Preferences panel, changes the background color, but then is disappointed to find that the color of the existing windows doesn't change. When the user sends you an e-mail about this problem, you reply, "The defaults are read only when the document window is created. Just save the document, close it, and open it again." In response, the user sends you a mean e-mail. It would be better to update all the existing windows. But how many are there? Will you have to keep a list of all open documents?

What Notifications Are

The task is much easier than that. Every running application has an instance of **NSNotificationCenter**, which functions much like a bulletin board. Objects register as interested in certain notifications ("Please write me if anyone finds a lost dog"); we call the registered object an *observer*. Other objects can then post notifications to the center ("I have found a lost dog"). That notification is subsequently forwarded to all objects that are registered as interested. We call the object that posted the notification a *poster*.

Lots of standard Cocoa classes post notifications: Windows send notifications that they have changed size. When the selection of a table view changes, the table view sends a notification. The notifications sent by standard Cocoa objects are listed in the online documentation.

In our example, you will register all your **MyDocument** objects as observers. Your preference controller will post a notification when the user chooses a new color. When sent the notification, the **MyDocument** objects will change the background color.

Before the **MyDocument** object is deallocated, you must remove it from the notification center's list of observers. Typically, this is done in the **dealloc** method.

What Notifications Are Not

When programmers first hear about the notification center, they sometimes think that it is a form of interprocess communications. They think, "I will create an observer in one application and post notifications from an object in another." This scheme doesn't work, however: A notification center allows objects in an application to send notifications to other objects *in that same application*. Notifications do not travel between applications.

NSNotification and NSNotificationCenter

Notification objects are very simple. A notification is like an envelope into which the poster will place information for the observers. A notification has two important instance variables: name and object. Nearly always, object is a pointer to the object that posted the notification. (It is analogous to a return address.)

Thus, the notification also has two interesting methods:

- (NSString *)**name**
- (id)**object**

The **NSNotificationCenter** is the brains of the operation. It allows you to register observer objects, post notifications, and unregister observers.

Here are some commonly used methods implemented by **NSNotificationCenter**:

+ (NSNotificationCenter *)**defaultCenter**

Returns the notification center.

- (void)**addObserver:**(id)anObserver
        selector:(SEL)aSelector
            name:(NSString *)notificationName
          object:(id)anObject

Registers anObserver to receive notifications with the name notificationName and containing anObject (Figure 14.1). When a notification of the name notificationName containing the object anObject is posted, anObserver is sent an aSelector message with this notification as the argument.

- ▪ If notificationName is nil, the notification center sends the observer all notifications with an object matching anObject.

An object registers to receive notifications named "SomeNotificationName"...

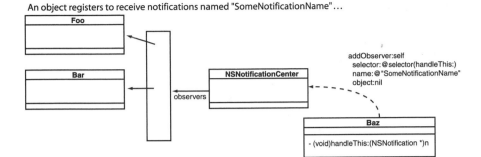

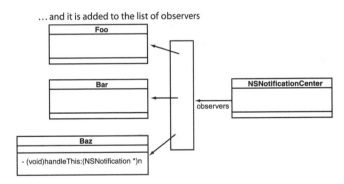

Figure 14.1   Registering for Notifications

- If anObject is nil, the notification center sends the observer all notifications with the name notificationName.

The observer is *not* retained by the notification center. Note that the method takes a selector.

```
- (void)postNotification:(NSNotification *)notification
```
Posts a notification to the notification center (Figure 14.2).

```
- (void)postNotificationName:(NSString *)aName
                      object:(id)anObject
```
Creates and posts a notification.

```
- (void)removeObserver:(id)observer
```
Removes observer from the list of observers.

An object posts a notification named "SomeNotificationName" ...

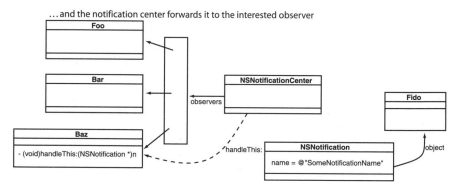

Figure 14.2   Posting a Notification

Posting a Notification

Posting a notification is the easiest step, so you will start there. When it receives a **changeBackgroundColor:** message, your **PreferenceController** object will post a notification with the new color.

You are going to name the notification @"BNRColorChanged", but you are going to create a global variable for the constant. (Experienced programmers put a prefix on the notification so that it doesn't conflict with other notifications that may be flying around the application.) Open PreferenceController.h and add the declaration with the other string constants:

```
extern NSString * const BNRColorChangedNotification;
```

In PreferenceController.m, define the constant:

```
NSString * const BNRColorChangedNotification = @"BNRColorChanged";
```

Make your **changeBackgroundColor:** method in PreferenceController.m look like this:

```
- (IBAction)changeBackgroundColor:(id)sender
{
    NSColor *color = [colorWell color];
    NSData *colorAsData =
                [NSKeyedArchiver archivedDataWithRootObject:color];
    [[NSUserDefaults standardUserDefaults] setObject:colorAsData
                                        forKey:BNRTableBgColorKey];

    NSNotificationCenter *nc = [NSNotificationCenter defaultCenter];
    NSLog(@"Sending notification");
    [nc postNotificationName:BNRColorChangedNotification object:self];
}
```

Registering as an Observer

To register as an observer, you must supply several things: the object that is the observer, the names of the notifications in which it is interested, and the message that you want sent when an interesting notification arrives. You can also specify that you are interested only in notifications with a certain object attached to them. (Remember that this is often the object that posted the notification. Thus, when you specify that you want resize notifications with a certain window attached, you are saying that you are interested only in the resizing of that particular window.)

Edit your **MyDocument** class's **init** method as follows:

```
- (id)init
{
    if (![super init])
        return nil;

    employees = [[NSMutableArray alloc] init];

    NSNotificationCenter *nc = [NSNotificationCenter defaultCenter];
    [nc addObserver:self
            selector:@selector(handleColorChange:)
                name:BNRColorChangedNotification
             object:nil];
    NSLog(@"Registered with notification center");
    return self;
}
```

In the **dealloc** method, remove the instance of **MyDocument** from the notification center:

```
- (void)dealloc
{
    [self setEmployees:nil];
    NSNotificationCenter *nc = [NSNotificationCenter defaultCenter];
    [nc removeObserver:self];
    [super dealloc];
}
```

Handling the Notification When It Arrives

When the notification arrives, the method **handleColorChange:** is called. For now, simply log its arrival. Add this method to your MyDocument.m file:

```
- (void)handleColorChange:(NSNotification *)note
{
    NSLog(@"Received notification: %@", note);
}
```

Build and run the application. Note that the notifications are sent and received when the color is edited in the Preferences panel.

The userInfo Dictionary

If you wanted to include more than just the poster with the notification, you would use the user info dictionary. Every notification has a variable called userInfo that can be attached to an **NSDictionary** filled with other information that you want to pass to the observers. In this case, we want to add the color to the userInfo dictionary. **MyDocument** will use the color when the notification arrives. In PreferenceController.m, add a userInfo dictionary to the notification:

```
- (IBAction)changeBackgroundColor:(id)sender
{
    NSColor *color = [sender color];
    NSData *colorAsData;
    colorAsData = [NSKeyedArchiver archivedDataWithRootObject:color];
    [[NSUserDefaults standardUserDefaults] setObject:colorAsData
                                    forKey:BNRTableBgColorKey];

    NSNotificationCenter *nc = [NSNotificationCenter defaultCenter];
    NSLog(@"Sending notification");
```

```
    NSDictionary *d = [NSDictionary dictionaryWithObject:color
                                              forKey:@"color"];
    [nc postNotificationName:BNRColorChangedNotification
                      object:self
                    userInfo:d];
}
```

In MyDocument.m, read the color out of the userInfo dictionary:

```
- (void)handleColorChange:(NSNotification *)note
{
    NSLog(@"Received notification: %@", note);
    NSColor *color = [[note userInfo] objectForKey:@"color"];
    [tableView setBackgroundColor:color];
}
```

Open several windows and change the preferred background color. Note that they all of them receive the notification and change color immediately.

For the More Curious: Delegates and Notifications

An object that has made itself the delegate of a standard Cocoa object is probably interested in receiving notifications from that object as well. For example, if you have implemented a delegate to handle the **windowShouldClose:** delegate method for a window, that same object is likely to be interested in the NSWindowDidResizeNotification from that same window.

If a standard Cocoa object has a delegate and posts notifications, it is automatically registered as an observer for the methods the object implements. If you are implementing such a delegate, how would you know what to call the method?

The naming convention is simple: Start with the name of the notification. Remove NS from the beginning, and make the first letter lowercase. Remove Notification from the end. Add a colon. For example, to be notified that the window has posted an NSWindowDidResizeNotification, the delegate would implement the following method:

```
- (void)windowDidResize:(NSNotification *)aNotification
```

This method will be called automatically after the window resizes. You can also find this method listed in the documentation and header files for the class **NSWindow.**

Challenge

Make your application beep when it gives up its active status. **NSApplication** posts an NSApplicationDidResignActiveNotification notification. Your **AppController** is a delegate of **NSApplication**. **NSBeep()** will cause a system beep.

Chapter 15

Using Alert Panels

Occasionally, you will want to warn the user about something by means of an Alert panel. Alert panels are easy to create. Most things in Cocoa are object oriented, but showing a modal Alert panel is typically done with a C function: **NSRunAlertPanel()**. Here is the declaration:

```
int NSRunAlertPanel(NSString *title, NSString *msg,
        NSString *defaultButton, NSString *alternateButton,
        NSString *otherButton, ...);
```

The code

```
int choice = NSRunAlertPanel(@"Fido", @"Rover",
                             @"Rex", @"Spot", @"Fluffy");
```

would result in the Alert panel shown in Figure 15.1.

Figure 15.1 Example Alert Panel

Note that the icon on the panel will be the icon for the responsible application. The second and third buttons are optional. To prevent a button from appearing, replace its label with nil.

The **NSRunAlertPanel()** function returns an int that indicates which button the user clicked. There are global variables for these constants: NSAlertDefaultReturn, NSAlertAlternateReturn, and NSAlertOtherReturn.

Note that **NSRunAlertPanel()** takes a variable number of arguments. The second string may include `printf`-like tokens. Values supplied after the `otherButton` label will be substituted in. Thus, the code

```
int choice = NSRunAlertPanel(@"Fido", @"Rover is %d",
                             @"Rex", @"Spot", nil, 8);
```

would result in the Alert panel shown in Figure 15.2.

Figure 15.2   Another Example Alert Panel

Alert panels run *modally*; that is, other windows in the application don't receive events until the Alert panel has been dismissed.

Alerts can also be run as a *sheet*. A sheet is a window that drops down in front of another window. Until the sheet is dismissed, no keyboard or mouse events will be dispatched to the obscured window.

Make the User Confirm the Deletion

If the user clicks the Delete button, an Alert panel should appear as a sheet before the records are deleted (Figure 15.3).

To enable this behavior, open MyDocument.nib, select the table view, and open the Inspector. Allow the user to make multiple selections (Figure 15.4).

You now want the Delete button to send to **MyDocument** a message that will ask the user to confirm the deletion. If the user confirms this choice, **MyDocument** will send the **removeEmployee:** message to the array controller to remove the selected **Person** objects.

In Xcode, open the MyDocument.h file and add the method that will be triggered by the Delete button:

```
- (IBAction)removeEmployee:(id)sender;
```

Figure 15.3   Completed Application

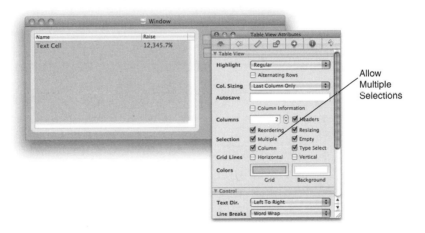

Figure 15.4   Inspect TableView

In MyDocument.m, implement the **removeEmployee:** method, which will start the Alert panel as a sheet:

```
- (IBAction)removeEmployee:(id)sender
{
    NSArray *selectedPeople = [employeeController selectedObjects];
    NSAlert *alert = [NSAlert alertWithMessageText:@"Delete?"
            defaultButton:@"Delete"
        alternateButton:@"Cancel"
            otherButton:nil
informativeTextWithFormat:@"Do you really want to delete %d people?",
                        [selectedPeople count]];
```

```
    NSLog(@"Starting alert sheet");
    [alert beginSheetModalForWindow:[tableView window]
                     modalDelegate:self
                   didEndSelector:@selector(alertEnded:code:context:)
                      contextInfo:NULL];
}
```

This method will start the sheet. When the user clicks a button, the document object will get sent the **alertEnded:code:context:** message:

```
- (void)alertEnded:(NSAlert *)alert
             code:(int)choice
          context:(void *)v
{
    NSLog(@"Alert sheet ended");
    // If the user chose "Delete", tell the array controller to
    // delete the people
    if (choice == NSAlertDefaultReturn) {
        // The argument to remove: is ignored
        // The array controller will delete the selected objects
        [employeeController remove:nil];
    }
}
```

Open MyDocument.nib. Control-drag from the Delete button to the File's Owner icon to make File's Owner be the new target. Set the action to **removeEmployee:** (Figure 15.15.

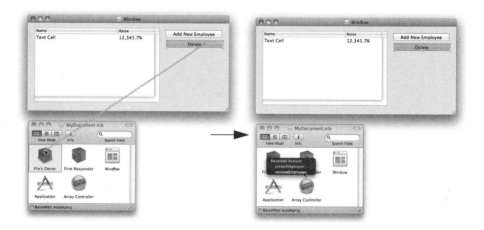

Figure 15.5   Change target/action of Delete Button

Build and run your application.

Challenge

Add to the Alert sheet another button that says Keep, but no raise. Instead of deleting the employees, this button will simply set the raises of the selected employees to zero.

Chapter 16
LOCALIZATION

If the application you create is useful, you will want to share it with all the people of the world. Unfortunately, we don't all speak the same language. Suppose that you wish to make your RaiseMan application available to French speakers. We would say, "You are going to *localize* RaiseMan for French speakers."

If you are creating an application for the world, you should plan on localizing it for at least the following languages: English, French, Spanish, German, Dutch, Italian, and Japanese. Clearly, you do not want to have to rewrite the entire app for each language. In fact, our goal is to ensure that you don't have to rewrite any Objective-C code for each language. That way, all the nations of the world can use a single executable in peace and harmony.

Instead of creating multiple executables, you will localize resources and create string tables. Inside your project directory, an `English.lproj` directory holds all the resources for English speakers: nib files, images, and sounds. To localize the app for French speakers, you will add a `French.lproj` directory. The nibs, images, and sounds in this directory will be appropriate for French speakers. At runtime, the app will automatically use the version of the resource appropriate to the user's language preference.

What about the places in your application where you use the language programmatically? For example, in `MyDocument.m`, you have the following line of code:

```
NSAlert *alert = [NSAlert alertWithMessageText:@"Delete
            defaultButton:@"Delete"
        alternateButton:@"Cancel"
            otherButton:nil
 informativeTextWithFormat:@"Do you really want to delete %d people?",
                            [selectedPeople count]];
```

That Alert sheet is not going to bring about world peace. For each language, you will have a table of strings. You will ask **NSBundle** to look up the string, and it will automatically use the version appropriate to the user's language preference (Figure 16.1).

Figure 16.1 Completed Application

Localizing a Nib File

In Xcode, select—but do not open—MyDocument.nib, and bring up the Info panel. Click the Add Localization button (Figure 16.2).

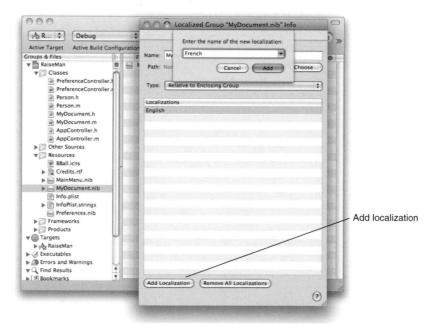

Figure 16.2 Create a French Version of MyDocument.nib

You will be prompted for a locale. Choose French.

If you look in Finder, you will see that a copy of English.lproj/MyDocument.nib has been created in French.lproj. You will francophize this copy. In Xcode, under the Resources group, you will have two versions of MyDocument.nib: English and French, as shown in Figure 16.3. Double-click on the French version to open it in Interface Builder.

Figure 16.3 Completed Application

Make your window look like Figure 16.4.

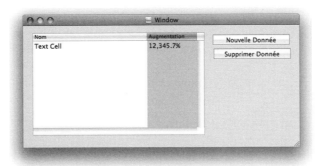

Figure 16.4 Completed Interface

To type in characters with accents, you will need to use the Option key. For example, to type é, type the e, while holding down the Option key, and then type e again. (In the International page of System Preferences, you can add the Keyboard Viewer to your input menu. If you are using a lot of unusual characters, the Keyboard Viewer can help you learn which key combinations create which characters.)

At this point, you have created a localized resource. Note that if you make a lot of changes to your program, you may need to update both nib files (the French version and the English version). For this reason, it is a good idea to wait until the application is completed and tested before localizing it.

Build your app. Before running it, bring up the International page of the System Preferences application. Set Français as your preferred language. Now run your application. Note that the French version of the nib is used automatically.

Also, note that the document architecture takes care of some localization for you. For example, if you try to close an unsaved document, you will be asked in French whether you want to save the changes.

String Tables

For each language, you can create several string tables. A string table is a file with the extension `.strings`. For example, if you had a Find panel, you might create a `Find.strings` file for each language. This file would have the phrases used by the Find panel, such as None found.

The string table is simply a collection of key-value pairs. The key and the value are strings surrounded by quotes, and the pair is terminated with a semicolon:

```
"Key1" = "Value1";
"Key2" = "Value2";
```

To find a value for a given key, you use **NSBundle**:

```
NSBundle *main = [NSBundle mainBundle];
NSString *aString = [main localizedStringForKey:@"Key1"
                                          value:@"DefaultValue1"
                                          table:@"Find"];
```

This would search for the value for "Key1" in the Find.strings file. If it is not found in the user's preferred language, the second-favorite language is searched, and so on. If the key is not found in any of the user's languages, "DefaultValue1" is returned. If you do not supply the name of the table, Localizable is used. Most simple applications have just one string table—Localizable.strings— for each language.

Creating String Tables

To create a Localizable.strings file for English speakers, choose the New File... menu item in Xcode. Create an empty file, and name it Localizable.strings. Save it in the English.lproj directory (Figure 16.5).

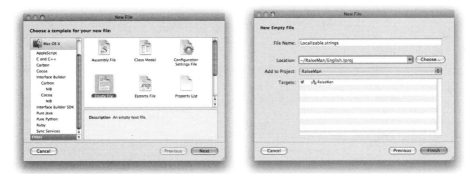

Figure 16.5   Create an English String Table

Edit the new file to have the following text:

```
"DELETE" = "Delete";
"SURE_DELETE" = "Do you really want to delete %d people?";
"CANCEL" = "Cancel";
```

Save it. (Don't forget the semicolons!)

Now create a localized version of that file for French. Select the Localizable.strings file in Xcode, bring up the Info panel, and create a localized variant (Figure 16.6).

Figure 16.6   Create a French String Table

Edit the file to look like this:

```
"DELETE" = "Supprimer";
"SURE_DELETE" =
     "Etes-vous sûr de vouloir effacer ces %d personnes ?";
"CANCEL" = "Annuler";
```

(To create the u with the circumflex, type i while holding down the Option key, and then type u. To type é, type e while holding down the Option key, and then type e again.)

When saving a file with unusual characters, you should use the Unicode (UTF-8) file encoding. In the Info panel for French.lproj/Localizable.strings, set the file encoding to UTF-8. When you are presented with a panel asking whether you wish to convert the file to UTF-8, click the Convert button (Figure 16.7).

Save the file.

Figure 16.7   Change the File Encoding

Using the String Table

In an app with only one string table, you would probably do this:

```
NSString *deleteString;
deleteString = [[NSBundle mainBundle]
                    localizedStringForKey:@"DELETE"
                                    value:@"Delete?"
                                    table:nil];
```

Fortunately, there is a macro defined in NSBundle.h for this purpose:

```
#define NSLocalizedString(key, comment)
        [[NSBundle mainBundle] localizedStringForKey:(key)
                                               value:@""
                                               table:nil]
```

(Note that the comment is completely ignored by this macro. It is, however, used by a tool called *genstrings*, which scans through your code for calls to the macro **NSLocalizedString** and creates a skeleton string table. This string table includes the comment.)

In MyDocument.m, find the place where you run the Alert panel. Replace that line with this one:

```
NSAlert *alert = [NSAlert
    alertWithMessageText:NSLocalizedString(@"DELETE", @"Delete")
           defaultButton:NSLocalizedString(@"DELETE", @"Delete")
         alternateButton:NSLocalizedString(@"CANCEL", @"Cancel")
             otherButton:nil
informativeTextWithFormat:NSLocalizedString(@"SURE_DELETE",
                      @"Do you really want to delete %d people?"),
                      [selectedPeople count]];
```

Build the app. Change your preferred language back to French in System Preferences, and run the app again. When you delete a row from the table, you should get an Alert panel in French.

For the More Curious: ibtool

Clearly, as you develop and localize many applications, you will develop a set of common translations. It would be handy to have an automated way to get the translated strings into a nib file. This is one of several uses for ibtool.

The ibtool command, which is run from the terminal, can list the classes or objects in a nib file and can also dump the localizable strings into a plist. Here is how you would dump the localizable strings from the English.lproj/MyDocument.nib file into a file named Doc.strings:

```
> cd RaiseMan/English.lproj
> ibtool --generate-stringsfile Doc.strings MyDocument.nib
```

The resulting Doc.strings file would have a bunch of entries something like this:

```
/* Class="NSTableColumn";headerCell.title="Name";ObjectID="100026"; */
"100026.headerCell.title" = "Name";
```

To create a Spanish dictionary for this nib file, you could edit the file to have Spanish entries:

```
/* Class="NSTableColumn";headerCell.title="Name";ObjectID="100026"; */
"100026.headerCell.title" = "Nombre";
```

To substitute the strings in a nib file with their Spanish equivalents from this dictionary, you could create a new nib file like this:

```
> mkdir ../Spanish.lproj
> ibtool --strings-file Doc.strings
        --write ../Spanish.lproj/MyDocument.nib MyDocument.nib
```

To learn more about `ibtool`, use Unix's `man` command:

```
> man ibtool
```

For the More Curious: Explicit Ordering of Tokens in Format Strings

As text is moved from language to language, the words change, as does their order. For example, in one language, the words may be laid out like this: "Ted wants a scooter." In another, the order might be "A scooter is what Ted wants." Suppose that you try to localize the format string to be used like this:

```
NSString * theFormat = NSLocalizedString(@"WANTS", @"%@ wants a %@");
x = [NSString stringWithFormat:theFormat, @"Ted", @"Scooter"];
```

For the first language, the following will work fine:

```
"WANTS" = "%@ wants a %@";
```

For the second language, you would need to explicitly indicate the index of the token you want to insert. This is done with a number and the dollar sign:

```
"WANTS" = "A %2$@ is what %1$@ wants".
```

Chapter 17
CUSTOM VIEWS

All visible objects in an application are either windows or views. In this chapter, you will create a subclass of **NSView**. From time to time, you may need to create a custom view to do custom drawing or event handling. Even if you do not plan to do custom drawing or event handling, you will learn a lot about how Cocoa works by learning how to create a new view class.

Windows are instances of the class **NSWindow**. Each window has a collection of views, each of which is responsible for a rectangle of the window. The view draws inside that rectangle and handles mouse events that occur there. A view may also handle keyboard events. You have worked with several subclasses of **NSView** already: **NSButton**, **NSTextField**, **NSTableView**, and **NSColorWell** are all views. (Note that a window is not a subclass of **NSView**.)

The View Hierarchy

Views are arranged in a hierarchy (Figure 17.1). The window has a content view that completely fills its interior. The content view usually has several subviews, each of which may have subviews of its own. Every view knows its superview, its subviews, and the window it lives on.

Here are the relevant methods from **NSView**:

```
- (NSView *)superview;
- (NSArray *)subviews;
- (NSWindow *)window;
```

Any view can have subviews, but most don't. The following five views commonly have subviews:

1. The content view of a window.

2. **NSBox**. The contents of a box are its subviews.

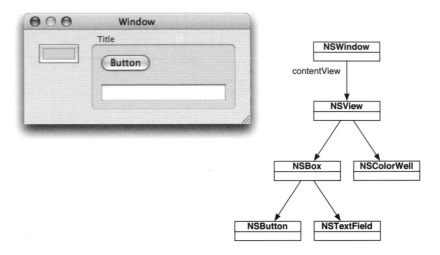

Figure 17.1   Views Hierarchy

3. **NSScrollView.** A view that appears in a scroll view is a subview of the scroll view. The scroll bars are also subviews of the scroll view.

4. **NSSplitView.** Each view in a split view is a subview (Figure 17.2).

Figure 17.2   A Scroll View in a Split View

5. **NSTabView.** As the user chooses different tabs, different subviews are swapped in and out (Figure 17.3).

Figure 17.3   A Tab View

Getting a View to Draw Itself

In this section, you will create a very simple view that will appear and paint itself green. It will look like Figure 17.4.

Figure 17.4   Completed Application

Create a new project of type Cocoa Application. Name the project ImageFun.

Using the File->New File menu item, create an Objective-C NSView subclass, and name it **StretchView**.

Create an Instance of a View Subclass

Open MainMenu.nib. Create an instance of your class by dragging out a CustomView placeholder from the Library (under Views & Cells -> Layout View) and dropping it on the window (Figure 17.5).

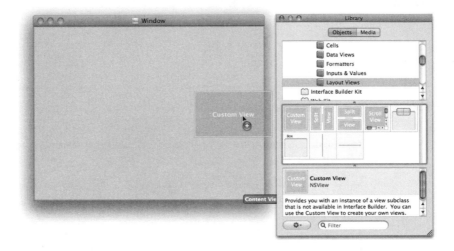

Figure 17.5   Drop a View on the Window

Resize the view to fill most of the window. Open the Info panel, and set the class of the view to be **StretchView** (Figure 17.6).

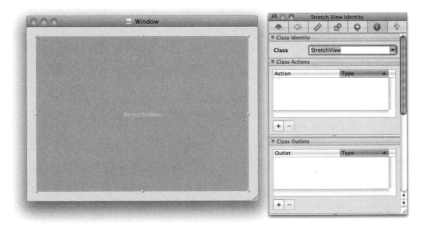

Figure 17.6   Set the Class of the View to StretchView

Size Inspector

Your **StretchView** object is a subview of the window's content view. This point raises an interesting question: What happens to the view when the superview resizes? A page in the Info panel allows you to specify that behavior. Open the Size Info panel, and set it as shown in Figure 17.7. Now it will grow and shrink as necessary to keep the distance from its edges to the edges of its superview constant.

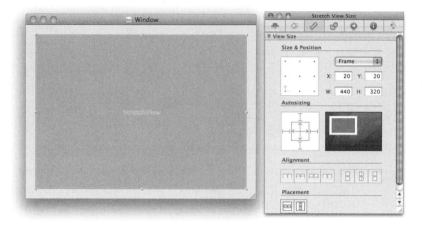

Figure 17.7   Make the View Resize with the Window

If you wanted the view to stay the same height, you could let the distance between the bottom of the view and the bottom of the superview grow and shrink. You could also let the distance between the right edge of the view and the right edge of the window grow and shrink. In this exercise, you do not want this behavior. But if you did want the view to stick to the upper-left corner of the window, the Inspector would look like Figure 17.8.

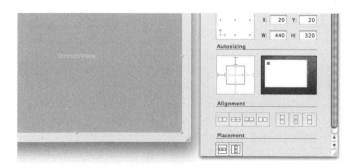

Figure 17.8   Not This!

Figure 17.9 is a complete diagram of what the Size Inspector means.

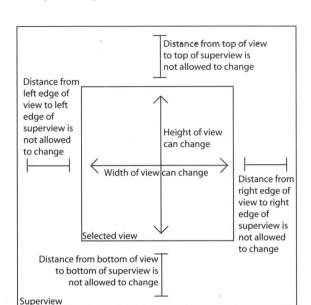

Figure 17.9   What the Red Lines in the Size Inspector Mean

Save and close the nib file.

drawRect:

When a view needs to draw itself, it is sent the message **drawRect:** with the rectangle that needs to be drawn or redrawn. The method is called automatically—you never need to call it directly. Instead, if you know that a view needs redrawing, you send the view the **setNeedsDisplay:** message:

```
[myView setNeedsDisplay:YES];
```

This message informs myView that it is "dirty." After the event has been handled, the view will be redrawn.

Before calling **drawRect:**, the system *locks focus* on the view. Each view has its own graphics context, which includes the view's coordinate system, its current color, its current font, and the clipping rectangle. When the focus is locked on a view, the view's graphics context is active. When the focus is unlocked, the graphics context is no longer active. Whenever you issue drawing commands, they will be executed in the current graphics context.

You can use **NSBezierPath** to draw lines, circles, curves, and rectangles. You can use **NSImage** to create composite images on the view. In this example, you will fill the entire view with a green rectangle.

Open StretchView.m and add the following code to the **drawRect:** method:

```
- (void)drawRect:(NSRect)rect
{
    NSRect bounds = [self bounds];
    [[NSColor greenColor] set];
    [NSBezierPath fillRect:bounds];
}
```

As shown in Figure 17.10, NSRect is a struct with two members: origin, which is an NSPoint, and size, which is an NSSize.

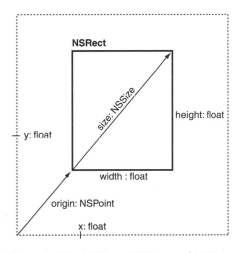

Figure 17.10   NSRect, NSSize, and NSPoint

NSSize is a struct with two members: width and height (both floats).

NSPoint is a struct with two members: x and y (both floats).

For performance reasons, structs are used in a few places instead of Objective-C classes. For completeness, here is the list of all the Cocoa structs that you are likely to use: NSSize, NSPoint, NSRect, NSRange, NSDecimal, and NSAffineTransformStruct. NSRange is used to define subranges. NSDecimal describes numbers with very specific precision and rounding behavior. NSAffineTransformStruct describes linear transformations of graphics.

Note that your view knows its location as an NSRect called bounds. In this method, you fetched the bounds rectangle, set the current color to green, and filled the entire bounds rectangle with the current color.

The NSRect that is passed as an argument to the view is the region that is "dirty" and needs redrawing. It may be less than the entire view. If you are doing very time-consuming drawing, redrawing only the dirty rectangle may speed up your application considerably.

Note that **setNeedsDisplay:** will trigger the entire visible region of the view to be redrawn. If you wanted to be more precise about which part of the view needs redrawing, you would use **setNeedsDisplayInRect:** instead:

```
NSRect dirtyRect;
dirtyRect = NSMakeRect(0, 0, 50, 50);
[myView setNeedsDisplayInRect:dirtyRect];
```

Build and run your app. Try resizing the window.

Drawing with NSBezierPath

If you want to draw lines, ovals, curves, or polygons, you can use **NSBezierPath**. In this chapter, you have already used the **NSBezierPath**'s **fillRect:** class method to color your view. In this section, you will use **NSBezierPath** to draw lines connecting random points (Figure 17.11).

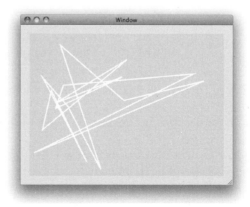

Figure 17.11 Completed Application

The first thing you will need is an instance variable to hold the instance of **NSBezierPath**. You will also create an instance method that returns a random point in the view. Open StretchView.h and make it look like this:

```
#import <Cocoa/Cocoa.h>

@interface StretchView : NSView
{
    NSBezierPath *path;
}
- (NSPoint)randomPoint;

@end
```

In StretchView.m, you will override **initWithFrame:**. As the designated initializer for **NSView, initWithFrame:** will be called automatically when an instance of your view is created. In your version of **initWithFrame:**, you will create the path object and fill it with lines to random points. Make StretchView.m look like this:

```
#import "StretchView.h"

@implementation StretchView

- (id)initWithFrame:(NSRect)rect
{
    if (![super initWithFrame:rect])
        return nil;

    // Seed the random number generator
    srandom(time(NULL));

    // Create a path object
    path = [[NSBezierPath alloc] init];
    [path setLineWidth:3.0];
    NSPoint p = [self randomPoint];
    [path moveToPoint:p];
    int i;
    for (i = 0; i < 15; i++) {
        p = [self randomPoint];
        [path lineToPoint:p];
    }
    [path closePath];
    return self;
}
- (void)dealloc
{
    [path release];
    [super dealloc];
}
```

```
// randomPoint returns a random point inside the view
- (NSPoint)randomPoint
{
    NSPoint result;
    NSRect r = [self bounds];
    result.x = r.origin.x + random() % (int)r.size.width;
    result.y = r.origin.y + random() % (int)r.size.height;
    return result;
}

- (void)drawRect:(NSRect)rect
{
    NSRect bounds = [self bounds];

    // Fill the view with green
    [[NSColor greenColor] set];
    [NSBezierPath fillRect: bounds];

    // Draw the path in white
    [[NSColor whiteColor] set];
    [path stroke];
}

@end
```

Build and run your app. Pretty, eh?

Okay, now try replacing [path stroke] with [path fill]. Build and run it.

NSScrollView

In the art world, a larger work is typically more expensive than a smaller one of equal quality. Your beautiful view is lovely, but it would be more valuable if it were larger. How can it be larger yet still fit inside that tiny window? You are going to put it in a scroll view (Figure 17.12).

A scroll view has three parts: the document view, the content view, and the scroll bars. In this example, your view will become the document view and will be displayed in the content view, which is an instance of **NSClipView**.

Although this change looks tricky, it is very simple to make. In fact, it requires no code at all. Open MainMenu.nib in Interface Builder. Select the view, and choose Embed Objects in Scroll View from the Layout menu (Figure 17.13).

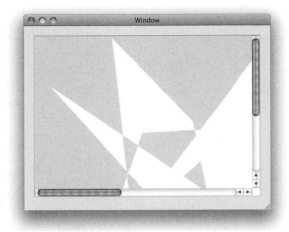

Figure 17.12   Completed Application

Figure 17.13   Embed the StretchView in a Scroll View

As the window resizes, you want the scroll view to resize, but you do not want your document to resize. Open the Size Inspector, select Scroll View, and set the Size Inspector so that it resizes with the window (Figure 17.14).

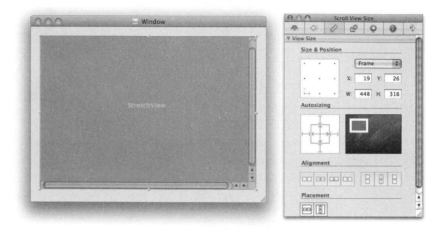

Figure 17.14   Make Scroll View Resize with Window

Note the width and height of the view.

To select the document view, double-click inside the scroll view. You should see the title of the inspector change to Stretch View Size. Make the view about twice as wide and twice as tall as the scroll view. Set the Size Inspector so that the view will stick to the lower-left corner of its superview and not resize (Figure 17.15). Build the application and run it.

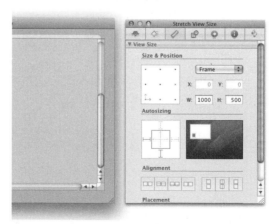

Figure 17.15   Make StretchView Larger and Nonresizing

Creating Views Programmatically

You will instantiate most of your views in Interface Builder. Every once in a while, you will need to create views programmatically. For example, assume that you have a pointer to a window and want to put a button on it. This code would create a button and put it on the window's content view:

```
NSView *superview = [window contentView];
NSRect frame = NSMakeRect(10, 10, 200, 100);
NSButton *button = [[NSButton alloc] initWithFrame:frame];
[button setTitle:@"Click me!"];
[superview addSubview:button];
[button release];
```

For the More Curious: Cells

NSControl inherits from **NSView**. With its graphics context, **NSView** is a relatively large and expensive object to create. When the **NSButton** class was created, the first thing someone did was to create a calculator with 10 rows and 10 columns of buttons. The performance was less than it could have been because of the 100 tiny views. Later, someone had the clever idea of moving the brains of the button into another object (not a view) and creating one big view (called an **NSMatrix**) that would act as the view for all 100 button brains. The class for the button brains was called **NSButtonCell** (Figure 17.16).

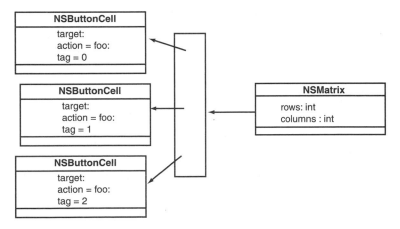

Figure 17.16   NSMatrix

In the end, **NSButton** became simply a view that had an **NSButtonCell**. The button cell does everything, and **NSButton** simply claims a space in the window (Figure 17.17).

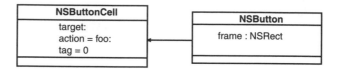

Figure 17.17   NSButton and NSButtonCell

Similarly, **NSSlider** is a view with an **NSSliderCell**, and **NSTextField** is a view with an **NSTextFieldCell**. **NSColorWell**, by contrast, has no cell.

To create an instance of **NSMatrix** in Interface Builder, you drop a control with a cell onto the window, choose Embed Objects In -> Matrix, and then Option-drag as if resizing until the matrix has the correct number of rows and columns (Figure 17.18).

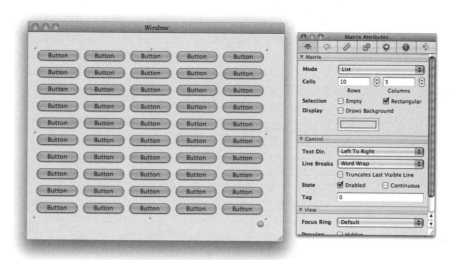

Figure 17.18   A Matrix of Buttons

An **NSMatrix** has a target and an action. A cell may also have a target and an action. If the cell is activated, the cell's target and action are used. If the target and action of the selected cell are not set, the matrix's target and action will be used.

When dealing with matrices, you will often ask which cell was activated. Cells can also be given a tag:

```
- (IBAction)myAction:(id)sender {
    id theCell = [sender selectedCell];
    int theTag = [theCell tag];
    ...
}
```

The cell's tag can be set in Interface Builder.

Cells are used in several other types of objects. The data in an **NSTableView**, for example, is drawn by cells.

For the More Curious: isFlipped

Both PDF and PostScript use the standard Cartesian coordinate system, whereby y increases as you move up the page. Quartz follows this model by default. The origin is usually at the lower-left corner of the view.

For some types of drawing, the math becomes easier if the upper-left corner is the origin and y increases as you move down the page. We say that such a view is *flipped*.

To flip a view, you override **isFlipped** in your view class to return YES:

```
- (BOOL)isFlipped
{
    return YES;
}
```

While we are discussing the coordinate system, note that x- and y-coordinates are measured in *points*. A point is typically defined as 72.0 points = 1 inch. In reality, by default 1.0 point = 1 pixel on your screen. You can, however, change the size of a point by changing the coordinate system:

```
// Make everything in the view twice as large
NSSize newScale;
newScale.width = 2.0;
newScale.height = 2.0;
[myView scaleUnitSquareToSize:newScale];
[myView setNeedsDisplay:YES];
```

Challenge

NSBezierPath can also draw Bezier curves. Replace the straight lines with randomly curved ones. (*Hint:* Look in the documentation for **NSBezierPath**.)

Chapter 18
IMAGES AND MOUSE EVENTS

In the previous chapter, you drew lines connecting random points. A more interesting application would have been to write a drawing application. To write this sort of application, you will need to be able to get and handle mouse events.

NSResponder

NSView inherits from NSResponder. All the event-handling methods are declared in NSResponder. We discuss keyboard events in the next chapter. For now, we are interested only in mouse events. NSResponder declares these methods:

```
- (void)mouseDown:(NSEvent *)theEvent;
- (void)rightMouseDown:(NSEvent *)theEvent;
- (void)otherMouseDown:(NSEvent *)theEvent;

- (void)mouseUp:(NSEvent *)theEvent;
- (void)rightMouseUp:(NSEvent *)theEvent;
- (void)otherMouseUp:(NSEvent *)theEvent;

- (void)mouseDragged:(NSEvent *)theEvent;
- (void)scrollWheel:(NSEvent *)theEvent;
- (void)rightMouseDragged:(NSEvent *)theEvent;
- (void)otherMouseDragged:(NSEvent *)theEvent;
```

Note that the argument is always an NSEvent object.

NSEvent

An event object has all the information about what the user did to trigger the event. When you are dealing with mouse events, you might be interested in the following methods:

```
- (NSPoint)locationInWindow
```

This method returns the location of the mouse event.

```
- (unsigned int)modifierFlags
```

The integer tells you which modifier keys the user is holding down on the keyboard. This enables the programmer to tell a Control-click from a Shift-click, for example. The code would look like this:

```
- (void)mouseDown:(NSEvent *)e
{
    unsigned int flags;
    flags = [e modifierFlags];
    if (flags & NSControlKeyMask) {
        ...handle control click...
    }
    if (flags & NSShiftKeyMask) {
        ...handle shift click...
    }
}
```

Here are the constants that you commonly AND (&) against the modifier flags:

```
NSShiftKeyMask
NSControlKeyMask
NSAlternateKeyMask
NSCommandKeyMask
```

```
- (NSTimeInterval)timestamp
```

This method gives the time interval in seconds between the time the machine booted and the time of the event. NSTimeInterval is a double.

```
- (NSWindow *)window
```

This method returns the window associated with the event.

```
- (int)clickCount
```

Was it a single-, double-, or triple-click?

```
- (float)pressure
```

If the user is using an input device that gives pressure (a tablet, for example), this method returns the pressure. It is between 0 and 1.

```
- (float)deltaX;
- (float)deltaY;
- (float)deltaZ;
```

These methods give the change in the position of the mouse or scroll wheel.

Getting Mouse Events

To get mouse events, you need to override the mouse event methods in
StretchView.m:

```
#pragma mark Events

- (void)mouseDown:(NSEvent *)event
{
    NSLog(@"mouseDown: %d", [event clickCount]);
}

- (void)mouseDragged:(NSEvent *)event
{
    NSPoint p = [event locationInWindow];
    NSLog(@"mouseDragged:%@", NSStringFromPoint(p));
}

- (void)mouseUp:(NSEvent *)event
{
    NSLog(@"mouseUp:");
}
```

Build and run your application. Try double-clicking, and check the click count.
Note that the first click is sent and then the second click. The first click has a
click count of 1; the second click has a click count of 2.

Note the use of #pragma mark. At the top of any Xcode editing window there is
a pop-up that enables you to jump to any of the declarations and definitions in
the file. #pragma mark puts a label into that pop-up. Stylish programmers (like
you, dear reader) use it to group their methods.

Using NSOpenPanel

It would be fun to composite an image onto the view, but first, you need to create
a controller object that will read the image data from a file. This is a good
opportunity to learn how to use **NSOpenPanel**. Note that the RaiseMan
application used the **NSOpenPanel**, but it was done automatically by the
NSDocument class. Here, you will use the **NSOpenPanel** explicitly. Figure 18.1
shows what your application will look like once the user has chosen an image.

The slider at the bottom of the window will control how opaque the image is.
Figure 18.2 shows the object diagram.

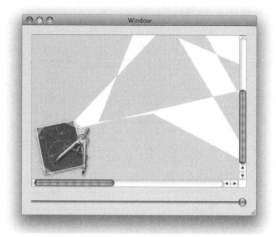

Figure 18.1 Completed Application

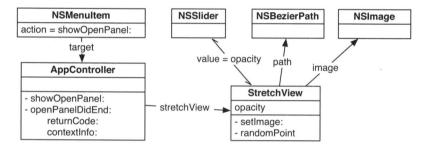

Figure 18.2 Object Diagram

Change the Nib File

In Xcode, create a new Objective-C class named **AppController**. In AppController.h, add an outlet for the **StretchView** and an action that will start the Open panel:

```
#import <Cocoa/Cocoa.h>
@class StretchView;

@interface AppController : NSObject
{
    IBOutlet StretchView *stretchView;
}
- (IBAction)showOpenPanel:(id)sender;
```

Open `MainMenu.nib`. Drag an object from the Library to the doc window. In the Identity Inspector, set its class to **AppController**, as shown in Figure 18.3.

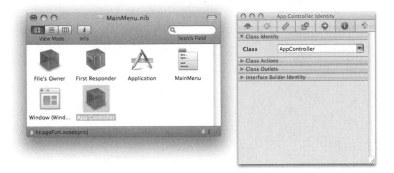

Figure 18.3   Create an AppController

Drop a slider on the window. In the Inspector, set its range from 0 to 1. Also, check the box labeled Continuous. This slider will control how opaque the image is (Figure 18.4).

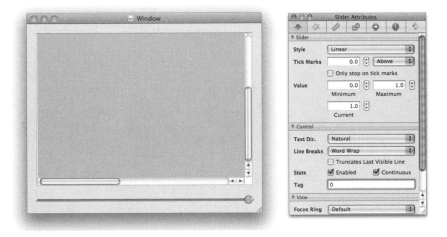

Figure 18.4   Inspect the Slider

Bind the value of the slider to the **AppController**'s `stretchView.opacity` Key Path (Figure 18.5).

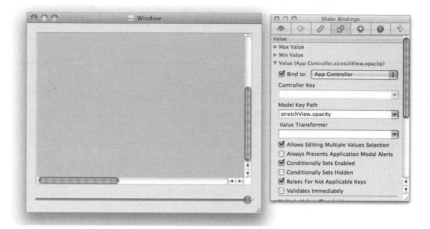

Figure 18.5   Bind the Slider's Value

Control-click on the **AppController.** Connect the stretchView outlet to the **StretchView** on the window (Figure 18.6).

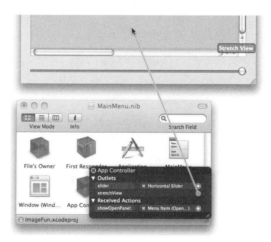

Figure 18.6   Connect the stretchView Outlet

Look at the main menu in your nib. Open the File menu and delete all menu items except Open. Control-drag to connect the menu item to the **AppController**'s **showOpenPanel:** action (Figure 18.7).

Save the file.

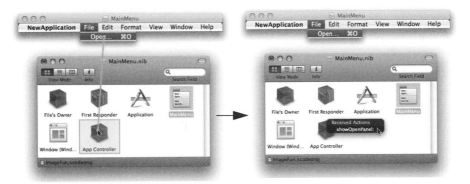

Figure 18.7   Connect the Menu Item

Edit the Code

Edit AppController.m:

```
#import "AppController.h"
#import "StretchView.h"

@implementation AppController

- (void)openPanelDidEnd:(NSOpenPanel *)openPanel
            returnCode:(int)returnCode
            contextInfo:(void *)x
{
    // Did they choose "Open"?
    if (returnCode == NSOKButton) {
        NSString *path = [openPanel filename];
        NSImage *image = [[NSImage alloc] initWithContentsOfFile:path];
        [stretchView setImage:image];
        [image release];
    }
}

- (IBAction)showOpenPanel:(id)sender
{
    NSOpenPanel *panel = [NSOpenPanel openPanel];

    // Run the open panel
    [panel beginSheetForDirectory:nil
                             file:nil
                            types:[NSImage imageFileTypes]
                  modalForWindow:[stretchView window]
                   modalDelegate:self
                   didEndSelector:
        @selector(openPanelDidEnd:returnCode:contextInfo:)
                      contextInfo:NULL];
}

@end
```

Look at the line where you start the sheet. This is a very handy method:

```
- (void)beginSheetForDirectory:(NSString *)path
                          file:(NSString *)name
                         types:(NSArray *)types
                  modalForWindow:(NSWindow *)docWindow
                   modalDelegate:(id)delegate
                  didEndSelector:(SEL)didEndSelector
                     contextInfo:(void *)contextInfo
```

This method brings up an Open panel as a sheet attached to the docWindow. The didEndSelector should have the following signature:

```
- (void)openPanelDidEnd:(NSWindow *)sheet
              returnCode:(int)returnCode
             contextInfo:(void *)contextInfo;
```

It should be implemented in the modal delegate. The path is the place where the file browser will open initially. The name is the name of the file that will be chosen initially. Both the path and the name may be nil.

Composite an Image onto Your View

You will also need to change **StretchView** so that it uses the opacity and image. First, declare variables and methods in your StretchView.h file:

```
#import <Cocoa/Cocoa.h>

@interface StretchView : NSView
{
    NSBezierPath *path;
    NSImage *image;
    float opacity;
}
@property (readwrite) float opacity;
- (void)setImage:(NSImage *)newImage;
- (NSPoint)randomPoint;

@end
```

Now implement these methods in your StretchView.m file:

```
#pragma mark Accessors

- (void)setImage:(NSImage *)newImage
{
    [newImage retain];
```

```
        [image release];
        image = newImage;
        [self setNeedsDisplay:YES];
}

- (float)opacity
{
    return opacity;
}

- (void)setOpacity:(float)x
{
    opacity = x;
    [self setNeedsDisplay:YES];
}
```

At the end of each of the methods, you inform the view that it needs to redraw itself. Near the end of the **initWithFrame** method, set opacity to be 1.0:

```
        [path closePath];
        opacity = 1.0;
        return self;
}
```

Also in StretchView.m, you need to add compositing of the image to the **drawRect:** method:

```
- (void)drawRect:(NSRect)rect
{
    NSRect bounds = [self bounds];
    [[NSColor greenColor] set];
    [NSBezierPath fillRect:bounds];
    [[NSColor whiteColor] set];
    [path fill];
    if (image) {
        NSRect imageRect;
        imageRect.origin = NSZeroPoint;
        imageRect.size = [image size];
        NSRect drawingRect = imageRect;
        [image drawInRect:drawingRect
                 fromRect:imageRect
                operation:NSCompositeSourceOver
                 fraction:opacity];
    }
}
```

Note that the **drawInRect:fromRect:operation:fraction:** method composites the image onto the view. The fraction determines the image's opacity.

You should release the image in your **dealloc** method:

```
- (void)dealloc
{
    [path release];
    [image release];
    [super dealloc];
}
```

Build and run your application. You will find a few images in /Developer/ Examples/AppKit/Sketch . When you open an image, it will appear in the lower-left corner of your **StretchView** object.

The View's Coordinate System

The final bit of fun comes from being able to choose the location and dimensions of the image, based on the user's dragging. The **mouseDown** will indicate one corner of the rectangle where the image will appear, and the **mouseUp** will indicate the opposite corner. The final application will look something like Figure 18.8.

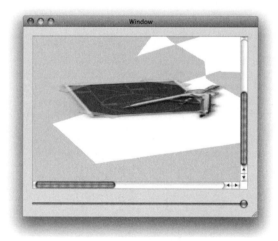

Figure 18.8   Completed Application

Each view has its own coordinate system. By default, (0, 0) is in the lower-left corner. This is consistent with PDF and PostScript. If you wish, you can change the coordinate system of the view. You can move the origin, change the scale, or rotate the coordinates. The window also has a coordinate system.

If you have two views, a and b, and you need to translate an NSPoint p from b's coordinate system to a's coordinate system, it would look like this:

```
NSPoint q = [a convertPoint:p fromView:b];
```

If b is nil, the point is converted from the window's coordinate system.

Mouse events have their locations in the window's coordinate system, so you will nearly always have to convert the point to the local coordinate system. You are going to create variables to hold onto the corners of the rectangle where the image will be drawn.

Add these instance variables to StretchView.h:

```
NSPoint downPoint;
NSPoint currentPoint;
```

The location of the **mouseDown:** will be downPoint and currentPoint will be updated by **mouseDragged:** and **mouseUp:**.

Edit the mouse event-handling methods to update downPoint and currentPoint:

```
- (void)mouseDown:(NSEvent *)event
{
    NSPoint p = [event locationInWindow];
    downPoint = [self convertPoint:p fromView:nil];
    currentPoint = downPoint;
    [self setNeedsDisplay:YES];
}

- (void)mouseDragged:(NSEvent *)event
{
    NSPoint p = [event locationInWindow];
    currentPoint = [self convertPoint:p fromView:nil];
    [self setNeedsDisplay:YES];
}

- (void)mouseUp:(NSEvent *)event
{
    NSPoint p = [event locationInWindow];
    currentPoint = [self convertPoint:p fromView:nil];
    [self setNeedsDisplay:YES];
}
```

Add a method to calculate the rectangle based on the two points:

```
- (NSRect)currentRect
{
    float minX = MIN(downPoint.x, currentPoint.x);
```

```
    float maxX = MAX(downPoint.x, currentPoint.x);
    float minY = MIN(downPoint.y, currentPoint.y);
    float maxY = MAX(downPoint.y, currentPoint.y);

    return NSMakeRect(minX, minY, maxX minX, maxY minY);
}
```

(I don't know why, but many people mistype that last method. Look at yours once more before going on. If you get it wrong, the results are disappointing.)

Declare the **currentRect** method in StretchView.h.

So that the user will see something even if he or she has not dragged, initialize downPoint and currentPoint in the **setImage:** method:

```
- (void)setImage:(NSImage *)newImage
{
    [newImage retain];
    [image release];
    image = newImage;
    NSSize imageSize = [newImage size];
    downPoint = NSZeroPoint;
    currentPoint.x = downPoint.x + imageSize.width;
    currentPoint.y = downPoint.y + imageSize.height;
    [self setNeedsDisplay:YES];
}
```

In the **drawRect:** method, composite the image inside the rectangle:

```
- (void)drawRect:(NSRect)rect
{
    NSRect bounds = [self bounds];
    [[NSColor greenColor] set];
    [NSBezierPath fillRect:bounds];
    [[NSColor whiteColor] set];
    [path stroke];
    if (image) {
        NSRect imageRect;
        imageRect.origin = NSZeroPoint;
        imageRect.size = [image size];
        NSRect drawingRect = [self currentRect];
        [image drawInRect:drawingRect
                 fromRect:imageRect
                operation:NSCompositeSourceOver
                 fraction:opacity];
    }
}
```

Build and run your application. Note that the view doesn't scroll when you drag past the edge. It would be nice if the scroll view would move to allow users to see where they have dragged to, a technique known as *autoscrolling*.

Autoscrolling

To add autoscrolling to your application, you will send the message **autoscroll:** to the clip view when the user drags. You will include the event as an argument. Open StretchView.m and add the following line to the **mouseDragged:** method:

```
- (void)mouseDragged:(NSEvent *)event
{
    NSPoint p = [event locationInWindow];
    currentPoint = [self convertPoint:p fromView:nil];
    [self autoscroll:event];
    [self setNeedsDisplay:YES];
}
```

Build and run your application.

Note that autoscrolling happens only as you drag. For smoother autoscrolling, most developers will create a timer that sends the view the **autoscroll:** method periodically while the user is dragging. Timers are discussed in Chapter 24.

For the More Curious: NSImage

In most cases, it suffices to read in an image, resize it, and composite it onto a view, as you did in this exercise.

An **NSImage** object has an array of representations. For example, your image might be a drawing of a cow. That drawing can be in PDF, a color bitmap, and a black-and-white bitmap. Each of these versions is an instance of a subclass of **NSImageRep**. You can add representations to and remove representations from your image. When you sit down to rewrite Adobe Photoshop, you will be manipulating the image representations.

Here is a list of the subclasses of **NSImageRep**:

- **NSBitmapImageRep**
- **NSEPSImageRep**
- **NSPICTImageRep**
- **NSCachedImageRep**
- **NSCustomImageRep**
- **NSPDFImageRep**

Although **NSImageRep** has only five subclasses, it is important to note that **NSImage** knows how to read approximately two dozen types of image files, including all the common formats: PICT, GIF, JPG, PNG, PDF, BMP, TIFF, and so on.

Challenge

Create a new document-based application that allows the user to draw ovals in arbitrary locations and sizes. **NSBezierPath** has the following method:

+ (NSBezierPath *)**bezierPathWithOvalInRect:**(NSRect)rect;

If you are feeling ambitious, add the ability to save and read files.

If you are feeling extra ambitious, add undo capabilities.

Chapter 19
KEYBOARD EVENTS

When the user types, where are the corresponding events sent? First, the window manager gets the event and forwards it to the active application. The active application forwards the keyboard events to the key window. The key window forwards the event to the "active" view. Which view, then, is the active one? Each window has an outlet, called firstResponder, that points to one view of that window. That view is the "active" one for that window. For example, when you click on a text field, it becomes the firstResponder of that window (Figure 19.1).

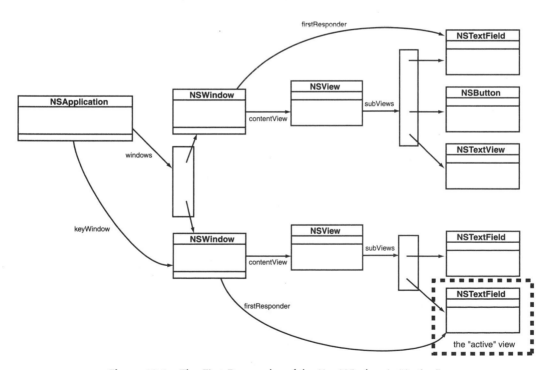

Figure 19.1 The First Responder of the Key Window Is "Active"

When the user tries to change the firstResponder by tabbing or clicking another view, the views go through a certain ritual before the firstResponder outlet is changed. First, the view that may become the firstResponder is asked whether it accepts first-responder status. A return of NO means that the view is not interested in keyboard events. For example, you can't type into a slider, so it refuses to accept first-responder status. If the view does accept first-responder status, the view that is currently the first responder is asked whether it resigns its role as the first responder. If the editing is not done, the view can refuse to give up first-responder status. For example, if the user had not typed in his or her entire phone number, the text field could refuse to resign this status. Finally, the view is told that it is becoming the first responder. Often, this triggers a change in its appearance (Figure 19.2).

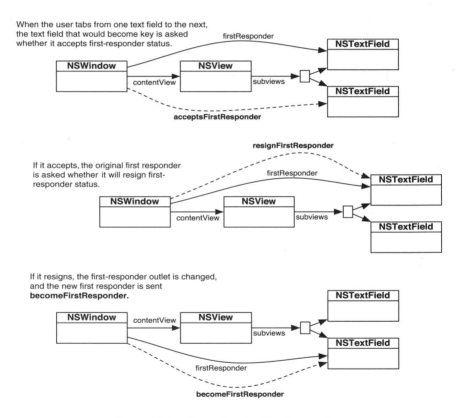

Figure 19.2   Becoming the First Responder

Note that each window has its own first responder. Several windows may be open, but only the first responder of the key window gets the keyboard events.

NSResponder

We are interested in the following methods that are inherited from
NSResponder:

- (BOOL)**acceptsFirstResponder**

Overridden by a subclass to return YES if it handles keyboard events.

- (BOOL)**resignFirstResponder**

Asks the receiver whether it is willing to give up first-responder status.

- (BOOL)**becomeFirstResponder**

Notifies the receiver that has become first responder in its **NSWindow**.

- (void)**keyDown:**(NSEvent *)theEvent

Informs the receiver that the user has pressed a key.

- (void)**keyUp:**(NSEvent *)theEvent

Informs the receiver that the user has released a key.

- (void)**flagsChanged:**(NSEvent *)theEvent

Informs the receiver that the user has pressed or released a modifier key
(e.g., Shift or Control).

NSEvent

In the previous chapter, we discussed **NSEvent** in terms of mouse events. Here
are some of the methods commonly used when getting information about a
keyboard event:

- (NSString *)**characters**

Returns the characters created by the event.

- (BOOL)**isARepeat**

Returns YES if the key event is a repeat caused by the user's holding the key
down; returns NO if the key event is new.

- (unsigned short)**keyCode**

Returns the code for the keyboard key that caused the event.

```
- (unsigned int)modifierFlags
```

Returns an integer bit field indicating the modifier keys in effect for the receiver. For information about what the bits of the integer mean, refer to the discussion in Chapter 18.

Create a New Project with a Custom View

Create a new project of type Cocoa Application. Name the project TypingTutor.

In Xcode, create an Objective-C NSView subclass and name it **BigLetterView.**

Lay Out the Interface

Open `MainMenu.nib`. Create an instance of your class by dragging out a CustomView placeholder (under Views & Cells -> Layout Views) and dropping it on the window (Figure 19.3).

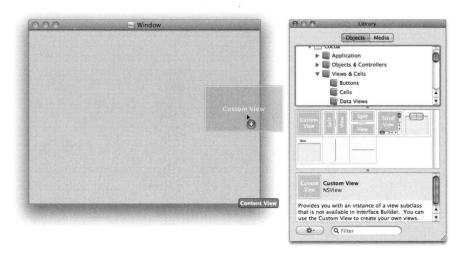

Figure 19.3   Drop a View on the Window

In the Identity Inspector, set the class of the view to be **BigLetterView** (Figure 19.4).

Drop two text fields (under Views & Cells -> Input & Values) on the window (Figure 19.5).

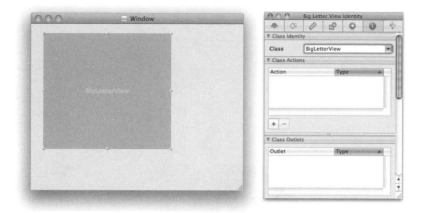

Figure 19.4   Set the Class of the View to BigLetterView

Figure 19.5   Completed Interface

Make Connections

Now you need to create the loop of key views for your window. That is, you are setting the order in which the views will be selected as the user tabs from one element to the next. The order will be the text field on the left, the text field on the right, the **BigLetterView**, and then back to the text field on the left.

Set the left-hand text field's nextKeyView to be the right-hand text field (Figure 19.6).

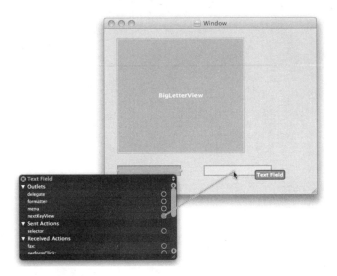

Figure 19.6 Set nextKeyView of Left-Hand Text Field

Set the right-hand text field's nextKeyView to be the **BigLetterView** (Figure 19.7).

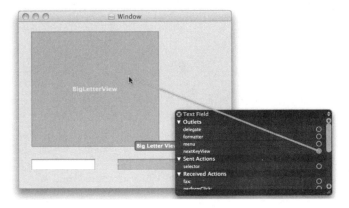

Figure 19.7 Set nextKeyView of Right-Hand Text Field

Finally, set the nextKeyView of the **BigLetterView** to be the left-hand text field (Figure 19.8). This will enable the user to tab between the three views. Shift-tabbing will move the selection in the opposite direction.

Which view, then, should be the firstResponder when the window first appears? To make the **BigLetterView** be the initial FirstResponder, right click

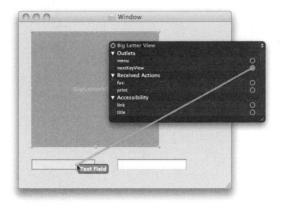

Figure 19.8 Set nextKeyView of the BigLetterView

on the window icon in the doc window and set the `initialFirstResponder` outlet to the **BigLetterView** (Figure 19.9).

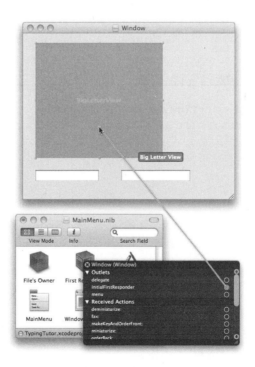

Figure 19.9 Set the initialFirstResponder of the Window

Save and close the nib file.

Write the Code

In this section, you will make your **BigLetterView** respond to key events. You will also make it accept first-responder status. The characters typed by the user will appear in the console. The completed application will look like Figure 19.10.

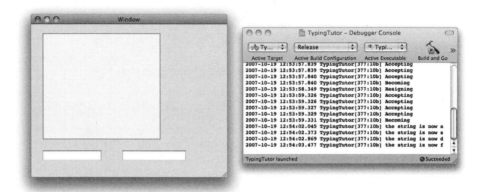

Figure 19.10   Completed Application

In BigLetterView.h

Your **BigLetterView** will have two instance variables and accessor methods for those variables. The bgColor variable will identify the background color of the view and will be an **NSColor** object. The string variable will hold on to the letter that the user most recently typed and will be an **NSString** object:

```
#import <Cocoa/Cocoa.h>

@interface BigLetterView : NSView
{
    NSColor *bgColor;
    NSString *string;
}
@property (retain, readwrite) NSColor *bgColor;
@property (copy, readwrite) NSString *string;
@end
```

In BigLetterView.m

The designated initializer for a view is **initWithFrame:**. In this method, you will call the superclass's **initWithFrame:** method and initialize bgColor and string to default values. Add the following method to BigLetterView.m:

```
- (id)initWithFrame:(NSRect)rect
{
    if (![super initWithFrame:rect])
        return nil;

    NSLog(@"initializing view");
    bgColor = [[NSColor yellowColor] retain];
    string = @" ";
    return self;
}
- (void)dealloc
{
    [bgColor release];
    [string release];
    [super dealloc];
}
```

Create accessor methods for bgColor and string:

```
#pragma mark Accessors

- (void)setBgColor:(NSColor *)c
{
    [c retain];
    [bgColor release];
    bgColor = c;
    [self setNeedsDisplay:YES];
}

- (NSColor *)bgColor
{
    return bgColor;
}

- (void)setString:(NSString *)c
{
    c = [c copy];
    [string release];
    string = c;
    NSLog(@"The string is now %@", string);
}

- (NSString *)string
{
    return string;
}
```

Add the following code to the **drawRect:** method. The code will fill the view with bgColor. If it is the window's firstResponder, the view will stroke a blue rectangle around its bounds to show the user that it will be the view receiving keyboard events:

```objc
- (void)drawRect:(NSRect)rect
{
    NSRect bounds = [self bounds];
    [bgColor set];
    [NSBezierPath fillRect:bounds];

    // Am I the window's first responder?
    if ([[self window] firstResponder] == self) {
        [[NSColor keyboardFocusIndicatorColor] set];
        [NSBezierPath setDefaultLineWidth:4.0];
        [NSBezierPath strokeRect:bounds];
    }
}
```

The system can optimize your drawing a bit if it knows that the view is completely opaque. Override **NSView**'s **isOpaque** method:

```objc
- (BOOL)isOpaque
{
    return YES;
}
```

The methods to become firstResponder are as follows:

```objc
- (BOOL)acceptsFirstResponder
{
    NSLog(@"Accepting");
    return YES;
}
```

```objc
- (BOOL)resignFirstResponder
{
    NSLog(@"Resigning");
    [self setNeedsDisplay:YES];
    return YES;
}
```

```objc
- (BOOL)becomeFirstResponder
{
    NSLog(@"Becoming");
    [self setNeedsDisplay:YES];
    return YES;
}
```

Once it becomes the first responder, the view will handle key events. For most **keyDowns**, the view will simply change string to be whatever the user typed. If, however, the user presses Tab or Shift-Tab, the view will ask the window to change the first responder.

NSResponder (from which **NSView** inherits) has a method called
interpretKeyEvents:. For most key events, it simply tells the view to insert
the text. For events that might do something else (e.g., Tab or Shift-Tab), it calls
methods on itself.

In **keyDown:**, you simply call **interpretKeyEvents:**

```
- (void)keyDown:(NSEvent *)event
{
    [self interpretKeyEvents:[NSArray arrayWithObject:event]];
}
```

Then you need to override the methods that **interpretKeyEvents:** will call:

```
- (void)insertText:(NSString *)input
{
    // Set string to be what the user typed
    [self setString:input];
}

- (void)insertTab:(id)sender
{
    [[self window] selectKeyViewFollowingView:self];
}
// Be careful with capitalization here "backtab" is considered
// one word.
- (void)insertBacktab:(id)sender
{
    [[self window] selectKeyViewPrecedingView:self];
}
- (void)deleteBackward:(id)sender
{
    [self setString:@" "];
}
```

```
@end
```

Build and run your program. You should see that your view becomes the first
responder. While it is first responder, it should take keyboard events and log
them to the terminal. Also, note that you can Tab and Shift-Tab between the
views (Figure 19.11).

(Yes, **acceptsFirstResponder** gets called more times than you might expect
each time the view is selected.)

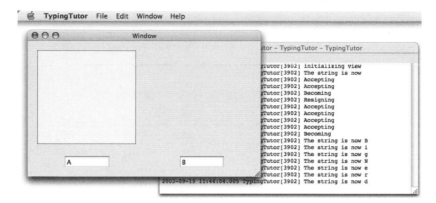

Figure 19.11   Completed Application

For the More Curious: Rollovers

Three mouse events were not discussed in Chapter 18: **mouseMoved:**, **mouseEntered:**, and **mouseExited:**.

```
- (void)mouseMoved:(NSEvent *)event
```

To receive **mouseMoved:**, the view's window needs to accept "mouse-moved" events. If it does, the **mouseMoved:** message is sent to the window's first responder. To set the window to get mouse-moved events, you send it the message **setAcceptsMouseMovedEvents:**

```
[[self window] setAcceptsMouseMovedEvents:YES];
```

At this point, the view will be sent the message every time the mouse moves. This is a lot of events. When people ask me about mouse-moved events, I ask them why they want it. They usually say, "Uh, rollovers."

Rollovers are very popular in Web browsers. As you roll over a region, its appearance changes to make it clear that if you clicked now, that region would accept the click. Bookmarks in Safari, for example, become highlighted when you roll over them.

To do rollovers, you don't typically use **mouseMoved:**. Instead, you set up a tracking area and override **mouseEntered:** and **mouseExited:**.

When a view is put on a window, **viewDidMoveToWindow** gets called. This is a pretty good place to create tracking areas. By passing the NSTrackingInVisibleRect, the tracking area will automatically match the visible rect of the owner:

```
- (void)viewDidMoveToWindow
{
    int options = NSTrackingMouseEnteredAndExited |
                  NSTrackingActiveAlways |
                  NSTrackingInVisibleRect;
    NSTrackingArea *ta;
    ta = [[NSTrackingArea alloc] initWithRect:NSZeroRect
                                      options:options
                                        owner:self
                                     userInfo:nil];
    [self addTrackingArea:ta];
    [ta release];
}
```

Then, you change the appearance when **mouseEntered:** and **mouseExited:** are called. Assuming that you have a variable called isHighlighted of type BOOL, here is the code:

```
- (void)mouseEntered:(NSEvent *)theEvent
{
    isHighlighted = YES;
    [self setNeedsDisplay:YES];
}

- (void)mouseExited:(NSEvent *)theEvent
{
    isHighlighted = NO;
    [self setNeedsDisplay:YES];
}
```

You would then check isHighlighted in your **drawRect:** method and draw the view appropriately.

The Fuzzy Blue Box

Your **BigLetterView** gets a blue box around its edge when it is firstResponder. Note, however, that the box isn't nice and fuzzy like the box around text fields. You want the fuzzy blue box? It takes a little work.

See where you draw the blue box in **drawRect:** in BigLetterView.m? Change the code to look like this:

```
if (([[self window] firstResponder] == self) &&
        [NSGraphicsContext currentContextDrawingToScreen]) {
    [NSGraphicsContext saveGraphicsState];
    NSSetFocusRingStyle(NSFocusRingOnly);
    [NSBezierPath fillRect:bounds];
    [NSGraphicsContext restoreGraphicsState];
}
```

Now, when you lose first-responder status, you need to redraw the view *and the area occupied by the fuzzy blue glow around it*:

```
- (BOOL)resignFirstResponder
{
    NSLog(@"Resigning");
    [self setKeyboardFocusRingNeedsDisplayInRect:[self bounds]];
    return YES;
}
```

Build and run your application.

Chapter 20

Drawing Text with Attributes

The next step is to get the string to appear in our view. At the end of the chapter, your application will look like Figure 20.1. The character being displayed will change as you type.

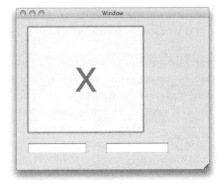

Figure 20.1   Completed Application

NSFont

Overall, the class **NSFont** has basically only two types of methods:

1. Class methods for getting the font you want

2. Methods for getting metrics on the font, such as letter height

The following are commonly used methods in **NSFont**.

+ (NSFont *)**fontWithName:**(NSString *)fontName **size:**(float)fontSize

This method returns a font object. fontName is a family-face name, such as HelveticaBoldOblique or Times-Roman. If you use a fontSize of 0.0, this method uses the default user font size.

```
+ (NSFont *)userFixedPitchFontOfSize:(float)fontSize

+ (NSFont *)userFontOfSize:(float)fontSize

+ (NSFont *)messageFontOfSize:(float)fontSize

+ (NSFont *)toolTipsFontOfSize:(float)fontSize

+ (NSFont *)titleBarFontOfSize:(float)fontSize
```

These methods return the user's default font for the corresponding string types. Once again, a size of 0.0 will get a font of the default size.

NSAttributedString

Sometimes, you want to display a string that has certain attributes for a range of characters. For example, suppose that you want to display the string "Big Nerd Ranch" and want the letters 0 through 2 to be underlined, the letters 0 through 7 to be green, and the letters 9 through 13 to be subscripts.

When dealing with a range of numbers, Cocoa uses the struct NSRange, which has two members—location and length—both of which are integers. The location is the index of the first item, and the length is the number of items in the range. You can use the function **NSMakeRange()** to create an NSRange.

To create strings with attributes that remain in effect over a range of characters, Cocoa has **NSAttributedString** and **NSMutableAttributedString**. Here is how you could create the **NSAttributedString** just described:

```
NSMutableAttributedString *s;
s = [[NSMutableAttributedString alloc]
        initWithString:@"Big Nerd Ranch"];

[s addAttribute:NSFontAttributeName
        value:[NSFont userFontOfSize:22]
        range:NSMakeRange(0, 14)];

[s addAttribute:NSUnderlineStyleAttributeName
        value:[NSNumber numberWithInt:1]
        range:NSMakeRange(0,3)];

[s addAttribute:NSForegroundColorAttributeName
        value:[NSColor greenColor]
        range:NSMakeRange(0, 8)];

[s addAttribute:NSSuperscriptAttributeName
        value:[NSNumber numberWithInt:-1]
        range:NSMakeRange(9,5)];
```

Once you have an attributed string, you can do lots of stuff with it.

```
[s drawInRect:[self bounds]];

// Put it in a text field
[textField setAttributedStringValue:s];

// Put it on a button
[button setAttributedTitle:s];
```

Figure 20.2 shows the result of this code's execution.

Figure 20.2   Using the Attributed String

Here are the names of the global variables for the most commonly used
attributes, the type of object they correspond to, and their default values:

NSFontAttributeName	Font object; 12-point Helvetica
NSForegroundColorAttributeName	Color; black
NSParagraphStyleAttributeName	NSParagraphStyle object; the standard paragraph style
NSUnderlineColorAttributeName	Color; the same as the foreground
NSUnderlineStyleAttributeName	Number; 0, or no underline
NSSuperscriptAttributeName	Number; 0, or no superscripting or subscripting
NSShadowAttributeName	**NSShadow** object; nil (no shadow)

A list of all the attribute names can be found in <AppKit/NSAttributedString.h>.

The easiest way to create attributed strings is from a file. **NSAttributedString** can read and write the following file formats:

- *A string:* You read a text file.

- *RTF:* Rich Text Format is a standard for text with multiple fonts and colors. In this case, you will read and set the contents of the attributed string with an instance of **NSData**.

- *RTFD:* This is RTF with attachments. Besides the multiple fonts and colors of RTF, you can have images.

- *HTML:* The attributed string can do basic HTML layout, but you probably want to use the **WebView** for best quality.

- *Word:* The attributed string can read and write simple .doc files.

- *OpenOffice*

When you read a document in, you may want to know some things about it, such as the paper size. If you supply a place where the method can put a pointer to a dictionary, the dictionary will have all the extra information that it could get from the data. For example:

```
NSDictionary *myDict;
NSData *data = [NSData dataWithContentsOfFile:@"myfile.rtf"];
NSAttributedString *aString;
aString = [[NSAttributedString alloc] initWithRTF:data
                                documentAttributes:&myDict];
```

If you don't care about the document attributes, supply NULL.

Drawing Strings and Attributed Strings

Both **NSString** and **NSAttributedString** have methods that cause them to be drawn onto a view. **NSAttributedString** has the following methods:

- (void)**drawAtPoint:**(NSPoint)aPoint

Draws the receiver, with aPoint the lower-left corner of the string.

- (void)**drawInRect:**(NSRect)rect

Draws the receiver. All drawing occurs inside rect. If rect is too small for the string to fit, the drawing is clipped to fit inside rect.

- (NSSize)**size**

Returns the size that the receiver would be if drawn.

NSString has analogous methods. With **NSString**, you need to supply a
dictionary of attributes to be applied for the entire string:

```
- (void)drawAtPoint:(NSPoint)aPoint
       withAttributes:(NSDictionary *)attribs
```

Draws the receiver with the attributes in `attribs`.

```
- (void)drawInRect:(NSRect)aRect
      withAttributes:(NSDictionary *)attribs
```

Draws the receiver with the attributes in `attribs`.

```
- (NSSize)sizeWithAttributes:(NSDictionary *)attribs
```

Returns the size that the receiver would be if drawn with the atttributes in
`attribs`.

Making Letters Appear

Open `BigLetterView.h`. Add an instance variable to hold the attributes
dictionary:

```
#import <Cocoa/Cocoa.h>

@interface BigLetterView : NSView
{
    NSColor *bgColor;
    NSString *string;
    NSMutableDictionary *attributes;
}
```

Open `BigLetterView.m`. Create a method that creates the `attributes`
dictionary with a font and a foreground color:

```
- (void)prepareAttributes
{
    attributes = [[NSMutableDictionary alloc] init];

    [attributes setObject:[NSFont fontWithName:@"Helvetica"
                                          size:75]
                   forKey:NSFontAttributeName];

    [attributes setObject:[NSColor redColor]
                   forKey:NSForegroundColorAttributeName];
}
```

In the **initWithFrame:** method, call the new method:

```
- (id)initWithFrame:(NSRect)rect
{
    if (![super initWithFrame:rect])
        return nil;

    NSLog(@"initializing view");
    [self prepareAttributes];
    bgColor = [[NSColor yellowColor] retain];
    string = @" ";
    return self;
}
- (void)dealloc
{
    [bgColor release];
    [string release];
    [attributes release];
    [super dealloc];
}
```

In the **setString:** method, tell the view that it needs to redisplay itself:

```
- (void)setString:(NSString *)c
{
    c = [c copy];
    [string release];
    string = c;
    NSLog(@"The string: %@", string);
    [self setNeedsDisplay:YES];
}
```

Create a method that will display the string in the middle of a rectangle:

```
- (void)drawStringCenteredIn:(NSRect)r
{
    NSSize strSize = [string sizeWithAttributes:attributes];
    NSPoint strOrigin;
    strOrigin.x = r.origin.x + (r.size.width - strSize.width)/2;
    strOrigin.y = r.origin.y + (r.size.height - strSize.height)/2;
    [string drawAtPoint:strOrigin withAttributes:attributes];
}
```

Call that method from inside your **drawRect:** method:

```
- (void)drawRect:(NSRect)rect
{
    NSRect bounds = [self bounds];
    [bgColor set];
    [NSBezierPath fillRect:bounds];
```

```
    [self drawStringCenteredIn:bounds];

    if ((([[self window] firstResponder] == self) &&
```

Build and run the application. Note that keyboard events go to your view unless they trigger a menu item. Try pressing Command-w: The window should close even if your view is the first responder for the key window.

Getting Your View to Generate PDF Data

All the drawing commands can be converted into PDF by the AppKit framework. The PDF data can be sent to a printer or to a file. Note that the PDF will always look as good as possible on any device, because it is resolution independent.

You have already created a view that knows how to generate PDF data to describe how it is supposed to look. Getting the PDF data into a file is quite easy. **NSView** has the following method:

```
- (NSData *)dataWithPDFInsideRect:(NSRect)aRect
```

This method creates a data object and then calls **drawRect:**. The drawing commands that would usually go to the screen instead go into the data object. Once you have this data object, you simply save it to a file.

Open BigLetterView.m, and add a method that will create a Save panel as a sheet:

```
- (IBAction)savePDF:(id)sender
{
    NSSavePanel *panel = [NSSavePanel savePanel];
    [panel setRequiredFileType:@"pdf"];
    [panel beginSheetForDirectory:nil
                             file:nil
                  modalForWindow:[self window]
                   modalDelegate:self
                   didEndSelector:
                     @selector(didEnd:returnCode:contextInfo:)
                     contextInfo:NULL];
}
```

When the user has chosen the filename, the following method will be called:

didEnd:returnCode: contextInfo:

Implement this method in `BigLetterView.m`:

```
- (void)didEnd:(NSSavePanel *)sheet
    returnCode:(int)code
    contextInfo:(void *)contextInfo
{
    if (code != NSOKButton)
        return;

    NSRect r = [self bounds];
    NSData *data = [self dataWithPDFInsideRect:r];
    NSString *path = [sheet filename];
    NSError *error;
    BOOL successful = [data writeToFile:path
                               options:0
                                 error:&error];
    if (!successful) {
        NSAlert *a = [NSAlert alertWithError:error];
        [a runModal];
    }
}
```

Also, declare the action method in the `BigLetterView.h` file:

```
- (IBAction)savePDF:(id)sender;
```

Open the nib file. Select Save As... under the File menu. Relabel the menu item Save PDF.... (You may delete all the other menu items from the menu, if you wish.) Make the Save PDF... menu item trigger the **BigLetterView**'s **savePDF:** method (Figure 20.3).

Save and build the application. You should be able to generate a PDF file and view it in Preview (Figure 20.4).

You will notice that multikeystroke characters (e.g., "é") are not handled by your **BigLetterView**. To make this possible, you would need to add several methods that the **NSInputManager** uses. This topic is beyond the scope of this book (I simply wanted to show you how to get keyboard events), but you can learn about it in Apple's discussion of **NSInputManager** (/Developer/Documentation/ Cocoa/Conceptual/InputManager/index.html).

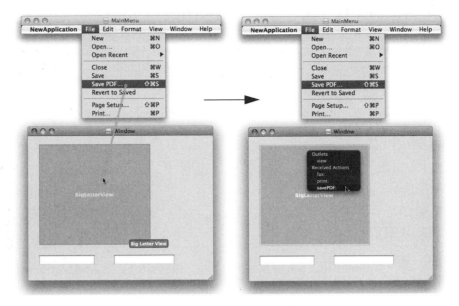

Figure 20.3 Connect Menu Item

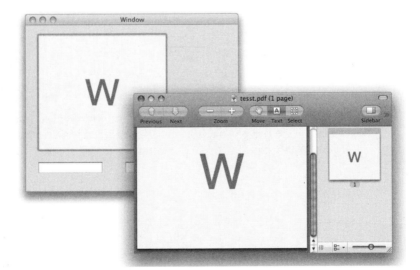

Figure 20.4 Completed Application

For the More Curious: NSFontManager

Sometimes, you will have a font that is good but would be perfect if it were bold or italicized or condensed. **NSFontManager** can be used to make this sort of conversion. You can also use a font manager to change the size of the font.

For example, imagine that you have a font and would like a similar font but bold. Here is the code:

```
fontManager = [NSFontManager sharedFontManager];
boldFont = [fontManager convertFont:aFont toHaveTrait:NSBoldFontMask];
```

Challenge 1

Give the letter a shadow. The **NSShadow** class has the following methods:

- (id)**init**;
- (void)**setShadowOffset:**(NSSize)offset;
- (void)**setShadowBlurRadius:**(float)val;
- (void)**setShadowColor:**(NSColor *)color;

Challenge 2

Add the Boolean variables bold and italic to your **BigLetterView**. Add check boxes that toggle these variables. If bold is YES, make the letter appear in boldface; if italic is YES, make the letter appear in italics.

Chapter 21
PASTEBOARDS AND NIL-TARGETED ACTIONS

The pasteboard server (/usr/bin/pboard) is a process that runs on your Mac. Applications use the **NSPasteboard** class to write data into and to read data from that process. The pasteboard server makes possible such operations as copying, cutting, and pasting between applications.

An application can copy the same data onto the pasteboard in several formats. For example, an image can be copied onto the pasteboard as a PDF document and as a bitmapped image. Then the application that reads the data can choose the format that it prefers.

When putting data on the pasteboard, your application typically declares the types it will put on the pasteboard and then immediately copies that data to the pasteboard. The receiving application will first ask the pasteboard what types are available and then read the data in its preferred format.

You can also copy data to the pasteboard in a lazy manner. To do so, simply declare all the types of data you could put on the pasteboard, and then supply the data when it is requested. We will talk about lazy copying at the end of the chapter.

Multiple pasteboards are available: one for copy-and-paste operations and another for drag-and-drop tasks. Another pasteboard stores the last string that the user searched for. One pasteboard is for copying rulers; another, for copying fonts.

In this section, you will add cut, copy, and paste capabilities to your **BigLetterView**. First, you will implement the methods that will read from and write to the pasteboard. Then we will discuss how those methods get called.

NSPasteboard

The **NSPasteboard** class acts as an interface to the pasteboard server. Following are some of the commonly used methods of **NSPasteboard**:

+ (NSPasteboard *)**generalPasteboard**

Returns the general **NSPasteboard**. You will use this pasteboard to copy, cut, and paste.

+ (NSPasteboard *)**pasteboardWithName:**(NSString *)name

Returns the pasteboard identified by name. Here are the global variables that contain the names of the standard pasteboards:

NSGeneralPboard	NSFindPboard
NSFontPboard	NSDragPboard
NSRulerPboard	

- (int)**declareTypes:**(NSArray *)types **owner:**(id)theOwner

Clears whatever was on the pasteboard before and declares the types of data that theOwner will put on the pasteboard. Here are the global variables for the standard types:

NSColorPboardType	NSRTFPboardType
NSFileContentsPboardType	NSRTFDPboardType
NSFilenamesPboardType	NSStringPboardType
NSFontPboardType	NSTabularTextPboardType
NSPDFPboardType	NSVCardPboardType
NSPICTPboardType	NSTIFFPboardType
NSPostScriptPboardType	NSURLPboardType
NSRulerPboardType	

You can also create your own pasteboard types.

- (BOOL)**setData:**(NSData *)aData **forType:**(NSString *)dataType
- (BOOL)**setString:**(NSString *)s **forType:**(NSString *)dataType

Write data to the pasteboard.

- (NSArray *)**types**

Returns an array containing the types of data available to be read from the pasteboard.

- (NSString *)**availableTypeFromArray:**(NSArray *)types

Returns the first type found in types available for reading from the pasteboard. The list types identifies all types that you would be able to read.

- (NSData *)**dataForType:**(NSString *)dataType

- (NSString *)**stringForType:**(NSString *)dataType

Read data from the pasteboard.

Add Cut, Copy, and Paste to BigLetterView

You will create methods named **cut:**, **copy:**, and **paste:** in the **BigLetterView** class. To make these methods easier to write, you will first create methods for putting data onto and reading data off a pasteboard. Add these methods to BigLetterView.m:

```
- (void)writeToPasteboard:(NSPasteboard *)pb
{
    // Declare types
    [pb declareTypes:[NSArray arrayWithObject:NSStringPboardType]
            owner:self];

    // Copy data to the pasteboard
    [pb setString:string forType:NSStringPboardType];
}

- (BOOL)readFromPasteboard:(NSPasteboard *)pb
{
    // Is there a string on the pasteboard?
    NSArray *types = [pb types];
    if ([types containsObject:NSStringPboardType]) {

        // Read the string from the pasteboard
        NSString *value = [pb stringForType:NSStringPboardType];

        // Our view can handle only one letter
        if ([value length] == 1) {
            [self setString:value];
            return YES;
        }
    }
    return NO;
}
```

Add **cut:**, **copy:**, and **paste:** to `BigLetterView.m`:

```
- (IBAction)cut:(id)sender
{
    [self copy:sender];
    [self setString:@""];
}

- (IBAction)copy:(id)sender
{
    NSPasteboard *pb = [NSPasteboard generalPasteboard];
    [self writeToPasteboard:pb];
}

- (IBAction)paste:(id)sender
{
    NSPasteboard *pb = [NSPasteboard generalPasteboard];
    if(![self readFromPasteboard:pb]) {
        NSBeep();
    }
}
```

Declare these methods in `BigLetterView.h`:

```
- (IBAction)cut:(id)sender;

- (IBAction)copy:(id)sender;

- (IBAction)paste:(id)sender;
```

Nil-Targeted Actions

How is the right view sent the **cut:**, **copy:**, or **paste:** message? After all, there are many, many views. If you select a text field, it should get the message. When you select another view and then choose the Copy or Paste menu item, the message should go to the newly selected view.

To solve this problem, the clever engineers at NeXT came up with *nil-targeted actions*. If you set the target of a control to `nil`, the application will try to send the action message to several objects until one of them responds. The application first tries to send the message to the first responder of the key window. This is exactly the behavior that you want for Cut and Paste. You can have several windows, each of which can have several views. The active view on the active window gets sent the cut-and-paste messages.

The beauty of targeted actions doesn't end there. **NSView**, **NSApplication**, and **NSWindow** all inherit from **NSResponder**, which has an instance variable called nextResponder. If an object doesn't respond to a nil-targeted action, its `nextResponder` gets a chance. The `nextResponder` for a view is usually its superview. The `nextResponder` of the content view of the window is the window. Thus, the responders are linked together in what we call the *responder chain*.

Note that `nextResponder` has nothing to do with `nextKeyView`. For example, one menu item closes the key window. It has a target of `nil`. The action is **performClose:**. None of the standard objects respond to **performClose:** except **NSWindow**. Thus, the selected text field, for example, refuses to respond to **performClose:**. Then the superview of the text field refuses, and on up the view hierarchy. Ultimately, the window (the key window) accepts the **performClose:** method. So, to the user, the "active" window is closed.

As was mentioned in Chapter 12, a panel can become the key window but not the main window. If the key window and the main window are different, both windows get a chance to respond to the nil-targeted action.

How the Responder Chain Is Searched

In what order will the objects be tested before a nil-targeted action is discarded?

1. The `firstResponder` of the `keyWindow` and its responder chain. The responder chain would typically include the superviews and, finally, the key window.

2. The `delegate` of the key window

3. If it is a document-based application, the **NSWindowController** and then **NSDocument** object for the key window.

4. If the main window is different from the key window, it then goes through the same ritual with the main window:

   - The `firstResponder` of the main window and its responder chain, including the main window itself

   - The main window's `delegate`

   - The **NSWindowController** and then **NSDocument** object for the main window

5. The instance of **NSApplication**

6. The `delegate` of the **NSApplication**

7. The **NSDocumentController**

This series of objects is known as the *responder chain*. Figure 21.1 presents an example. The numbers indicate the order in which the objects would be asked whether they respond to the nil-targeted action.

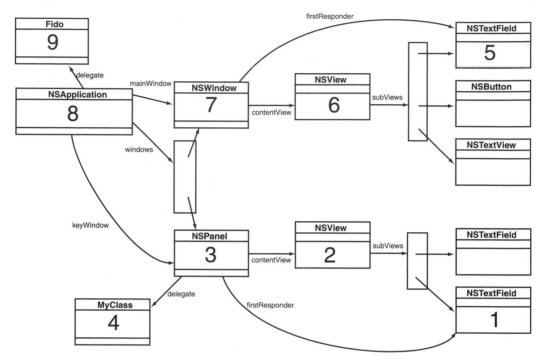

Figure 21.1 An Example of the Order in Which Responders Get a Chance to Respond

Note that in document-based applications, such as RaiseMan, the **NSDocument** object gets a chance to respond to the nil-targeted action. It receives the messages from the following menu items: Save, Save As…, Revert To Saved, Print…, and Page Layout….

Looking at the Nib File

Open the nib file. Note that the cut, copy, and paste items are connected to the icon labeled First Responder. The First Responder icon represents nil. It gives you something to drag to when you want an object to have a nil target (Figure 21.2).

The actions that appear in the Inspector when you drag to the First Responder are in the Identity Inspector under Class Actions. If you want an action to appear there, simply add it to the list.

Build and run your application. Note that cut, copy, and paste now work with your view. The keyboard equivalents also work. You can copy into the **BigLetterView** only strings that have one character.

Figure 21.2 Check Menu Item

For the More Curious: Which Object Sends the Action Message?

The target on the cut, copy, and paste menu items is `nil`. We know that sending a message to `nil` will not do anything. In fact, all target/action messages are handled by **NSApplication**. It has the following method:

```
- (BOOL)sendAction:(SEL)anAction to:(id)aTarget from:(id)sender
```

When the target is `nil`, **NSApplication** knows to try to send messages to the objects in the responder chain.

For the More Curious: Lazy Copying

An application can implement copying to a pasteboard in a lazy manner. For example, imagine a graphics application that copies large images to the pasteboard in several formats: PICT, TIFF, PDF, and so on. You can imagine that copying all these formats onto the pasteboard would be hard on the application and the pasteboard server. Instead, such an application might do a lazy copy. That is, the application will declare all the types that it could put on the pasteboard but will put off copying such data until another application asks for it.

Essentially, the application puts an IOU (instead of the data) on the pasteboard and gives an object that will provide the data when it is needed. When another application asks for the data, the pasteboard server calls back for the data.

The declaration works the same as earlier:

```
- (int)declareTypes:(NSArray *)types owner:(id)theOwner
```

But theOwner must implement the following method:

```
- (void)pasteboard:(NSPasteboard *)sender
        provideDataForType:(NSString *)type
```

When another application needs the data, this method will be called. At that point, the application must copy the data it promised onto the supplied pasteboard.

As you can imagine, a problem would arise if the pasteboard server asked for the data after the application had terminated. If an application that is terminating has an IOU currently on the pasteboard, it will be asked to supply all the data promised before terminating. Thus, it is not uncommon for an IOU owner to be sent **pasteboard:provideDataForType:** several times while the application is in the process of terminating.

The trickiest part of a lazy copy is that when copying data to the pasteboard and later pasting it into another application, the user doesn't want the most recent state of the data, but rather, the data *the way it was when the user copied it*. Most developers, when implementing a lazy copy, will take some sort of a snapshot of the information when declaring the types. When providing the data, the developer will copy the snapshot, instead of the current state, onto the pasteboard.

Of course, when the user does a copy somewhere else, your object will no longer be responsible for keeping the snapshot.

```
- (void)pasteboardChangedOwner:(NSPasteboard *)sender;
```

If you implement this method, it will be called when you are no longer responsible for keeping the snapshot.

Challenge 1

You are putting the string on the pasteboard. Create the PDF for the view, and put that on the pasteboard, too. Now you will be able to copy the image of the letter into graphics programs. Test it using Preview's New from Clipboard menu item. (Don't break the string copy and paste: Put both the string and the PDF on the pasteboard.)

Challenge 2

In the RaiseMan project, add a menu item that triggers the **removeEmployee:** method in **MyDocument**.

Chapter 22
CATEGORIES

Although the engineers at Apple are very wise, one day you will think, "Golly, if only they had put that method on that class, my life would be so much easier." When this happens, you will want to create a *category*, a collection of methods that you would like added to an existing class. The category concept is very useful, and I find it surprising that so few object-oriented languages include this powerful idea.

Creating categories is easier than talking about them. In the previous chapter, you added pasting capabilities to your **BigLetterView**. Note, however, that if the string on the pasteboard has more than one letter, the paste attempt will fail, because **BigLetterView** is capable of displaying only one letter at a time. Let's extend the example to take only the first letter of the string instead of failing.

Add a Method to NSString

It would be nice if every **NSString** object had a method that returned its first letter. It does not, so you will use a category to add it.

Open your project and create a new file of type Objective-C class. You are not in fact creating a class, but this is a good starting place for the creation of a category.

Name the file FirstLetter.m. Also create FirstLetter.h.

Change FirstLetter.h to declare your category. Here is what it looks like:

```
#import <Foundation/Foundation.h>

@interface NSString (FirstLetter)

- (NSString *)BNR_firstLetter;

@end
```

You appear to be declaring the class **NSString**, but you are not giving it any instance variables or a superclass. Instead, you are naming the category **FirstLetter** and declaring a method. A category cannot add instance variables to the class, only methods.

Now implement the method **BNR_firstLetter** in the file FirstLetter.m. Make the file look like this:

```
#import "FirstLetter.h"

@implementation NSString (FirstLetter)

- (NSString *)BNR_firstLetter
{
    if ([self length] < 2) {
        return self;
    }
    NSRange r;
    r.location = 0;
    r.length = 1;
    return [self substringWithRange:r];
}
@end
```

Now you can use this method as if it were part of **NSString**. In BigLetterView.m, change **readFromPasteboard:** to look like this:

```
- (BOOL)readFromPasteboard:(NSPasteboard *)pb
{
    // Is there a string on the pasteboard?
    NSArray *types = [pb types];
    if ([types containsObject:NSStringPboardType]) {

        // Read the string from the pasteboard
        NSString *value = [pb stringForType:NSStringPboardType];

        [self setString:[value BNR_firstLetter]];
        return YES;
    }
    return NO;
}
```

At the beginning of the BigLetterView.m, import the header:

```
#import "FirstLetter.h"
```

Build and run your application. You will be able to copy strings with more than one letter into **BigLetterView**. Only the first letter of the string will be copied.

In this example, you added only one method, but note that you can add as many methods to the class as you wish. Also, you used only the methods of the class here, but you can also access the class's instance variables directly.

Note that I added a prefix, BNR_ to the method name in my category. I would like to name the method **firstLetter**. But what if Apple adds a **firstLetter** method to **NSString** in Mac OS X 10.9? There would be a conflict. For safety, I added the prefix.

Cocoa itself has many categories. For example, **NSAttributedString** is part of the Foundation framework. However, **NSAttributedString**'s **drawInRect:** method is part of a category from the AppKit framework. As a result, the documention for the methods on **NSAttributedString** are distributed between the two frameworks. There are also separate header files for **NSAttributedString** and its categories, which tends to cause some confusion.

For the More Curious: Declaring Private Methods

Often, you will have in your .m file methods defined that you do not want to advertise by declaring them in your .h file. These are known as *private methods*.

If you call a private method before you declare or define it, you will get a warning from the compiler. One common technique to prevent these warnings is to declare the private methods in a category at the beginning of the .m file:

```
#import  "Megatron.h"

// Declare the private methods
@interface Megatron ()
- (void)blowTheLidOff;
- (void)putTheLidBackOn;
@end

@implementation Megatron

...actually implement all the private and public methods...

@end
```

For the More Curious: Declaring Informal Protocols

With Objective-C 2.0, you can flag parts of a protocol as @optional, and this is how you would declare delegate methods in Objective-C 2.0. But we needed a way to declare them before Objective-C 2.0. What we did was ugly. And we called this bit of ugliness an *Informal Protocol*. If you look near the end NSWindow.h, you will see something like this:

```
@interface NSObject (NSWindow)
- (BOOL)windowShouldClose:(NSWindow *)w;
- (NSSize)windowWillResize:(NSWindow *)sender toSize:(NSSize)aSize;
...
@end
```

This is not really a category on **NSObject**. It is simply the ugly way that we used to declare delegate methods.

Chapter 23

DRAG-AND-DROP

Drag-and-drop is little more than a flashy copy-and-paste operation. When the drag starts, some data is copied onto the dragging pasteboard. When the drop occurs, the data is read off the dragging pasteboard. The only thing that makes this technique trickier than copy-and-paste is that users need feedback: an image that appears as they drag, a view that becomes highlighted when they drag into it, and maybe a big gulping sound when they drop the image.

Several things can happen when data is dragged from one application to another: Nothing may happen, a copy of the data may be created, or a link to the existing data may be created. Constants represent these operations:

    NSDragOperationNone

    NSDragOperationCopy

    NSDragOperationLink

There are several other operations that you see less frequently:

    NSDragOperationGeneric

    NSDragOperationPrivate

    NSDragOperationMove

    NSDragOperationDelete

    NSDragOperationEvery

Both the source and the destination must agree on the operation that will occur when the user drops the image.

When you add drag-and-drop to a view, the change involves both

1. Making it a drag source

2. Making it a drag destination

Let's take these steps separately. First, you will make your view be a drag source.
When that is working, you will make it be a drag destination.

Make BigLetterView a Drag Source

When you finish this section, you will be able to drag a letter off the
BigLetterView and drop it into any text editor. It will look like Figure 23.1.

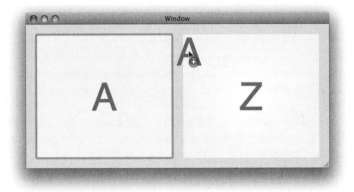

Figure 23.1   Completed Application

To be a drag source, your view must implement **draggingSourceOperationMask
ForLocal:**. This method declares what operations the view is willing to
participate in as a source. Add the following method to your BigLetterView.m:

```
- (NSDragOperation)draggingSourceOperationMaskForLocal:(BOOL)isLocal
{
    return NSDragOperationCopy;
}
```

This method is automatically called twice: once with isLocal as YES, which
determines what operations it is willing to participate in for destinations within
your application; and once with isLocal as NO, which determines what
operations it is willing to participate in for destinations in other applications.

To start a drag operation, you will use a method on **NSView**:

```
- (void)dragImage:(NSImage *)anImage
              at:(NSPoint)imageLoc
          offset:(NSSize)mouseOffset
           event:(NSEvent *)theEvent
```

```
   pasteboard:(NSPasteboard *)pboard
       source:(id)sourceObject
    slideBack:(BOOL)slideBack
```

You will supply it with the image to be dragged and the point at which you want the drag to begin. The event supplied should be the mouseDown event. The offset is completely ignored. The pasteboard is usually the standard drag pasteboard. If the drop does not occur, you can choose whether the icon should slide back to the place from which it came.

Add an instance variable to BigLetterView.h to hold the mouseDown event:

```
NSEvent *mouseDownEvent;
```

In **mouseDown:**, put the event into that instance variable. In BigLetterView.m:

```
- (void)mouseDown:(NSEvent *)event
{
    [event retain];
    [mouseDownEvent release];
    mouseDownEvent = event;
}
```

You will also need to create an image to drag. You can draw on an image just as you can on a view. To make the drawing appear on the image instead of on the screen, you must first lock focus on the image. When the drawing is complete, you must unlock the focus.

Here is the whole method to add to BigLetterView.m:

```
- (void)mouseDragged:(NSEvent *)event
{
    NSPoint down = [mouseDownEvent locationInWindow];
    NSPoint drag = [event locationInWindow];
    float distance = hypot(down.x - drag.x, down.y - drag.y);
    if (distance < 3) {
        return;
    }

    // Is the string of zero length?
    if ([string length] == 0) {
        return;
    }

    // Get the size of the string
    NSSize s = [string sizeWithAttributes:attributes];

    // Create the image that will be dragged
    NSImage *anImage = [[NSImage alloc] initWithSize:s];
```

```
    // Create a rect in which you will draw the letter
    // in the image
    NSRect imageBounds;
    imageBounds.origin = NSZeroPoint;
    imageBounds.size = s;

    // Draw the letter on the image
    [anImage lockFocus];
    [self drawStringCenteredIn:imageBounds];
    [anImage unlockFocus];

    // Get the location of the mouseDown event
    NSPoint p = [self convertPoint:down fromView:nil];

    // Drag from the center of the image
    p.x = p.x - s.width/2;
    p.y = p.y - s.height/2;

    // Get the pasteboard
    NSPasteboard *pb = [NSPasteboard pasteboardWithName:NSDragPboard];

    // Put the string on the pasteboard
    [self writeToPasteboard:pb];

    // Start the drag
    [self dragImage:anImage
                 at:p
             offset:NSMakeSize(0, 0)
              event:mouseDownEvent
         pasteboard:pb
             source:self
          slideBack:YES];
    [anImage release];
}
```

That's it. Build and run the application. You should be able to drag a letter off the view and into any text editor. (Try dragging it into Xcode.)

When a drop occurs, the drag source will be notified if you implement the following method:

```
- (void)draggedImage:(NSImage *)image
             endedAt:(NSPoint)screenPoint
           operation:(NSDragOperation)operation;
```

For example, to make it possible to clear the **BigLetterView** by dragging the letter to the trashcan in the dock, advertise your willingness in **draggingSourceOperationMaskForLocal:**

```
- (NSDragOperation)draggingSourceOperationMaskForLocal:(BOOL)isLocal
{
    return NSDragOperationCopy | NSDragOperationDelete;
}
```

Then implement **draggedImage:endedAt:operation:**

```
- (void)draggedImage:(NSImage *)image
            endedAt:(NSPoint)screenPoint
          operation:(NSDragOperation)operation
{
    if (operation == NSDragOperationDelete) {
        [self setString:@""];
    }
}
```

Build and run the application. Drag a letter into the trashcan. The letter should disappear from the view.

Make BigLetterView a Drag Destination

Being a drag destination involves several parts. First, you need to declare your view to be a destination for the dragging of certain types. **NSView** has a method for this purpose:

```
- (void)registerForDraggedTypes:(NSArray *)pboardTypes
```

You typically call this method in your **initWithFrame:** method.

Then you need to implement six methods. (Yes, six!) All six methods have the same argument: an **NSDraggingInfo** object. It has the dragging pasteboard. The six methods are invoked as follows:

1. As the image is dragged into the destination, the destination is sent a **draggingEntered:** message. Often, the destination view updates its appearance. For example, it might highlight itself.

2. While the image remains within the destination, a series of **draggingUpdated:** messages are sent. Implementing **draggingUpdated:** is optional.

3. If the image is dragged outside the destination, **draggingExited:** is sent.

4. If it is released on the destination, either the image slides back to its source and breaks the sequence, or a **prepareForDragOperation:** message is sent to the destination, depending on the value returned by the most recent invocation of **draggingEntered:** (or **draggingUpdated:** if the view implemented it).

5. If the **prepareForDragOperation:** message returns YES, a **performDragOperation:** message is sent. This is typically where the application reads data off the pasteboard.

6. Finally, if **performDragOperation:** returned YES, **concludeDragOperation:** is sent. The appearance may change. This is where you might generate the big gulping sound that implies a successful drop.

registerForDraggedTypes

Add a call to **registerForDraggedTypes:** to the **initWithFrame:** method in BigLetterView.m:

```
- (id)initWithFrame:(NSRect)rect
{
    [super initWithFrame:rect];
    NSLog(@"initializing view");
    [self prepareAttributes];
    bgColor = [[NSColor yellowColor] retain];
    string = @"";
    [self registerForDraggedTypes:
                    [NSArray arrayWithObject:NSStringPboardType]];
    return self;
}
```

Add Highlighting

To signal the user that the drop is acceptable, your view will highlight itself. Add a highlighted instance variable to BigLetterView.h:

```
@interface BigLetterView : NSView
{
    NSColor *bgColor;
    NSString *string;
    NSMutableDictionary *attributes;
    NSEvent *mouseDownEvent;
    BOOL highlighted;
}
...
```

Now, you are going to add highlighting to **drawRect:**. The class **NSGradient** makes it easy to draw with gradients. In this case, you are going to draw a radial gradient—white in the center fading into the bgColor:

```
- (void)drawRect:(NSRect)rect
{
 NSRect bounds = [self bounds];
 // Draw gradient background if highlighted
 if (highlighted) {
```

```
  NSGradient *gr;
  gr = [[NSGradient alloc] initWithStartingColor:[NSColor whiteColor]
                              endingColor:bgColor];
  [gr drawInRect:bounds relativeCenterPosition:NSZeroPoint];
  [gr release];
} else {
  [bgColor set];
  [NSBezierPath fillRect:bounds];
}
[self drawStringCenteredIn:bounds];
...
```

Implement the Dragging-Destination Methods

So far, we have seen two ways to declare a pointer to an object. If the pointer can refer to any type of object, we would declare it like this:

```
id foo;
```

If the pointer should refer to an instance of a particular class, we can declare it like this:

```
MyClass *foo;
```

A third possibility also exists. If we have a pointer that should refer to an object that conforms to a particular protocol, we can declare it like this:

```
id <MyProtocol> foo;
```

NSDraggingInfo is in fact a protocol, not a class. All the dragging-destination methods expect an object that conforms to the **NSDraggingInfo** protocol.

Add the following methods to BigLetterView.m:

```
#pragma mark Dragging Destination

- (NSDragOperation)draggingEntered:(id <NSDraggingInfo>)sender
{
    NSLog(@"draggingEntered:");
    if ([sender draggingSource] == self) {
        return NSDragOperationNone;
    }

    highlighted = YES;
    [self setNeedsDisplay:YES];
    return NSDragOperationCopy;
}
```

```objc
- (void)draggingExited:(id <NSDraggingInfo>)sender
{
    NSLog(@"draggingExited:");
    highlighted = NO;
    [self setNeedsDisplay:YES];
}

- (BOOL)prepareForDragOperation:(id <NSDraggingInfo>)sender
{
    return YES;
}

- (BOOL)performDragOperation:(id <NSDraggingInfo>)sender
{
    NSPasteboard *pb = [sender draggingPasteboard];
    if(![self readFromPasteboard:pb]) {
        NSLog(@"Error: Could not read from dragging pasteboard");
        return NO;
    }
    return YES;
}

- (void)concludeDragOperation:(id <NSDraggingInfo>)sender
{
    NSLog(@"concludeDragOperation:");
    highlighted = NO;
    [self setNeedsDisplay:YES];
}
```

Test

Open the nib file, and add another **BigLetterView** to the window. Delete the text fields. Make sure to set the nextKeyView for each **BigLetterView** so that you can tab between them (Figure 23.2).

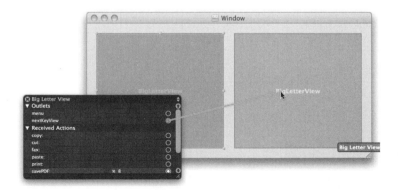

Figure 23.2   Set nextKeyView for Each BigLetterView

Build and run the application. Note that you can drag characters between the views and from other applications.

For the More Curious: Operation Mask

For some apps, the negotiations of what operation will occur when the user drops can be quite complicated. After all, the source advertises its willingness to participate in some kinds of operations through **draggingSourceOperation-MaskForLocal:**. The user may also indicate preferences by holding down the Control, Option, or Command key. It is the job of the destination to determine what happens.

The dragging info object will do most of the work for you. It will get the source's advertised operation mask and filter it, depending on what modifier keys the user holds down. To see this, implement **draggingUpdated:**, and log out the dragging info's operation mask:

```
- (NSDragOperation)draggingUpdated:(id <NSDraggingInfo>)sender
{
    NSDragOperation op = [sender draggingSourceOperationMask];
    NSLog(@"operation mask = %d", op);
    if ([sender draggingSource] == self) {
        return NSDragOperationNone;
    }
    return NSDragOperationCopy;
}
```

Now build and run the application. Try dragging text from different sources and holding down different modifier keys. Note what happens to the mask and the cursor.

Chapter 24
NSTIMER

An instance of **NSButton** has a target and an action (selector). When the button is clicked, the action message is sent to the target. Timers work in a similar way. A timer is an object that has a target, a selector, and a delay, which is given in seconds (Figure 24.1).

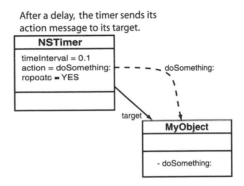

Figure 24.1   NSTimer

After the delay, the selector message is sent to the target. The timer sends itself as an argument to the message. The timer can also be set to send the message repeatedly.

To play with timers a bit, you will create a typing-tutor application. The application will have two **BigLetterView** objects. One will display what the user should type, and the other will display what the user has typed (Figure 24.2).

An **NSProgressIndicator** will display how much time is left. After 2 seconds, the application will beep to indicate that the user took too long. Then the user is given 2 more seconds.

You will create an **AppController** class. When the user clicks the Go button, an instance of **NSTimer** will be created. The timer will send a message every 0.2 second.

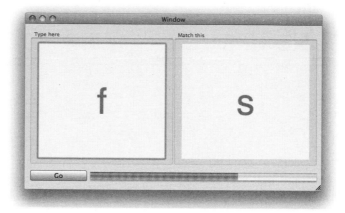

Figure 24.2   Completed Application

The method triggered will check whether the two views match. If so, the user is given a new letter to type. Otherwise, the progress indicator is incremented. If the user pauses the application, the timer is invalidated. Figure 24.3 shows the object diagram.

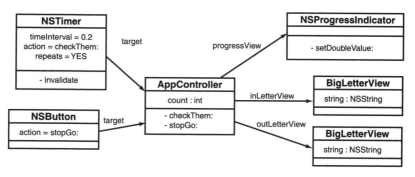

Figure 24.3   Object Diagram

Go back to your TypingTutor project in Xcode. Create a new Objective-C class called **AppController**. In AppController.h, give it two outlets and an action. You will also need a timer, an array for the letters, the index of the last letter displayed, and a count that indicates how long the current letter has been visible:

```
#import <Cocoa/Cocoa.h>
@class BigLetterView;

@interface AppController : NSObject
{
    // Outlets
```

```
    IBOutlet BigLetterView *inLetterView;
    IBOutlet BigLetterView *outLetterView;

    // Data
    NSArray *letters;
    int lastIndex;

    // Time
    NSTimer *timer;
    int count;
}
- (IBAction)stopGo:(id)sender;
- (void)incrementCount;
- (void)resetCount;
- (void)showAnotherLetter;
@end
```

Lay Out the Interface

Open the MainMenu.nib. Create an instance of **AppController** by dragging an Object into the doc window (from under Objects & Controllers). Set the class to be **AppController** (Figure 24.4).

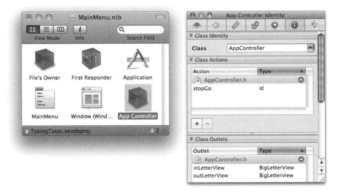

Figure 24.4   Create an Instance of AppController

Select the **BigLetterView** on the left. From the Layout menu, choose the Embed Objects in -> Box menu item. Relabel the box Type here. Embed the other **BigLetterView** in a box, and relabel that box Match this.

Drop an **NSProgressIndicator** on the window. Use the Inspector to make it not indeterminate. Set its range to be 0 to 100 (Figure 24.5).

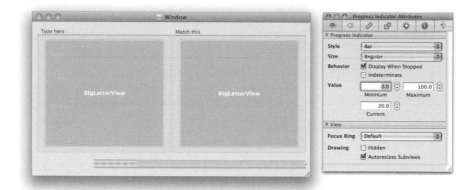

Figure 24.5   Inspect the Progress Indicator

Put a button on the window. Using the Inspector, set its title to Go and its alternative title to Pause. Make the button style Round Textured, and set its mode to Toggle. Also, set it to be unselected (Figure 24.6).

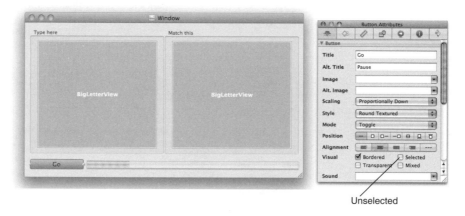

Figure 24.6   Inspect the Button

Make Connections

Control-drag from the button to the **AppController** object. Set the action to be **stopGo:** (Figure 24.7).

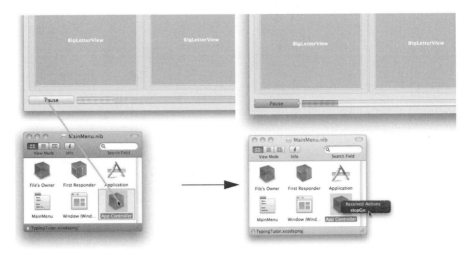

Figure 24.7   Connect the Button to the AppController

Bind the value of the **NSProgressIndicator** to the count attribute of
AppController (Figure 24.8).

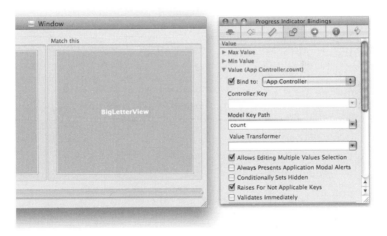

Figure 24.8   Connect the inLetterView Outlet

Control-click on the **AppController** to display the Connection panel. Drag
from inLetterView to the **BigLetterView** on the left. Drag from outLetterView
to the **BigLetterView** on the right (Figure 24.9).

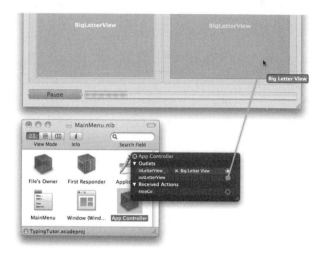

Figure 24.9 Connect the inLetterView Outlet

Adding Code to AppController

Implement the following methods in AppController.m:

```objc
#import "AppController.h"
#import "BigLetterView.h"

#define MAX_COUNT (100)
#define COUNT_STEP (5)

@implementation AppController

- (id)init
{
    [super init];

    // Create an array of letters
    letters = [[NSArray alloc] initWithObjects:@"a", @"s",
                    @"d",@"f", @"j", @"k", @"l", @";",nil];

    // Seed the random number generator
    srandom(time(NULL));
    return self;

}

- (void)awakeFromNib
{
    [self showAnotherLetter];
}
```

```
- (void)resetCount
{
    [self willChangeValueForKey:@"count"];
    count = 0;
    [self didChangeValueForKey:@"count"];
}

- (void)incrementCount
{
    [self willChangeValueForKey:@"count"];
    count = count + COUNT_STEP;
    if (count > MAX_COUNT) {
        count = MAX_COUNT;
    }
    [self didChangeValueForKey:@"count"];
}

- (void)showAnotherLetter
{
    //Choose random numbers until you get a different
    // number than last time
    int x = lastIndex;
    while (x == lastIndex){
        x = random() % [letters count];
    }
    lastIndex = x;
    [outLetterView setString:[letters objectAtIndex:x]];

    // Start the count again
    [self resetCount];
}

- (IBAction)stopGo:(id)sender
{
    if (timer == nil) {
        NSLog(@"Starting");

        // Create a timer
        timer = [[NSTimer scheduledTimerWithTimeInterval:0.1
                                      target:self
                                    selector:@selector(checkThem:)
                                    userInfo:nil
                                     repeats:YES] retain];
    } else {
        NSLog(@"Stopping");

        // Invalidate and release the timer
        [timer invalidate];
        [timer release];
        timer = nil;
    }
}
```

```
- (void)checkThem:(NSTimer *)aTimer
{
    if ([[inLetterView string] isEqual:[outLetterView string]]) {
        [self showAnotherLetter];
    }
    if (count == MAX_COUNT) {
        NSBeep();
        [self resetCount];
    } else {
        [self incrementCount];
    }
}
@end
```

Build and run your application.

Note, once again, that we have separated our classes into views (**BigLetterView**) and controllers (**AppController**). If I were creating a full-featured application, I would probably also create model classes, such as **Lesson** and **Student**.

For the More Curious: NSRunLoop

NSRunLoop is an object that waits. It waits for events to arrive and then forwards them to **NSApplication**. It waits for timer events to arrive and then forwards them to **NSTimer**. You can even attach a network socket to the run loop, and it will wait for data to arrive on that socket.

Challenge

Change your ImageFun application so that autoscrolling is timer driven. Delete your **mouseDragged:** method from **StretchView**. In **mouseDown:**, create a repeating timer that invokes a method in the view every tenth of a second. In the invoked method, autoscroll using the current event. To get the current event, use **NSApplication**'s **currentEvent** method:

```
NSEvent *e = [NSApp currentEvent];
```

(Remember that NSApp is a global variable that points to the instance of **NSApplication**.) Invalidate and release the timer in **mouseUp:**. Note that the autoscrolling becomes much smoother and more predictable.

Chapter 25
SHEETS

A sheet is simply an **NSWindow** instance that is attached to another window. The sheet comes down over the window, and the window stops getting events until the sheet is dismissed. Typically, you will compose a sheet as an offscreen window in your nib file.

NSApplication has several methods that make sheets possible:

```
// Start a sheet
- (void)beginSheet:(NSWindow *)sheet
     modalForWindow:(NSWindow *)docWindow
      modalDelegate:(id)modalDelegate
     didEndSelector:(SEL)didEndSelector
        contextInfo:(void *)contextInfo;

// End the sheet
- (void)endSheet:(NSWindow *)sheet returnCode:(int)returnCode;
```

Besides the sheet window and the window to which it is attached, you supply a modal delegate, a selector, and a pointer when you start the sheet. The modalDelegate will be sent the didEndSelector, and the sheet, its return code, and the contextInfo will be sent as arguments. Thus, the method triggered by the didEndSelector should have a signature like this:

```
- (void)rex:(NSWindow *)sheet
        fido:(int)returnCode
       rover:(void *)contextInfo;
```

The dog names are used here to indicate that you could name the method anything you wish. Most programmers name the method something more meaningful, such as **sheetDidEnd:returnCode:contextInfo:**.

Adding a Sheet

You are going to add a sheet that will allow the user to adjust the speed of the TypingTutor application. You will bring up the sheet when the user selects the Adjust speed... menu item. You will end the sheet when the user clicks the OK button. The final application will look like Figure 25.1.

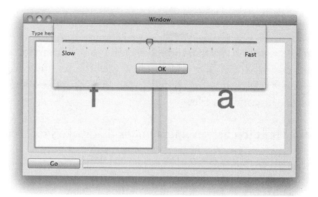

Figure 25.1   Completed Application

Your **AppController** will control the slider and the window, so you will need to add outlets for them. Also, your **AppController** will be sent a message when the user selects the Adjust speed... menu item or clicks the OK button, so you will need to add two action methods to the **AppController**.

Figure 25.2 presents the object diagram.

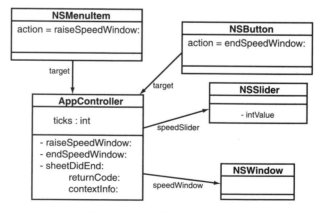

Figure 25.2   Object Diagram

Add Outlets and Actions

Edit AppController.h as follows:

```
#import <Cocoa/Cocoa.h>
@class BigLetterView;

@interface AppController : NSObject
{
    // Outlets
    IBOutlet BigLetterView *inLetterView;
    IBOutlet BigLetterView *outLetterView;
    IBOutlet NSWindow *speedSheet;

    // Data
    NSArray *letters;
    int lastIndex;

    // Time
    NSTimer *timer;
    int count;
    int stepSize;
}
- (IBAction)stopGo:(id)sender;
- (IBAction)showSpeedSheet:(id)sender;
- (IBAction)endSpeedSheet:(id)sender;
- (void)incrementCount;
- (void)resetCount;
- (void)showAnotherLetter;

@end
```

Save the file.

Lay Out the Interface

Open MainMenu.nib. Add a menu item to the main menu for your application by dragging it out of the Library (under Application -> Menus) (Figure 25.3).

Change the title of the menu item to Adjust Speed.... Control-drag from the menu item to the **AppController**. Set the action to be **showSpeedSheet:** (Figure 25.4).

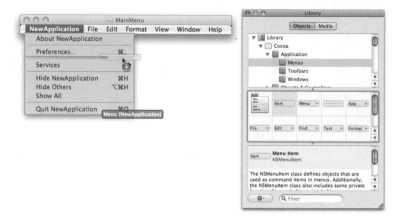

Figure 25.3   Add a Menu Item

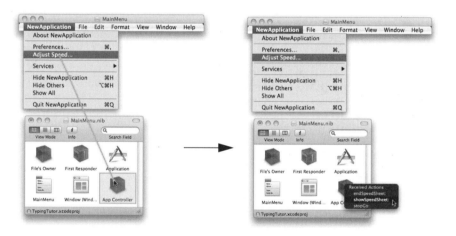

Figure 25.4   Connect the Menu Item

Create a new window by dragging one out of the Library (under Application -> Windows). Disable resizing for the window; make it not Visible at launch (Figure 25.5).

Put a slider on the new window. To label the left end of the slider as Slow and the right end as Fast, drop two uneditable text fields onto the window. Add a button and change its title to OK. Inspect the slider, and set its range to be 1 to 10 (Figure 25.6).

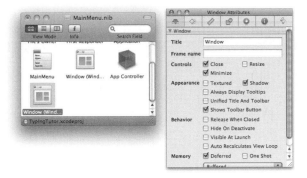

Figure 25.5   Inspect New Window

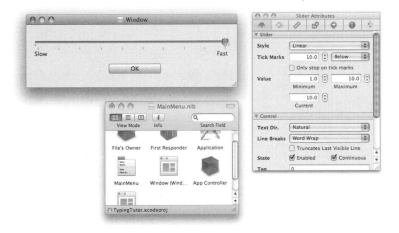

Figure 25.6   Inspect Slider

Bind the Value of the slider to the **AppController**'s stepSize, as shown in Figure 25.7.

When the user clicks the OK button, it should send the **AppController** a message that will end the sheet. Control-drag from the button to the **AppController**, and choose **endSpeedSheet:** as the action (Figure 25.8).

To raise the window as a sheet, your **AppController** must have a pointer to it. Control-click on the **AppController** to get the Connection panel. Connect the speedSheet outlet to the window (Figure 25.9).

Save and close the nib file.

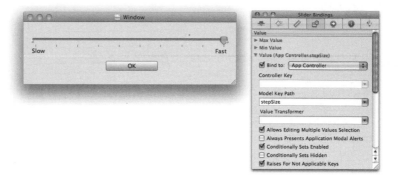

Figure 25.7   Bind the Slider's Value to stepSize

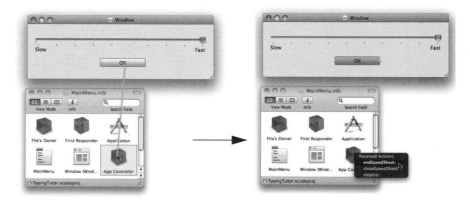

Figure 25.8   Set the target of the Button

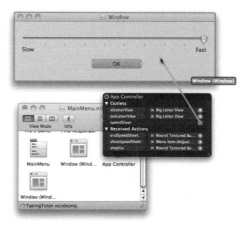

Figure 25.9   Connect speedSheet Outlet

Add Code

In AppController.m, you defined a constant called COUNT_STEP. In the last section, the user went from 0 to 100 in steps of 5. In this section, you will make the step size a variable. If playing Fast, the user will get bigger steps than if playing Slow. The step size is bound to the slider.

In AppController.m, delete the line that says #define COUNT_STEP (5).

In the **init** method, initialize stepSize to be 5:

```
- (id)init
{
    [super init];

    // Create an array of letters
    letters = [[NSArray alloc] initWithObjects:@"a", @"s",
                    @"d",@"f", @"j", @"k", @"l", @";",nil];

    // Seed the random number generator
    srandom(time(NULL));
    stepSize = 5;
    return self;
}
```

In **incrementCount**, replace COUNT_STEP with stepSize:

```
- (void)incrementCount
{
    [self willChangeValueForKey:@"count"];
    count = count + stepSize;
    if (count > MAX_COUNT) {
        count = MAX_COUNT;
    }
    [self didChangeValueForKey:@"count"];
}
```

When the user chooses the Adjust Speed... menu item, the sheet will run. Add the following method to AppController.m:

```
- (IBAction)showSpeedSheet:(id)sender
{
    [NSApp beginSheet:speedSheet
       modalForWindow:[inLetterView window]
        modalDelegate:nil
       didEndSelector:NULL
          contextInfo:NULL];
}
```

Note that you are attaching the sheet to the window that the inLetterView is on. Also, when the sheet is dismissed, you will not get any sort of callback.

The sheet will end when the user clicks the OK button. Add the following method to AppController.m:

```
- (IBAction)endSpeedSheet:(id)sender
{
  // Return to normal event handling
  [NSApp endSheet:speedSheet];

  // Hide the sheet
  [speedSheet orderOut:sender];

}
```

Build and run your application. Bring up the sheet, adjust the speed, and dismiss the sheet.

For the More Curious: contextInfo

The contextInfo parameter is a pointer to some data. You can supply this parameter when you start the sheet, and the delegate will get the pointer when you end the sheet. Here, for example, the developer has started a sheet and inserted a phone number for the context info:

```
[NSApp beginSheet:aWindow
   modalForWindow:someOtherWindow
    modalDelegate:self
   didEndSelector:@selector(didEnd:returnCode:phone:)
      contextInfo:@"703-555-6513"];
```

Later, in the **didEnd:returnCode:phone:** method, the phone number will be supplied as the third argument:

```
- (void)didEnd:(NSWindow *)sheet
   returnCode:(int)returnCode
        phone:(NSString *)phoneNumber
{
  NSLog(@"sheetDidEnd: Phone number = %@", phoneNumber);
}
```

Note that the context info and the **NSNotification**'s user info dictionary serve similar purposes.

For the More Curious: Modal Windows

When a sheet is active, the user is prevented from sending events to the window to which it is attached. When an Alert panel is run, it is modal—that is, the user is prevented from sending events to any other window.

To make a window modal, use the following method of NSApp:

- (int)**runModalForWindow:**(NSWindow *)aWindow

Only events destined for aWindow will make it through this method. When you are ready to make the aWindow nonmodal, send this message to the **NSApplication** object:

- (void)**stopModalWithCode:**(int)returnCode

At that point, **runModalForWindow:** will end and return returnCode.

Chapter 26
CREATING NSFORMATTERS

A formatter takes a string and makes another object, typically so that the user can type something that is more than simply a string. For example, when passed the string "3/17/1975", the **NSDateFormatter** converts it into an **NSDate** object that represents the seventeenth day of March in the year 1975 (Figure 26.1).

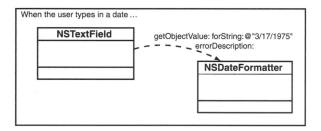

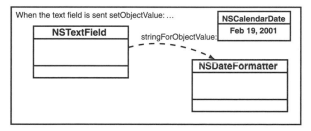

Figure 26.1   NSDateFormatter

Also, a formatter can take an object and create a string for the user to see. For example, imagine a text field that has an **NSDateFormatter**. When the text field is sent **setObjectValue:** with an **NSCalendarDate** object, the date formatter will create a string that represents that date. The user will then see that string.

All formatters are subclasses of the **NSFormatter** class. Two of these subclasses come with Cocoa: **NSDateFormatter** and **NSNumberFormatter**. You used **NSNumberFormatter** in Chapter 8 to format the expected raise as a percentage.

The most basic formatter will implement two methods:

```
- (BOOL)getObjectValue:(id *)anObject
            forString:(NSString *)aString
      errorDescription:(NSString **)errorPtr
```

This message is sent by the control (like a text field) to the formatter when it has to convert aString—what the user typed in—into an object. The formatter can return YES and set anObject to point to the new object. If the return is NO, the string could not be converted, and the errorPtr is set to indicate what went wrong. Note that errorPtr is a pointer to a pointer; that is, it is a location where you can put a pointer to the string. Similarly, anObject is a pointer to a pointer.

```
- (NSString *)stringForObjectValue:(id)anObject
```

This message is sent by the control to the formatter when it has to convert anObject into a string. The control will display the string that is returned for the user (Figure 26.2).

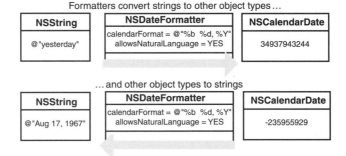

Figure 26.2   NSFormatter

Often, the object that is created from the string also is a string. For example, you might have a **TelephoneNumberFormatter** that properly inserts the parentheses and dashes into a telephone number.

A Basic Formatter

In this chapter, you will write your own formatter class. You will create a formatter that allows the user to type in the name of a color, and the formatter will in turn create the appropriate **NSColor** object. Then you will set the background of the **BigLetterView** with that color object. Figure 26.3 shows what the application will look like when you are done.

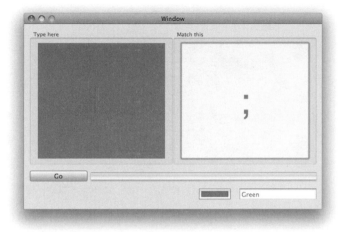

Figure 26.3   Completed Application

Create ColorFormatter.h

In Xcode, create a new Objective-C class. Name it **ColorFormatter**.

In ColorFormatter.h, change the superclass to **NSFormatter**, and add an instance variable:

```
#import <Cocoa/Cocoa.h>

@interface ColorFormatter : NSFormatter
{
    NSColorList *colorList;
}
@end
```

Save the file.

Edit the Nib File

Open MainMenu.nib. Drop a color well and a text field on the window (Figure 26.4).

Bind the value of the color well to the **AppController**'s inLetterView.bgColor (Figure 26.5).

Bind the value of the text field to the same Key Path (Figure 26.6).

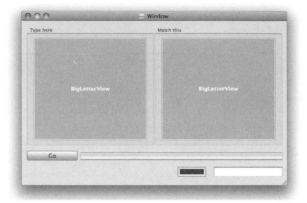

Figure 26.4   Add Color Well and Text Field

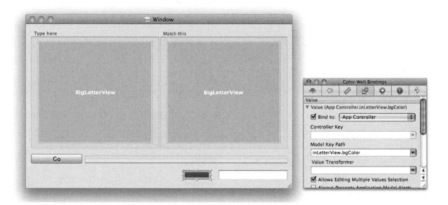

Figure 26.5   Bind Value of Color Well to bgColor of inLetterView

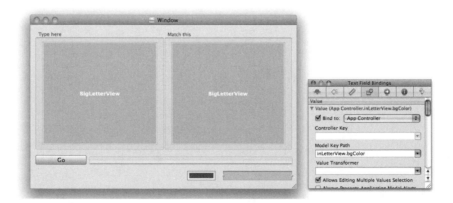

Figure 26.6   Bind Value of Text Field to bgColor of inLetterView

Drop an **NSObject** in the doc window. Set its class to be **ColorFormatter** (Figure 26.7).

Figure 26.7   Create an Instance of ColorFormatter

Control-click on the text field to bring up its Connection panel. Set the formatter outlet to point to the **ColorFormatter** object (Figure 26.8).

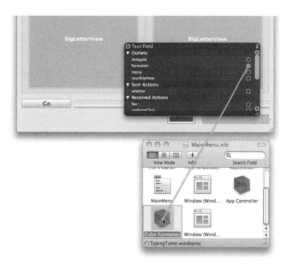

Figure 26.8   Set the Text Field's Formatter Outlet

NSColorList

For this exercise, you will use an **NSColorList**, a dictionary of color objects that maps a name to an instance of **NSColor** objects. Several color lists come standard with Mac OS X. In particular, the color list named "Apple" includes many of the standard colors, such as purple and yellow.

NSColorList is not a particularly useful class, but it makes this exercise very elegant. We will not spend much time discussing it.

Search Strings for Substrings

When you have a string such as "dakakookookakoo," and are searching through it for a shorter string, such as "ka," the result will be an NSRange. The location is the first letter of the matching substring in the longer string. The length is the length of the substring.

Of course, you might want to set a couple of options. For example, you might want to do a case-insensitive search or a backward search—from the end of the string instead of the beginning. To search backward for the string "KA" in "abbakachakaza" in a case-insensitive manner, you would use the following code:

```
NSRange aRange;
NSString *big = @"abbakachakazazzz";
NSString *small = @"KA";

aRange = [big rangeOfString:small
            options:(NSCaseInsensitiveSearch | NSBackwardsSearch)];
```

After this code executes, aRange.location would be 9, and aRange.length would be 2. If the substring is not found, the length will be 0.

Implement the Basic Formatter Methods

Edit ColorFormatter.m to look like this:

```
#import "ColorFormatter.h"

@interface ColorFormatter ()
- (NSString *)firstColorKeyForPartialString:(NSString *)string;
@end

@implementation ColorFormatter

- (id)init
{
    [super init];
    colorList = [[NSColorList colorListNamed:@"Apple"] retain];
    return self;
}
- (void)dealloc
{
    [colorList release];
    [super dealloc];
}
```

```objc
- (NSString *)firstColorKeyForPartialString:(NSString *)string
{
    // Is the key zero-length?
    if ([string length] == 0) {
        return nil;
    }

    // Loop through the color list
    for (NSString *key in [colorList allKeys]) {
        NSRange whereFound = [key rangeOfString:string
                                    options:NSCaseInsensitiveSearch];
        // Does the string match the beginning of the color name?
        if ((whereFound.location == 0) && (whereFound.length > 0)) {
            return key;
        }
    }
    // If no match is found, return nil
    return nil;
}

- (NSString *)stringForObjectValue:(id)obj
{
    // Not a color?
    if (![obj isKindOfClass:[NSColor class]]) {
        return nil;
    }

    // Convert to an RGB Color Space
    NSColor *color;
    color = [obj colorUsingColorSpaceName:NSCalibratedRGBColorSpace];

    // Get components as floats between 0 and 1
    CGFloat red, green, blue;
    [color getRed:&red
            green:&green
             blue:&blue
            alpha:NULL];

    // Initialize the distance to something large
    float minDistance = 3.0;
    NSString *closestKey = nil;

    // Find the closest color
    for (NSString *key in [colorList allKeys]) {
        NSColor *c = [colorList colorWithKey:key];
        CGFloat r, g, b;
        [c getRed:&r
            green:&g
             blue:&b
            alpha:NULL];

        // How far apart are 'color' and 'c'?
        float dist;
        dist = pow(red - r, 2) + pow(green -g, 2) + pow(blue - b, 2);
```

```
            // Is this the closest yet?
            if (dist < minDistance) {
                minDistance = dist;
                closestKey = key;
            }
        }
        // Return the name of the closest color
        return closestKey;
}

- (BOOL)getObjectValue:(id *)obj
             forString:(NSString *)string
      errorDescription:(NSString **)errorString
{
    // Look up the color for 'string'
    NSString *matchingKey = [self firstColorKeyForPartialString:string];
    if (matchingKey) {
      *obj = [colorList colorWithKey:matchingKey];
      return YES;
    } else {
      // Occasionally, 'errorString' is NULL
      if (errorString != NULL) {
          *errorString = [NSString stringWithFormat:
                                   @"'%@' is not a color", string];
      }
      return NO;
    }
}
@end
```

Build and run your application. You should be able to type in color names and see the background of the **BigLetterView** change accordingly. Also, if you use the color well, you should see the name of the color change in the text field. Try typing in string that is not a color.

The delegate of the NSControl

Note that bindings mechanism makes a nice Alert sheet when the formatting fails. The text field's delegate can also be informed of the failed formatting. If the formatter decides that the string is invalid, the delegate is sent the following error message:

```
- (BOOL)control:(NSControl *)control
      didFailToFormatString:(NSString *)string
            errorDescription:(NSString *)error
```

The delegate can override the opinion of the formatter. If YES is returned, the control displays the string as is. If NO is returned, the delegate agrees with the formatter: The string is invalid.

Implement the following method in AppController.m:

```
- (BOOL)control:(NSControl *)control
    didFailToFormatString:(NSString *)string
        errorDescription:(NSString *)error
{
    NSLog(@"AppController told that formatting of %@ failed: %@",
            string, error);
    return NO;
}
```

Now open the nib file, and make the **AppController** the delegate of the text field (Figure 26.9).

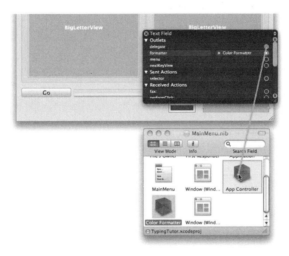

Figure 26.9   Connect the Text Field's delegate Outlet

Build and run your application. When validation fails, you will see on the console a message indicating what the string was and why it failed.

Checking Partial Strings

You might want to create a formatter that prevents the user from typing letters that are not part of a color name. To make the formatter check the string after every keystroke, implement the following method:

```
- (BOOL)isPartialStringValid:(NSString *)partial
        newEditingString:(NSString **)newString
        errorDescription:(NSString **)errorString
```

Here, `partial` is the string, including the last keystroke. A return of NO indicates that the partial string is not acceptable. Also, a return of NO means that the formatter can supply the `newString` and an `errorString`. The `newString` will appear in the control. The `errorString` should give the user an idea of what she or he did wrong. If your formatter returns YES, the `newString` and the `errorString` are ignored.

Add the following method to your `ColorFormatter.m`:

```
- (BOOL)isPartialStringValid:(NSString *)partial
          newEditingString:(NSString **)newString
          errorDescription:(NSString **)error
{
    // Zero-length strings are OK
    if ([partial length] == 0){
        return YES;
    }
    NSString *match = [self firstColorKeyForPartialString:partial];
    if (match) {
        return YES;
    } else {
        if (error) {
            *error = @"No such color";
        }
        return NO;
    }
}
```

Build and run your application. You will not be able to type in anything except the color names.

Notice something annoying about this app: You can't see what color would be chosen until you tab out of the field. What you would like is a formatter that does autocompletion. To enable autocompletion, you need to control the range of the selection as well. Comment out the **isPartialStringValid:newEditingString:errorDescription:** method, and replace it with this method:

```
- (BOOL)isPartialStringValid:(NSString **)partial
      proposedSelectedRange:(NSRange *)selPtr
          originalString:(NSString *)origString
      originalSelectedRange:(NSRange)origSel
          errorDescription:(NSString **)error
{
    // Zero-length strings are fine
    if ([*partial length] == 0) {
        return YES;
    }
    NSString *match = [self firstColorKeyForPartialString:*partial];
```

```
        // No color match?
        if (!match) {
            return NO;
        }

        // If this would not move the beginning of the selection, it
        // is a delete
        if (origSel.location == selPtr->location) {
            return YES;
        }

        // If the partial string is shorter than the
        // match, provide the match and set the selection
        if ([match length] != [*partial length]) {
            selPtr->location = [*partial length];
            selPtr->length = [match length] - selPtr->location;
            *partial = match;
            return NO;
        }
        return YES;
    }
```

Build and run your application. Your formatter will now autocomplete color names as you type them.

Formatters That Return Attributed Strings

Sometimes, it is nice for the formatter to define not only the string that is to be displayed but also its attributes. For example, a number formatter might print the number in red if it is negative. For this purpose, you will use **NSAttributedString**.

Your formatter can implement the following method:

```
- (NSAttributedString *)attributedStringForObjectValue:(id)anObj
                    withDefaultAttributes:(NSDictionary *)aDict
```

If the method exists, it will be called instead of **stringForObjectValue:**. The dictionary that you are passed contains the default attributes for the view where the data will be displayed. It is a good idea to merge the dictionary with your added attributes. For example, use the font from the text field where the data will be displayed, but make the foreground color red to show that the profits are negative.

Implement the following method to display the name of the color in that color:

```
- (NSAttributedString *)attributedStringForObjectValue:(id)anObj
                    withDefaultAttributes:(NSDictionary *)attributes
{
```

```
    NSMutableDictionary *md = [attributes mutableCopy];
    NSString *match = [self stringForObjectValue:anObj];
    if (match) {
        [md setObject:anObj forKey:NSForegroundColorAttributeName];
    } else {
        match = @"";
    }
    NSAttributedString *atString;
    atString = [[NSAttributedString alloc] initWithString:match
                                        attributes:md];

    [md release];
    [atString autorelease];
    return atString;
}
```

Build and run the application. Note that the text field will not change colors
until it gives up first-responder status.

Chapter 27
PRINTING

Code to handle printing is always relatively hard to write. Many factors are at play: pagination, margins, and page orientation, or landscape versus portrait. This chapter is designed to get you started on your journey toward the perfect printout.

Compared to most operating systems, Mac OS X makes writing print routines considerably easier. After all, your views already know how to generate PDF, and Mac OS X knows how to print PDF. If you have a document-based application and a view that knows how to draw itself, you simply implement **printOperationWithSettings:error:**. In this method, you create an **NSPrintOperation** object using a view and return it. The code, in your **NSDocument** subclass, would look like this:

```
- (NSPrintOperation *)printOperationWithSettings:(NSDictionary *)ps
                                           error:(NSError **)e;
{
    NSPrintInfo *printInfo = [self printInfo];
    NSPrintOperation *printOp
            = [NSPrintOperation printOperationWithView:aView
                                             printInfo:printInfo];
    return printOp;
}
```

Dealing with Pagination

What about multiple pages? A view, after all, has only a single page. How will you get a view to print multiple-page documents? Offscreen, you will make a huge view that can display all the pages of the document simultaneously. The print system will ask the view how many pages it is displaying. Then the system will ask the view where each page can be found in the view (Figure 27.1).

Figure 27.1   Each Page as a Rectangle on the View

Your view, then, must override two methods:

```
// How many pages?
- (BOOL)knowsPageRange:(NSRange *)rptr;

// Where is each page?
- (NSRect)rectForPage:(int)pageNum;
```

As an example, you will add printing to the RaiseMan application. You will print the name and expected raise for as many people as will fit on the paper size that the user selected from the Print panel (Figure 27.2).

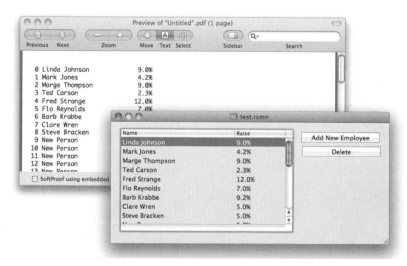

Figure 27.2   Completed Application

To do so, you will create a view that does the printing. Instead of making the view big enough to display all the people simultaneously, we will simply note which page the system is printing and draw only the names on that page in **drawRect:**.

The code in MyDocument.m is in fact pretty simple:

```
- (NSPrintOperation *)printOperationWithSettings:(NSDictionary *)ps
                                           error:(NSError **)e
{
    PeopleView *view = [[PeopleView alloc] initWithPeople:employees];
    NSPrintInfo *printInfo = [self printInfo];
    NSPrintOperation *printOp
            = [NSPrintOperation printOperationWithView:view
                                             printInfo:printInfo];
    [view release];
    return printOp;
}
```

Also, import PeopleView.h at the top of MyDocument.m.

In the MainMenu.nib file, note that the Print... menu item is nil-targeted, and its action is **printDocument:**. **printDocument:** will trigger **printOperationWith-Settings:error:** (Figure 27.3).

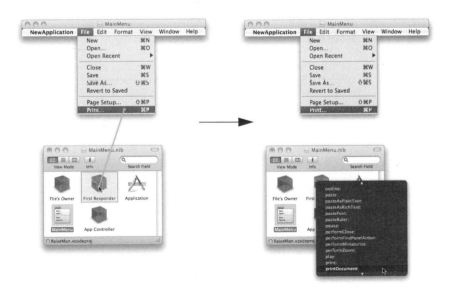

Figure 27.3 Connect Menu Item

Create a class called **PeopleView** that is a subclass of **NSView**. PeopleView.h would look like this:

```
#import <Cocoa/Cocoa.h>

@interface PeopleView : NSView {
    NSArray *people;
    NSMutableDictionary *attributes;
    float lineHeight;
    NSRect pageRect;
    int linesPerPage;
    int currentPage;
}
- (id)initWithPeople:(NSArray *)array;
@end
```

In PeopleView.m, you will implement the **initWithPeople:** method. This initializer will call **NSView**'s **initWithFrame:** method:

```
#import "PeopleView.h"
#import "Person.h"

@implementation PeopleView

- (id)initWithPeople:(NSArray *)persons
{
    // Call the superclass's designated initializer with some
    // dummy frame
    [super initWithFrame:NSMakeRect(0, 0, 700, 700)];
    people = [persons copy];
    // The attributes of the text to be printed
    attributes = [[NSMutableDictionary alloc] init];
    NSFont *font = [NSFont fontWithName:@"Monaco" size:12.0];
    lineHeight = [font capHeight] * 1.7;
    [attributes setObject:font
                   forKey:NSFontAttributeName];
    return self;
}
- (void)dealloc
{
    [people release];
    [attributes release];
    [super dealloc];
}

#pragma mark Pagination

- (BOOL)knowsPageRange:(NSRange *)range
{
    NSPrintOperation *po = [NSPrintOperation currentOperation];
    NSPrintInfo *printInfo = [po printInfo];
```

```
    // Where can I draw?
    pageRect = [printInfo imageablePageBounds];
    NSRect newFrame;
    newFrame.origin = NSZeroPoint;
    newFrame.size = [printInfo paperSize];
    [self setFrame:newFrame];

    // How many lines per page?
    linesPerPage = pageRect.size.height / lineHeight;

    // Pages are 1-based
    range->location = 1;

    // How many pages will it take?
    range->length = [people count] / linesPerPage;
    if ([people count] % linesPerPage) {
        range->length = range->length + 1;
    }
    return YES;
}

- (NSRect)rectForPage:(int)i
{
    // Note the current page
    currentPage = i - 1;

    // Return the same page rect everytime
    return pageRect;
}

#pragma mark Drawing

// The origin of the view is at the upper-left corner
- (BOOL)isFlipped
{
    return YES;
}

- (void)drawRect:(NSRect)r
{
    NSRect nameRect;
    NSRect raiseRect;
    raiseRect.size.height = nameRect.size.height = lineHeight;
    nameRect.origin.x = pageRect.origin.x;
    nameRect.size.width = 200.0;
    raiseRect.origin.x = NSMaxX(nameRect);
    raiseRect.size.width = 100.0;

    int i;
    for (i=0; i<linesPerPage; i++) {
        int index = (currentPage * linesPerPage) + i;
        if (index >= [people count]) {
            break;
```

```
        }
        Person *p = [people objectAtIndex:index];

        // Draw index and name
        nameRect.origin.y = pageRect.origin.y + (i * lineHeight);
        NSString *nameString = [NSString stringWithFormat:@"%2d %@",
                                              index, [p personName]];
        [nameString drawInRect:nameRect withAttributes:attributes];

        raiseRect.origin.y = nameRect.origin.y;
        NSString *raiseString=[NSString stringWithFormat:@"%4.1f%%",
                                              [p expectedRaise]];
        [raiseString drawInRect:raiseRect withAttributes:attributes];
    }
}

@end
```

Build and run the application. Note that multiple-pages-per-sheet setup (4-up, for example) works. Note that you can change the paper size and that more or fewer people subsequently appear on each page.

For the More Curious: Am I Drawing to the Screen?

Often in an application, you will want to draw things differently on the screen than on the printer. For example, in a drawing program, the view might show a grid onscreen but not when printed on paper.

In your **drawRect:** method, you can ask the current graphics context whether it is currently drawing to the screen:

```
if ([[NSGraphicsContext currentContext] isDrawingToScreen]) {
    ...draw grid...
}
```

Challenge

Add page numbers to the printout.

Chapter 28
WEB SERVICE

Web services are getting a lot of hype. In the end, however, they are simply an HTTP request and response whereby each may be carrying XML data. So using a Web service from Cocoa is simply a matter of being able to send HTTP requests and receive responses. It also may require generating and parsing XML. See Figure 28.1.

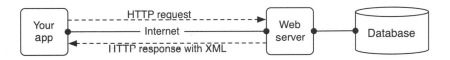

Figure 28.1   Your Average Web Service in Action

HTTP requests and responses are handled by **NSURL**, **NSURLRequest**, and **NSURLConnection** (Figure 28.2).

Figure 28.2   Classes for Making HTTP Requests

Generating and parsing XML are typically done by **NSXMLDocument** and **NSXMLNode**. Suppose that you have an **NSData** containing this XML:

```
<?xml version="1.0" encoding="UTF-8"?>
<person>
<first>Larry</first>
<last>Furg</last>
</person>
```

NSXMLDocument will parse it into a handy tree (Figure 28.3).

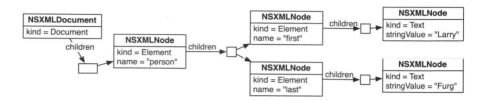

Figure 28.3 Parsed XML Document

AmaZone

In this exercise, you are going to write an application that uses the Amazon Web service to look up books by using keywords. The result of the search will be displayed in a table view. Double-clicking a row will open the page for that book in your Web brower. The app will look like Figure 28.4.

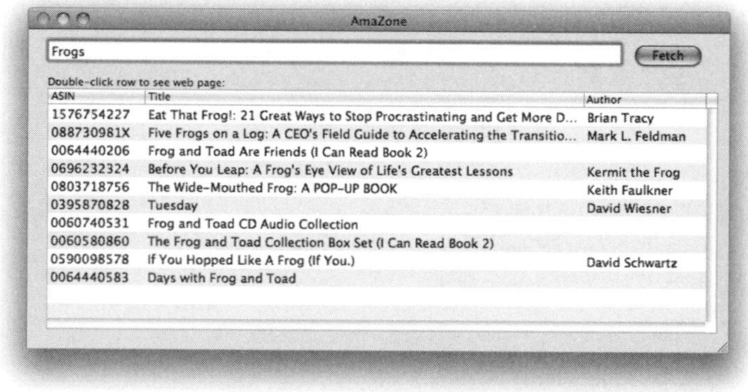

Figure 28.4 Completed Application

Create a new project of type Cocoa Application. Name the project AmaZone. Create an Objective-C class named **AppController**. In AppController.h, declare three outlets and an action:

```objc
#import <Cocoa/Cocoa.h>

@interface AppController : NSObject
{
    IBOutlet NSProgressIndicator *progress;
    IBOutlet NSTextField *searchField;
    IBOutlet NSTableView *tableView;
}
- (IBAction)fetchBooks:(id)sender;
@end
```

Lay Out the Interface

Open MainMenu.nib. Drop an **NSObject** in the doc window. In the Identity Inspector, set its class to be **AppController** (Figure 28.5).

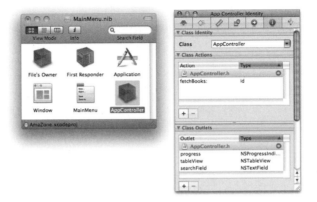

Figure 28.5   Creating the AppController

Drop a text field, a button, a progress indicator, and a table view (with three columns) on the window (Figure 28.6).

Figure 28.6   Basic Layout

Control-drag to set the target and the action of the button. It should trigger the **fetchBooks:** method of the **AppController**.

Control-click on the **AppController** to bring up the Connection panel, and connect all three outlets: tableView, searchField, and progress.

Control-click on the table view to bring up the Connection panel. Make **AppController** the data source for the table view. (Don't see the dataSource outlet? Did you select the scroll view instead of the table view?)

On pressing the Return key, the user will expect a fetch to occur. Control-drag from the text field to the button. Set the action to **performClick:**. In the text fields Attributes Inspector, set it to send its action only on Enter, as shown in Figure 28.7.

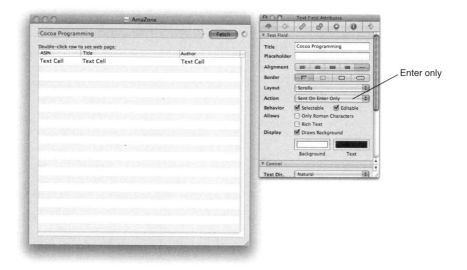

Figure 28.7   Attributes for Text Field

You can think of XML data as a tree made up of nodes. Once we have fetched the data from Amazon, we will have an array of **NSXMLNode** objects: one for each row in the table view. One way to get data out of an XML node is to use XPath (XPath is a little like Key Paths but uses / instead of .).

To make things easy on the coding end, we are going to set the identifier of each table column to be the XPath to the data we want to display in that column. Having read the Amazon Web services documentation, I can tell you that we will want the identifiers to be ASIN, ItemAttributes/Title, and ItemAttributes/Author.

Set the identifier of each column in the Attributes Inspector. While you are there, make each column not Editable (Figure 28.8).

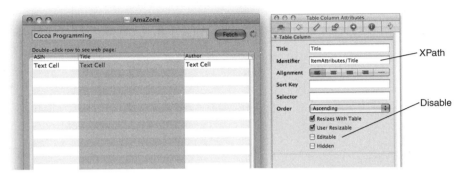

Figure 28.8 Setting Identifier for Columns

Write Code

In AppController.h, add instance variables to hold on to the entire XML document and an array of only the nodes that represent books:

```
NSXMLDocument *doc;
NSArray *itemNodes;
```

In AppController.m, the first thing you will need is my AWS ID. (If the ID stops working, it is because someone has abused it, thus ruining it for everyone else. In this case, you will need to apply for another at Amazon Developer Support.)

```
#define AWS_ID @"1CKE6MZ6S27EFQ458402"
```

(This is a preprocessor macro. Make sure that there is neither = nor ; on this line.)

Now you are going to put together a URL and a URL request. When you execute the request, you will get back an **NSData**. The data is XML, and you will parse it into an **NSXMLDocument**. Finally, you will use XPath to get the array of the nodes. Add this method to AppController.m:

```
- (IBAction)fetchBooks:(id)sender
{
    // Show the user that something is going on
    [progress startAnimation:nil];
```

```objectivec
// Put together the request
// See http://www.amazon.com/gp/aws/landing.html

// Get the string and percent-escape for insertion into URL
NSString *input = [searchField stringValue];
NSString *searchString =
                [input stringByAddingPercentEscapesUsingEncoding:
                                            NSUTF8StringEncoding];
NSLog(@"searchString = %@", searchString);

// Create the URL (Long string broken into several lines is OK)
NSString *urlString = [NSString stringWithFormat:
                @"http://ecs.amazonaws.com/onca/xml?"
                @"Service=AWSECommerceService&"
                @"AWSAccessKeyID=%@&"
                @"Operation=ItemSearch&"
                @"SearchIndex=Books&"
                @"Keywords=%@&"
                @"Version=2007-07-16",
                AWS_ID, searchString];

NSURL *url = [NSURL URLWithString:urlString];
NSURLRequest *urlRequest = [NSURLRequest requestWithURL:url
                cachePolicy:NSURLRequestReturnCacheDataElseLoad
                timeoutInterval:30];
// Fetch the XML response

NSData *urlData;
NSURLResponse *response;
NSError *error;
urlData = [NSURLConnection sendSynchronousRequest:urlRequest
                                returningResponse:&response
                                            error:&error];
if (!urlData) {
    NSAlert *alert = [NSAlert alertWithError:error];
    [alert runModal];
    return;
}

// Parse the XML response
[doc release];
doc = [[NSXMLDocument alloc] initWithData:urlData
                                  options:0
                                    error:&error];
NSLog(@"doc = %@", doc);
if (!doc) {
    NSAlert *alert = [NSAlert alertWithError:error];
    [alert runModal];
    return;
}

[itemNodes release];
itemNodes = [[doc nodesForXPath:@"ItemSearchResponse/Items/Item"
                        error:&error] retain];
```

```
        if (!itemNodes) {
            NSAlert *alert = [NSAlert alertWithError:error];
            [alert runModal];
            return;
        }
        // Update the interface
        [tableView reloadData];
        [progress stopAnimation:nil];
}
```

It would be good to test what you have so far. Put in a dummy table view data source method:

```
-(int)numberOfRowsInTableView:(NSTableView*)tv
{
    return 0;
}
```

Build and run the app. You will not see any titles in the table view but should see the XML on the console when you fetch. If you see book titles in the XML, continue. If you see an error message, use it to figure out what went wrong.

Now that you have an array of nodes, you need an easy way to get the data you need from them. Add a method to AppController.m:

```
- (NSString *)stringForPath:(NSString *)xp ofNode:(NSXMLNode *)n
{
    NSError *error;
    NSArray *nodes = [n nodesForXPath:xp error:&error];
    if (!nodes) {
        NSAlert *alert = [NSAlert alertWithError:error];
        [alert runModal];
        return nil;
    }
    if ([nodes count] == 0) {
        return nil;
    } else {
        return [[nodes objectAtIndex:0] stringValue];
    }
}
```

AppController is the data source for the table view. Add the data source methods to AppController.m:

```
#pragma mark TableView data source methods


- (int)numberOfRowsInTableView:(NSTableView *)tv
{
    return [itemNodes count];
}
```

```
- (id)tableView:(NSTableView *)tv
 objectValueForTableColumn:(NSTableColumn *)tableColumn
                        row:(int)row
{
    NSXMLNode *node = [itemNodes objectAtIndex:row];
    NSString *xPath = [tableColumn identifier];
    return [self stringForPath:xPath ofNode:node];
}
```

Build and run the application. You should be able to fetch titles from Amazon.

The last step is to make it possible for the user to double-click on a title to open it in his or her browser.

In **awakeFromNib**, set the doubleAction and target of the table view:

```
- (void)awakeFromNib
{
    [tableView setDoubleAction:@selector(openItem:)];
    [tableView setTarget:self];
}
```

Finally, implement **openItem:**. Here, you are using the **NSWorkspace** class, which represents the Finder.

```
- (void)openItem:(id)sender
{
    int row = [tableView clickedRow];
    if (row == -1) {
        return;
    }

    NSXMLNode *clickedItem = [itemNodes objectAtIndex:row];
    NSString *urlString = [self stringForPath:@"DetailPageURL"
                                       ofNode:clickedItem];
    NSURL *url = [NSURL URLWithString:urlString];
    [[NSWorkspace sharedWorkspace] openURL:url];
}
```

Build and run the application. Double-clicking on a title should open the Amazon page in your default browser.

In this example, you are blocking while waiting for the data to return. You can also make asynchronous URL requests. The delegate of the **NSURLConnection** object gets informed when the requested data arrives.

Challenge: Add a WebView

At the moment, you are using **NSWorkspace** to open the Web page in another application. Perhaps the user would like the Web page to appear in a sheet in the existing application (Figure 28.9).

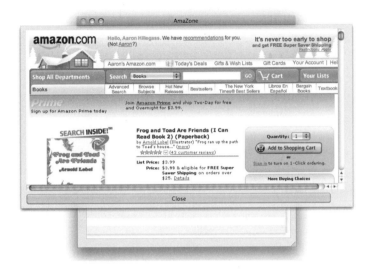

Figure 28.9   Use WebView to Display Details

The challenge, then, is to add a new window with a **WebView** to your application. Bring the window onto the screen as a sheet.

You will need to add the WebKit framework to your project.

If you have a string representing a URL, you can get a **WebView** to load that URL by sending it the message

```
- (void)setMainFrameURL:(NSString *)URLString;
```

That should be all you need. If you want a progress indicator, you will need to make your controller the "frame load delegate" of the Web view:

```
[webView setFrameLoadDelegate:self];
```

Then your controller can implement the following methods:

```
- (void)webView:(WebView *)wv
      didStartProvisionalLoadForFrame:(WebFrame *)wf;
```

```
- (void)webView:(WebView *)wv
     didFinishLoadForFrame:(WebFrame *)wf;

- (void)webView:(WebView *)wv
     didFailProvisionalLoadWithError:(NSError *)error
                            forFrame:(WebFrame *)wf;
```

Chapter 29

VIEW SWAPPING

Instead of bringing up a new window, you will often want to swap out a view and replace it with another. One easy way to do this is to change the content view of a box.

Putting each view in its own nib results in a more modular design. In Mac OS 10.5, Apple added the class **NSViewController** to Cocoa. We will make a subclass of **NSViewController** for each view that we want to swap in.

In the next chapter, this project will evolve into a relatively sophisticated Core Data application, so we will want each of our view controllers to have access to an **NSManagedObjectContext**. Figure 29.1 shows where we are going.

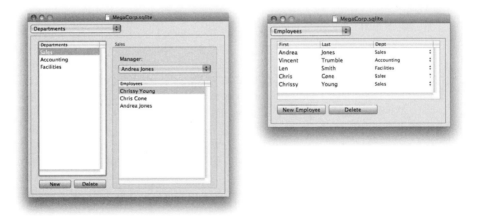

Figure 29.1 Completed Application

The pop-up button will enable the user to jump back and forth between the two views. In this chapter, you are going to make the jumping-back-and-forth part work. All the really useful parts of this app will be done in the next chapter.

Design

The views, controlled by view controllers, will become the content view of a box. Menu items in the pop-up button will trigger the view swapping. Figure 29.2 is a diagram of the objects involved.

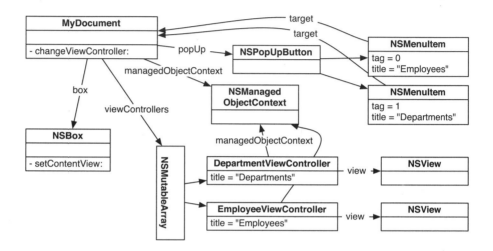

Figure 29.2   Object Diagram

Get Started

In Xcode, create a new Core Data Document-based Application, and name it Departments. Open up the MyDocument.nib file, and add a box and a pop-up button to the window (Figure 29.3).

Double-click on the pop-up button to open the menu and remove all the menu items from the pop-up button. You will create the menu items programmatically.

In MyDocument.h, add two outlets, an array, and an action:

```
#import <Cocoa/Cocoa.h>

@interface MyDocument : NSPersistentDocument {
    IBOutlet NSBox *box;
    IBOutlet NSPopUpButton *popUp;
    NSMutableArray *viewControllers;
}
- (IBAction)changeViewController:(id)sender;
@end
```

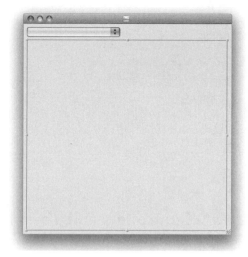

Figure 29.3   MyDocument.nib

Save the file.

Back in Interface Builder, Control-click on File's Owner to bring up the Connection panel, and set the two outlets.

Control-drag from the pop-up button to File's Owner to set its target. The action should be **changeViewController:**.

Save the nib file.

Create ManagedViewController Class

In Xcode, create a new Objective-C class, and name it **ManagingViewController**. We are subclassing **NSViewController** so that all our view controllers will have an **NSManagedObjectContext**. Edit ManagingViewController.h:

```
#import <Cocoa/Cocoa.h>

@interface ManagingViewController : NSViewController {
    NSManagedObjectContext *managedObjectContext;
}
@property (retain) NSManagedObjectContext *managedObjectContext;
@end
```

Add methods to handle this instance variable in `ManagingViewController.m`:

```
#import "ManagingViewController.h"

@implementation ManagingViewController
@synthesize managedObjectContext;

- (void)dealloc
{
    [managedObjectContext release];
    [super dealloc];
}
@end
```

Create ViewControllers and Their NIB files

Now you are going to create two separate views that will be swapped into the box you created. Each view has its own controller—a subclass of **ManagingViewController**. Thus, you are going to do the same basic steps twice:

- Create a subclass of **ManagingViewController** to act as File's Owner
- Create a nib for the view

One view will be for looking at departments in a company. The other view will be for looking at the employees of a company. You will do the Departments view first.

In Xcode, create an Objective-C class, and name it **DepartmentViewController**. In `DepartmentViewController.h`, make it a subclass of **ManagingViewController**:

```
#import "ManagingViewController.h"

@interface DepartmentViewController : ManagingViewController
```

In Xcode, create an Empty NIB file. Name it DepartmentView. Open Department-View.nib. From the Library, drag an **NSView** (labeled Custom View) into the doc window, as shown in Figure 29.4.

Put a few text fields and a couple of buttons on the view. (We aren't going to use these controls; I simply want you to see something interesting when the view appears in the box.)

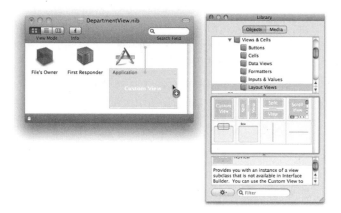

Figure 29.4   Creating an Instance of NSView

Set the class of File's Owner to be **DepartmentViewController**. Control-click on File's Owner, and drag to the view (labeled Custom View) to set the view outlet (Figure 29.5).

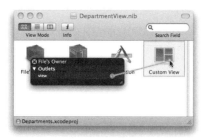

Figure 29.5   Introducing the View Controller to Its View

(The view outlet is defined in **NSViewController**.) Save the nib file.

Back in DepartmentViewController.m, give the controller a nib and a title in its **init** method:

```
- (id)init
{
    if (![super initWithNibName:@"DepartmentView"
                            bundle:nil]) {
        return nil;
    }
    [self setTitle:@"Departments"];
    return self;
}
```

Okay? Good. Do it again for **EmployeeViewController**:

- Create a class called **EmployeeViewController**, and make it a subclass of **ManagingViewController**.

- Make a nib file, named EmployeeView.nib, with a view.

- Put a text view—or something else pretty—on the view.

- Set the class of File's Owner to be **EmployeeViewController**.

- Set the view outlet of File's Owner to point to the view.

- Add an **init** method to EmployeeViewController.m:

```
- (id)init
{
    if (![super initWithNibName:@"EmployeeView"
                         bundle:nil]) {
        return nil;
    }
    [self setTitle:@"Employees"];
    return self;
}
```

Add View Swapping to MyDocument

Now you need to create instances of the controllers in **MyDocument** and add them to the viewControllers array. Add this to MyDocument.m:

```
#import "MyDocument.h"
#import "DepartmentViewController.h"
#import "EmployeeViewController.h"

@implementation MyDocument

- (id)init
{
    [super init];
    viewControllers = [[NSMutableArray alloc] init];

    ManagingViewController *vc;
    vc = [[DepartmentViewController alloc] init];
    [vc setManagedObjectContext:[self managedObjectContext]];
    [viewControllers addObject:vc];
    [vc release];

    vc = [[EmployeeViewController alloc] init];
    [vc setManagedObjectContext:[self managedObjectContext]];
    [viewControllers addObject:vc];
    [vc release];

    return self;
}
```

Release the `viewControllers` array in the **dealloc** method:

```
- (void)dealloc
{
    [viewControllers release];
    [super dealloc];
}
```

Create the method that swaps the view in:

```
- (void)displayViewController:(ManagingViewController *)vc
{
    // Try to end editing
    NSWindow *w = [box window];
    BOOL ended = [w makeFirstResponder:w];
    if (!ended) {
        NSBeep();
        return;
    }
    // Put the view in the box
    NSView *v = [vc view];
    [box setContentView:v];
}
```

Declare that method in MyDocument.h. (Also let the compiler know about the class **ManagingViewController**):

```
@class ManagingViewController;
...
- (void)displayViewController:(ManagingViewController *)vc;
...
```

A pop-up button is basically a button with a menu. When the nib file is loaded, you need to load the menu with an item for each controller. Add this code to MyDocument.m:

```
- (void)windowControllerDidLoadNib:(NSWindowController *)wc
{
    [super windowControllerDidLoadNib:wc];
    NSMenu *menu = [popUp menu];
    int i, itemCount;
    itemCount = [viewControllers count];

    for (i = 0; i < itemCount; i++) {
        NSViewController *vc = [viewControllers objectAtIndex:i];
        NSMenuItem *mi = [[NSMenuItem alloc] initWithTitle:[vc title]
                                action:@selector(changeViewController:)
                        keyEquivalent:@""];
        [mi setTag:i];
        [menu addItem:mi];
        [mi release];
    }
```

```
    // Initially show the first controller
    [self displayViewController:[viewControllers objectAtIndex:0]];
    [popUp selectItemAtIndex:0];
}
```

Note that the tag of the menu item is set to the index of the controller in the `viewControllers` array that the menu item represents. We can use the tag in the action method that the menu items trigger:

```
- (IBAction)changeViewController:(id)sender
{
    int i = [sender tag];
    ManagingViewController *vc = [viewControllers objectAtIndex:i];
    [self displayViewController:vc];
}
```

Build and run the application. The pop-up button should enable you to jump back and forth between the two views.

Resizing the Window

What if the two views are radically different sizes? Wouldn't it be nifty if the window would stretch and shrink to make the box fit the view perfectly? You are going to add that now.

Open the view nib files, and make the two views different sizes.

In MyDocument.nib, select the box, and use the Size Inspector to make it resize with the window (Figure 29.6).

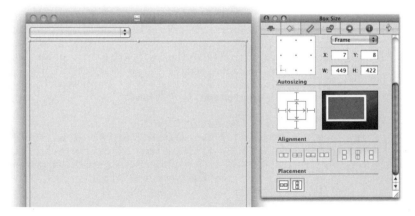

Figure 29.6   Size Inspector for Box

Select the window. In the Attributes Inspector, prevent the user from resizing the window (Figure 29.7).

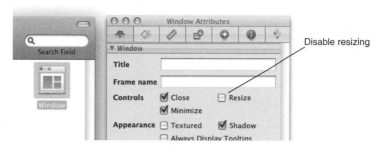

Figure 29.7   Disable Resizing for Window

In MyDocument.m, add the following lines to the **displayViewController:** method:

```
- (void)displayViewController:(ManagingViewController *)vc
{
    // End editing
    NSWindow *w = [box window];
    BOOL ended = [w makeFirstResponder:w];
    if (!ended) {
        NSBeep();
        return;
    }
    NSView *v = [vc view];

    // Compute the new window frame
    NSSize currentSize = [[box contentView] frame].size;
    NSSize newSize = [v frame].size;
    float deltaWidth = newSize.width - currentSize.width;
    float deltaHeight = newSize.height - currentSize.height;
    NSRect windowFrame = [w frame];
    windowFrame.size.height += deltaHeight;
    windowFrame.origin.y -= deltaHeight;
    windowFrame.size.width += deltaWidth;

    // Clear the box for resizing
    [box setContentView:nil];
    [w setFrame:windowFrame
        display:YES
        animate:YES];

    [box setContentView:v];
}
```

Build and run the app. When you change views, the window should resize to fit the new view.

Chapter 30
CORE DATA RELATIONSHIPS

It is time to delve a bit deeper into Core Data. In Chapter 11, you dealt with a single entity (**Car**). In most applications, you will have multiple entities and relationships between them. Core Data supports to-one relationships and unordered to-many relationships.

This exercise will have two entities: **Employee** and **Department**. An employee will work for one department. A department will have a set of employees. A department will also have one employee (chosen from its set) who will be a manager. Thus, there are three relationships, as shown in Figure 30.1.

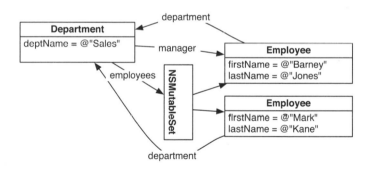

Figure 30.1 The Data Model

Edit the Model

In this section, you are going to be extending the Departments project that you started in the previous chapter. In Xcode, select MyDocument.xcdatamodel. Add two entities. Name one **Employee** and the other **Department**.

An **Employee** will have the attributes firstName and lastName, both strings, as well as a to-one relationship called department with **Department**. Add these properties (Figure 30.2). Note that you can't set the inverse until you have created it in the **Department** entity.

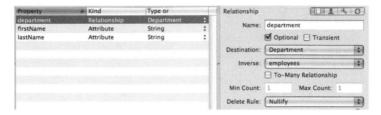

Figure 30.2   Employee Entity

A **Department** will have an attribute deptName, a string, as well as a to-many relationship called employees with **Employee**. Finally, a **Department** will have a to-one relationship called manager with **Employee**. Add these properties (Figure 30.3).

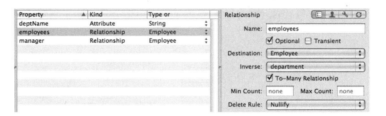

Figure 30.3   Department Entity

Note that the department relationship of **Employee** and the employees relationship of **Department** are inverses of each other. Be sure that the inverse is set for both of these relationships, as is shown in Figures 30.2 and 30.3.

The manager relationship will not have an inverse. You may get a warning about this when you compile; disregard the warning.

Create Custom NSManagedObject Classes

You will want to display an employee's full name, so you are going to create a custom class to hold employee data. This class will be a subclass of **NSManagedObject**.

A department can be managed only by an employee who works for that department. When an employee who is the manager leaves the department, you will need to set the manager to nil. This will be handled by the custom **NSManagedObject** subclass for the **Department** entity.

Make sure that your MyDocument.xcdatamodel file is open in the editor, and select one of the entities. In Xcode, select the File -> New File menu item. Select Managed Object Class. Create classes for **Employee** and **Department**. You don't need validation methods for these classes (Figure 30.4).

Figure 30.4   Creating Files

Employee

In Employee.h, declare the read-only property fullName:

```
#import <CoreData/CoreData.h>
@class Department;
@interface Employee :  NSManagedObject
{
}
@property (retain) NSString *firstName;
@property (retain) NSString *lastName;
@property (retain) Department *department;
@property (readonly) NSString *fullName;
@end
```

In Employee.m, implement the method **fullName**.

```
- (NSString *)fullName
{
    NSString *first = [self firstName];
```

```
    NSString *last = [self lastName];
    if (!first)
        return last;

    if (!last)
        return first;

    return [NSString stringWithFormat:@"%@ %@", first, last];
}
```

We are going to bind the column of a table to the fullName key. If firstName or lastName is changed, observers of fullName need to get informed that it also has changed. You are going to override a class method to specify what keys cause changes in fullName:

```
+ (NSSet *)keyPathsForValuesAffectingFullName
{
    return [NSSet setWithObjects:@"firstName", @"lastName", nil];
}
```

Department

In Department.h, specify that you are going to supply methods for adding and removing employees:

```
#import <CoreData/CoreData.h>
@class Employee;

@interface Department :  NSManagedObject
{
}
@property (retain) NSString *deptName;
@property (retain) Employee *manager;
@property (retain) NSSet *employees;
@end

@interface Department (CoreDataGeneratedAccessors)
- (void)addEmployeesObject*Employee *)value;
- (void)removeEmployeesObject:Employee *)value;
@end
```

Now implement those two methods in Department.m. (Although we care about only the method for removing, they come in pairs; the remove will be ignored unless we also implement the add.)

```
#import "Department.h"
#import "Employee.h"

@implementation Department
```

```
@dynamic deptName;
@dynamic manager;
@dynamic employees;

- (void)addEmployeesObject:(Employee *)value
{
    NSLog(@"Dept %@ adding employee %@",
                        [self deptName], [value fullName]);
    NSSet *s = [NSSet setWithObject:value];
    [self willChangeValueForKey:@"employees"
                withSetMutation:NSKeyValueUnionSetMutation
                    usingObjects:s];
    [[self primitiveValueForKey:@"employees"] addObject:value];
    [self didChangeValueForKey:@"employees"
                withSetMutation:NSKeyValueUnionSetMutation
                    usingObjects:s];
}

- (void)removeEmployeesObject:(Employee *)value
{
    NSLog(@"Dept %@ removing employee %@",
                        [self deptName], [value fullName]);
    Employee *manager = [self manager];
    if (manager == value) {
        [self setManager:nil];
    }
    NSSet *s = [NSSet setWithObject:value];
    [self willChangeValueForKey:@"employees"
                withSetMutation:NSKeyValueMinusSetMutation
                    usingObjects:s];
    [[self primitiveValueForKey:@"employees"] removeObject:value];
    [self didChangeValueForKey:@"employees"
                withSetMutation:NSKeyValueMinusSetMutation
                    usingObjects:s];
}
@end
```

Lay Out the Interface

Before you begin editing the nib files, a warning: There are a lot of bindings to make in this exercise. Be patient. Remember: In this book, you will never bind to a scroll view, a table view, or a cell. You will, however, bind to table columns. Watch the title of the Inspector window to be certain of what you are binding.

DepartmentView.nib

In DepartmentView.nib, put two buttons, two table views, and a pop-up button on the view. Place a label named Manager above the pop-up. Embed the label, the pop-up, and one table view in a box. Create three array controllers, and label them Depts, ManagerPopUp, and EmployeeList. See Figure 30.5.

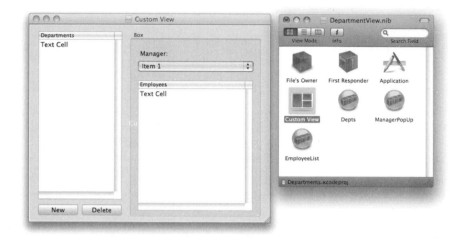

Figure 30.5   Basic Layout

Set the target of the two buttons to be the Depts array controller. The New button's action should be **add:**. The Delete button's action should be **remove:**.

The Depts array controller should be in Entity mode and pulling from the **Department** entity. Check the Prepares Content box to force it to fetch from the object store as soon as the nib file is loaded (Figure 30.6).

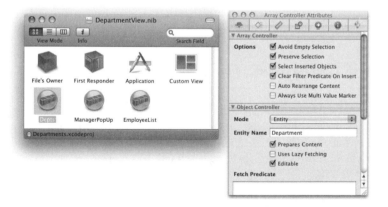

Figure 30.6   Depts Array Controller Attributes

Use Table 30.1 to set the bindings. Bindings are set in the *Bindings Inspector.*

Table 30.1   Bindings for DepartmentView.nib[a,b]

Object	Binding	To	Controller Key	Key Path
Depts AC	MOC	File's Owner		`managedObjectContext`
ManagerPopUp AC	Content set	Depts AC	`selection`	`employees`
EmployeeList AC	Content set	Depts AC	`selection`	`employees`
Departments column	Value	Depts AC	`arrangedObjects`	`deptName`
Delete button	Enabled	Depts AC	`canRemove`	
Employees column	Value	EmployeeList AC	`arrangedObjects`	`fullName`
Pop-up	Content	ManagerPopUp AC	`arrangedObjects`	
Pop-up	Content values	ManagerPopUp AC	`arrangedObjects`	`fullName`
Pop-up	Selected object	Depts AC	`selection`	`manager`
Box	Title	Depts AC	`selection`	`deptName`

a. AC = array controller
b. MOC = Managed Object Context

On the last binding, use No selection for the No Selection Placeholder. Use Unnamed Department as the Null Placeholder.

You can build and run your app. You should be able to add and remove departments.

EmployeeView.nib

Open `EmployeeView.nib`, and remove anything on the view. Add a table view with three columns. Put a pop-up cell on the third column. Add New Employee and Delete buttons. Add two array controllers and label them Employees and DeptPopUp. See Figure 30.7.

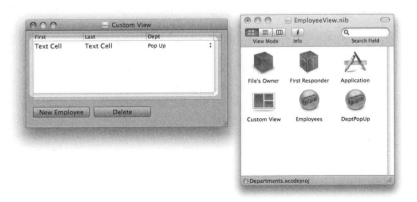

Figure 30.7   Basic Layout

Table 30.2   Bindings for EmployeeView.nib[a,b]

Object	Binding	To	Controller Key	Key Path
Employees AC	MOC	File's Owner		managedObjectContext
DeptPopUp AC	MOC	File's Owner		managedObjectContext
Delete button	Enabled	Employees AC	canRemove	
First column	Value	Employees AC	arrangedObjects	firstName
Last column	Value	Employees AC	arrangedObjects	lastName
Dept column	Content	DeptPopUp AC	arrangedObjects	
Dept column	Content values	DeptPopUp AC	arrangedObjects	deptName
Dept column	Selected object	Employees AC	arrangedObjects	department

a. AC = array controller
b. MOC = Managed Object Context

The Employees array controller should be in Entity mode and pulling from the **Employee** entity. The DeptPopUp array controller should be in Entity mode and pulling from the **Department** entity. Both should automatically prepare content.

Make the Employees array controller the target of the two buttons. The New Employee button should trigger **add:**. The Delete button should trigger **remove:**.

Set the bindings, as indicted in Table 30.2.

Build and run your app. You should now be able to add and remove employees. You should be able to set the manager of a department as well.

Events and nextResponder

The event methods (e.g., **mouseDown:** and **keyDown:**) defined in **NSResponder** typically simply forward the event on to the nextResponder. Thus, unhandled events flow up the responder chain.

So, for example, when someone selects a row in a table view and presses the Delete key, that flows up the responder chain until it is handled. Let's handle this case for the **EmployeeView** of the Departments project. The **NSViewController** is a subclass of **NSResponder**, so we can put it in the responder chain to handle unhandled keyboard events. Add these lines to the end of **displayViewController:** in MyDocument.m:

```
    [box setContentView:v];
    // Put the view controller in the responder chain
    [v setNextResponder:vc];
    [vc setNextResponder:box];
}
```

Now, if it gets a **keyDown:**, the view controller will check whether it is a delete. If so, the view controller will send the **remove:** message to the array controller. Add this method to EmployeeViewController.m:

```
// Take care of the delete key
- (void)keyDown:(NSEvent *)e
{
    if ([e keyCode] == 51) {
        [employeeController remove:nil];
    } else {
        [super keyDown:e];
    }
}
```

Now you need an outlet named employeeController. Add it in EmployeeViewController.h:

```
IBOutlet NSArrayController *employeeController;
```

Open EmployeeView.nib. Control-click on File's Owner. Drag from the employeeController outlet to the Employees array controller.

Build and run the application. Select an employee, and press the Delete key. It should disappear.

Chapter 31
GARBAGE COLLECTION

As long as you use only Objective-C objects, the garbage collector will do exactly what you want, without your needing to think about it. However, as soon as you start to **malloc** C data types and Core Foundation structures, you will need to be a bit more circumspect.

When the garbage collector runs, it is looking for unreachable objects. You can think of the objects in your applications as a directed graph: This object knows that object; it knows those objects; and they know those other objects. So, the garbage collector starts with the pointers on the stack and the global variables and wanders this directed graph until it has recorded every "reachable" object. The unreachable objects are deallocated. See Figure 31.1.

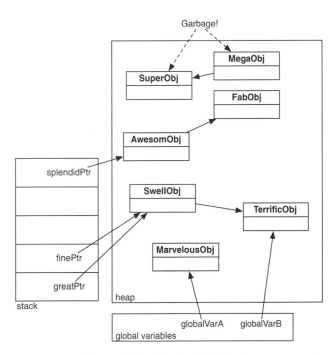

Figure 31.1   Reachable Objects

Before an object is deallocated by the garbage collector, it is sent the **finalize** message. Overall, you shouldn't need to implement **finalize** very often, but if you do, it looks like this:

```
- (void)finalize
{
    ...Do some last minute stuff here...
    [super finalize];
}
```

Throughout this book, you have been writing "dual-mode code" that will work with or without the garbage collector. In this chaper and the next, however, you will be writing code that is designed to work only with the garbage collector. Thus, you will see no calls to **retain** or **release**; nor will you see an implementation of **dealloc**.

Non-object Data Types

C Primitive

What if you have a buffer of integers that you would like freed by the garbage collector when it is unreachable? There is a **malloc()** replacement that will do this:

```
int *intBuff;
intBuff = NSAllocateCollectable(100 * sizeof(int), 0);
```

When one object "knows" another, we say that it has a reference. References can be either "strong" or "weak". Strong references are respected by the garbage collector. Weak references are ignored by the garbage collector. Thus, if you had only weak references to intBuff, it would be deallocated by the garbage collector immediately.

Instance variables of object types are, by default, strong. Instance variables of other types are, by default, weak. Thus, if you wanted an instance variable refering to the intBuff to be strong, you should explicitly mark it as strong:

```
__strong int *intBuff;
```

What is the second argument to **NSAllocateCollectable**? If the memory was going to be filled with pointers, and if the pointers should be treated as strong references, you would mark the buffer as Scanned. To do this, you would pass the NSScannedOption as the second argument:

```
char **words;
words = NSAllocateCollectable(100 * sizeof(char *), NSScannedOption);
```

Core Foundation

With Core Foundation (CF) data structures, there is a handy method for moving it under the control of the garbage collector:

```
CFString *str = CFCreate...
CFMakeCollectable(str);
```

Once again, if you want the reference to be strong, you will need to be explicit:

```
__strong CFStringRef str;
```

Polynomials Example

In this example, you are going to create a **Polynomial** class that has a C array of floats and a CGColorRef. The **Polynomial** will draw itself, using CoreGraphics. A PolynomialView will display an array of **Polynomial** objects, as shown in Figure 31.2.

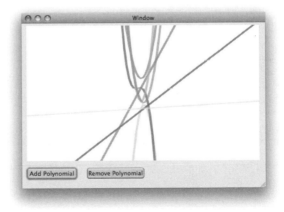

Figure 31.2 Running Application

The Cocoa classes that do drawing are a convenient wrapper for CoreGraphics. The data structures used in CoreGraphics are CF types. Thus, if you use this lower-level API directly, you need to ensure that the data structures stay around until you don't need them. Then, when you don't need them anymore, you will want them to be deallocated by the garbage collector.

In Xcode, create a new Cocoa Application project named Polynomials. In that project, create a new Objective-C class named **Polynomial**.

The **Polynomial** class will have strong references to both the C array and the CGColorRef. Edit Polynomial.h:

```
#import <Cocoa/Cocoa.h>

@interface Polynomial : NSObject {
    __strong CGFloat * terms;
    int termCount;
    __strong CGColorRef color;
}
- (float)valueAt:(float)x;
- (void)drawInRect:(CGRect)b
        inContext:(CGContextRef)ctx;
- (CGColorRef)color;
@end
```

Note that you explicitly marked the pointer to the C array and the CGColorRef as strong references. This will keep the garbage collector from deallocating them until you are done with them.

In Polynomial.m, these data structures need to be created so that they are under the control of the garbage collector:

```
#import "Polynomial.h"
#import <QuartzCore/QuartzCore.h>

// Number of segments drawn
#define HOPS (100)

// A random float between 0 and 1
#define RANDFLOAT() (random() % 128 / 128.0)

// The part of the x-y graph that will be drawn
static CGRect funcRect = {-20, -20, 40, 40};


@implementation Polynomial

// Create 'terms' and 'color' to be handled by CG
- (id)init
{
    [super init];
    // Create a color
    color = CGColorCreateGenericRGB(RANDFLOAT(), RANDFLOAT(),
                                    RANDFLOAT(), 0.5);
```

```objc
    // Put it under control of the GC
    CFMakeCollectable(color);

    // Create the coefficients of the polynomial between -5 and 5
    termCount = (random() % 3) + 2;
    terms = NSAllocateCollectable(termCount * sizeof(CGFloat), 0);

    // Set them to random values
    int i;
    for (i = 0; i < termCount; i++) {
        terms[i] = 5.0 - (random() % 100) / 10.0;
    }

    return self;
}
- (float)valueAt:(float)x
{
    float result = 0;
    int i;
    for (i = 0; i < termCount; i++) {
        result = (result * x) + terms[i];
    }
    return result;
}
// Draw using core graphics
- (void)drawInRect:(CGRect)b inContext:(CGContextRef)ctx
{
    NSLog(@"drawing");
    CGContextSaveGState(ctx);

    // Scale and translate coordinate system so drawing
    // in funcRect fills view
    CGAffineTransform tf =
        CGAffineTransformMake(b.size.width / funcRect.size.width, 0,
                            0, b.size.height / funcRect.size.height,
                            b.size.width/2, b.size.height/2);

    // Apply the affine transform to the graphics context
    CGContextConcatCTM(ctx, tf);
    CGContextSetStrokeColorWithColor(ctx, color);
    CGContextSetLineWidth(ctx, 0.4);
    float distance = funcRect.size.width / HOPS;
    float currentX = funcRect.origin.x;
    BOOL first = YES;
    while (currentX <= funcRect.origin.x + funcRect.size.width) {
        float currentY = [self valueAt:currentX];
        if (first) {
            CGContextMoveToPoint(ctx, currentX, currentY);
            first = NO;
        } else {
            CGContextAddLineToPoint(ctx, currentX, currentY);
        }
```

```
        currentX += distance;
    }
    CGContextStrokePath(ctx);

    // Remove the affine transform
    CGContextRestoreGState(ctx);

}
- (CGColorRef)color
{
    return color;
}

// Log during finalize
- (void)finalize
{
    NSLog(@"finalizing %@", self);
    [super finalize];
}

@end
```

What could have gone wrong?

- If you had forgotten the __strong directive, the CGColor and the C array would have been immediately deallocated by the garbage collector. This would have crashed your program in a sometimes strange and unpredictable manner.

- If you had forgotten to use **NSAllocateCollectable()** to create the C array or forgotten to mark the CGColor with **CFMakeCollectable()**, the garbage collector would never clean up that memory. Your application would have a memory leak.

Now create a **NSView** subclass to display the **Polynomial** objects. Name it **PolynomialView**:

```
#import <Cocoa/Cocoa.h>
@interface PolynomialView : NSView {
    NSMutableArray *polynomials;
}
- (IBAction)createNewPolynomial:(id)sender;
- (IBAction)deleteRandomPolynomial:(id)sender;
@end
```

In PolynomialView.m:

```
#import "PolynomialView.h"
#import "Polynomial.h"
#import <QuartzCore/QuartzCore.h>
```

```
@implementation PolynomialView

- (id)initWithFrame:(NSRect)frame {
    [super initWithFrame:frame];
    polynomials = [[NSMutableArray alloc] init];
    return self;
}

- (IBAction)createNewPolynomial:(id)sender
{
    Polynomial *p = [[Polynomial alloc] init];
    [polynomials addObject:p];
    [self setNeedsDisplay:YES];
}
- (IBAction)deleteRandomPolynomial:(id)sender
{
    if ([polynomials count] == 0) {
        NSBeep();
        return;
    }
    int i = random() % [polynomials count];
    [polynomials removeObjectAtIndex:i];
    [self setNeedsDisplay:YES];
}

- (void)drawRect:(NSRect)rect
{
    NSRect bounds = [self bounds];
    [[NSColor whiteColor] set];
    [NSBezierPath fillRect:bounds];
    // Get ahold of the core graphics context
    CGContextRef ctx = [[NSGraphicsContext currentContext]
                                                graphicsPort];
    CGRect cgBounds = *(CGRect *)&bounds;
    // Draw the polynomials
    for (Polynomial *p in polynomials) {
        [p drawInRect:cgBounds
            inContext:ctx];
    }
}

@end
```

Open MainMenu.nib. Drag two buttons and a custom view placeholder onto the window. Label one button Add Polynomial and the other Remove Polynomial. Set the class of the custom view to be **PolynomialView**. See Figure 31.3.

To set their targets, Control-drag from each button to the **PolynomialView**. Set their actions to be **createNewPolynomial:** and **deleteRandomPolynomial:**.

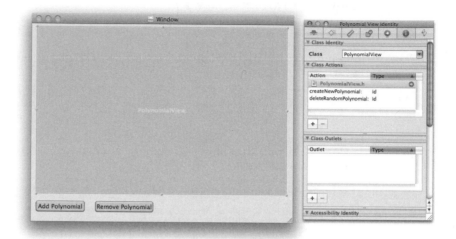

Figure 31.3   Basic Layout

Before building the application, make sure that the garbage collector is enabled. In Xcode, double-click on the target to bring up the Inspector panel. In the build settings, make sure that the garbage collector is required for all configurations (Figure 31.4).

Figure 31.4   Turn on Garbage Collector

Build and run the application. When you remove polynomials, you should see log statements from the **finalize** method of the instance that is being deallocated.

Okay, so you are now certain that the `Polynomial` objects are being correctly garbage collected. How do you know that the `CGColor` structures are? You can use Instruments.

Instruments

Instruments is a tool for analyzing a running program. The tool has many plug-ins, called instruments, that enable you to look at different aspects, usually performance related, of the running application.

In this example, you are going to use the ObjectAllocations instrument to monitor the creation and destruction of objects and other data structures. To start `Polynomials` in Instruments, use the Run -> Start with Performance Tool -> Object Allocations menu item in Xcode (Figure 31.5).

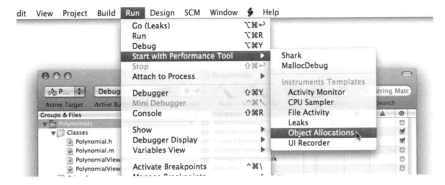

Figure 31.5   Starting Instruments

Instruments, which in many ways resembles GarageBand, will launch. If you click the Run button (with the red center), your application will launch. Along the top of the Instruments window is a graph of the total memory that your application is using. In the lower half is a list of the various data structures and how many instances are currently in memory. Create a couple of polynomials, and pause the application. Find `Polynomial` and `CGColor` on the list, and add them to the graph. Remove total allocations from the grap. See Figure 31.6.

Unpause the application. As you add and remove polynomials, you should see the Net # of **Polynomial** objects and `CGColor` structures rise and fall. If they never fall, you have a memory leak.

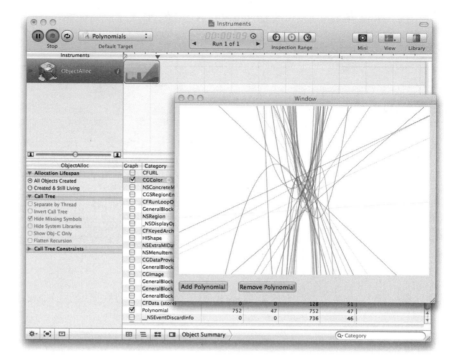

Figure 31.6   Running in Instruments

If you click on Polynomial in the Category column, you can inspect the individual instances of **Polynomial** and how they were created (Figure 31.7).

#	Object Address	Category	Creation Time	Size	Responsible Library	Responsible Caller
0	0x1038c70	Polynomial	00:07.104	16	Polynomials	-[PolynomialView createNew...
1	0x1031c80	Polynomial	00:08.247	16	Polynomials	-[PolynomialView createNew...
2	0x106de00	Polynomial	00:08.298	16	Polynomials	-[PolynomialView createNew...
3	0x1074ae0	Polynomial	00:08.347	16	Polynomials	-[PolynomialView createNew...
4	0x10796d0	Polynomial	00:08.397	16	Polynomials	-[PolynomialView createNew...
5	0x107ef90	Polynomial	00:08.448	16	Polynomials	-[PolynomialView createNew...
6	0x1084530	Polynomial	00:08.499	16	Polynomials	-[PolynomialView createNew...
7	0x1024fb0	Polynomial	00:08.547	16	Polynomials	-[PolynomialView createNew...
8	0x104b0d0	Polynomial	00:08.598	16	Polynomials	-[PolynomialView createNew...
9	0x10396a0	Polynomial	00:08.697	16	Polynomials	-[PolynomialView createNew...
10	0x103a500	Polynomial	00:08.865	16	Polynomials	-[PolynomialView createNew...
11	0x1029850	Polynomial	00:09.009	16	Polynomials	-[PolynomialView createNew...
12	0x10669e0	Polynomial	00:09.169	16	Polynomials	-[PolynomialView createNew...
13	0x107b0b0	Polynomial	00:09.329	16	Polynomials	-[PolynomialView createNew...
14	0x10796a0	Polynomial	00:09.529	16	Polynomials	-[PolynomialView createNew...
15	0x1084fc0	Polynomial	00:09.730	16	Polynomials	-[PolynomialView createNew...
16	0x10202e0	Polynomial	00:10.592	16	Polynomials	-[PolynomialView createNew...
17	0x1075aa0	Polynomial	00:10.686	16	Polynomials	-[PolynomialView createNew...
18	0x1083e10	Polynomial	00:10.753	16	Polynomials	-[PolynomialView createNew...
19	0x106d340	Polynomial	00:10.904	16	Polynomials	-[PolynomialView createNew...
20	0x1080840	Polynomial	00:13.249	16	Polynomials	-[PolynomialView createNew...

Figure 31.7   Running in Instruments

What about checking the leaking C arrays? Sadly, the C arrays you created are small general allocations, and there are a gazillion of those in your running application. Hunting them down would be difficult. Here is a stupid trick that will work: Make the allocations larger and of a specific size. Alter the code to allocate space for 100 floating-point numbers (400 bytes in 32-bit mode; 800 bytes in 64-bit mode):

```
terms = NSAllocateCollectable(100 * sizeof(CGFloat), NSScannedOption);
```

That allocation will show up in Instruments as GeneralBlock-400 (or GeneralBloc-800 in 64-bit mode). Now you can graph them. Are they getting collected?

Instruments is a very powerful tool, and we have only scratched the surface of its capabilities. As you work to improve the performance of your application, you will want to read Apple's documentation for Instruments.

For the More Curious: Weak References

Sometimes, you will want to have an object pointer that should point to that object as long as it exists, but you do not want that pointer to prevent the garbage collector from deallocating the object. In this case, you can use a weak reference:

```
__weak NSFont *favoriteFont;
```

The garbage collector will feel free to deallocate an object, even if favoriteFont is currently pointing to the object. If favoriteFont is pointing to an object when it is deallocated, favoriteFont is automatically set to nil.

There are also collections (e.g., **NSMapTable**, **NSHashTable**, and **NSPointerArray**) that can hold objects weakly. Also, in a garbage-collected application, the notification center has weak references to the observers.

Challenge: Do Bad Things

Create memory leaks: Leak the C array and the CGColor structures when you remove. Observe the leaks in Instruments. Then fix them again.

Crash your application: Make the garbage collector deallocate the C array and CGColor structure prematurely. Run in the debugger, and observe the resulting crash. Then fix it again.

Chapter 32
CORE ANIMATION

As Mac OS X has evolved, it has used OpenGL more and more to use the power of modern graphics processors. To make some of these capabilities convenient for all programmers, Apple created **CALayer** in Mac OS X 10.5. You can think of a **CALayer** as a buffer that you can draw into. Once it has been rendered, it can be moved, resized, and redrawn by the graphics processor at startling speeds.

Like views, layers are arranged in a hierarchy. A view can be covered with a layer, and that layer can have sublayers.

Once we have the **CALayer**, which can be manipulated at an amazing speed, we need something to drive the process. **CAAnimation** does this. **NSAnimationContext** can be used to group and synchronize multiple animations.

As an example, we are going to take the polynomial drawing program from Chapter 31 and move each polynomial onto its own **CALayer**. Then we can move the layers around the view at great speed. See Figure 32.1.

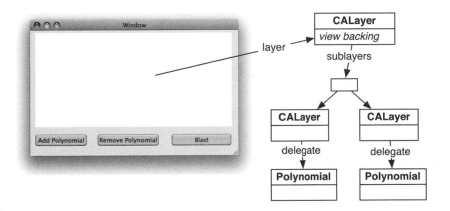

Figure 32.1 Object Diagram

Creating CALayer

Open up the `Polynomials` project in Xcode. The animation classes are part of the `QuartzCore` framework, so Control-click on Linked Frameworks to add an existing framework to your application (Figure 32.2).

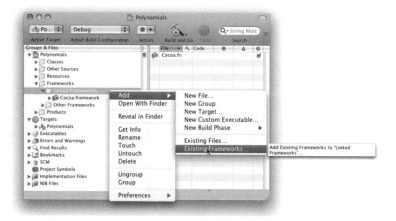

Figure 32.2   Add Framework

The framework is `/System/Library/Frameworks/QuartzCore.framework`.

Open the `MainMenu.nib` file. In the Animation Inspector, check the **PolynomialView** to make it **CALayer**-backed. (We say that the view wants a CALayer.) See Figure 32.3.

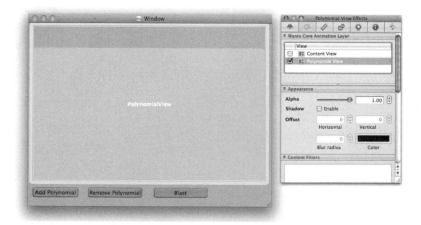

Figure 32.3   Polynomial View Wants CALayer

Add a button with the title Blast to the window (Figure 32.4).

Figure 32.4   Add Button

The Blast button will cause all the polynomials to move out of the view. Blasting a second time will bring them all back. Declare the method in PolynomialView.h. We are also going to need a BOOL to keep track of whether the polynomials have already been blasted off the screen:

```
#import <Cocoa/Cocoa.h>


@interface PolynomialView : NSView {
    NSMutableArray *polynomials;
    BOOL blasted;
}
- (IBAction)createNewPolynomial:(id)sender;
- (IBAction)deleteRandomPolynomial:(id)sender;
- (IBAction)blastem:(id)sender;

@end
```

In Interface Builder, connect the new button to the **blastem:** method.

In this exercise, you are going to let the layers do all the drawing. In PolynomialView.m, change the **drawRect:** method to create a white background:

```
- (void)drawRect:(NSRect)rect
{
    NSRect bounds = [self bounds];
    [[NSColor whiteColor] set];
    [NSBezierPath fillRect:bounds];
}
```

Create a stub for **blastem:** in `PolynomialView.m`:

```
#import "PolynomialView.h"
#import "Polynomial.h"
#import <QuartzCore/QuartzCore.h>

#define MARGIN (10)

@implementation PolynomialView

- (id)initWithFrame:(NSRect)frame {
    [super initWithFrame:frame];
    polynomials = [[NSMutableArray alloc] init];
    blasted = NO;
    return self;
}

- (IBAction)blastem:(id)sender
{
}
```

It doesn't do much, but build and run the application. Pretty white view? Good.

Using CALayer and CAAnimation

Now you will add layers containing the polynomials to the base layer. First, you need to create a method that will figure out a random off-view point. (You are going to slide the origin of the layer from that random point.) Add a method to `PolynomialView.m`:

```
- (NSPoint)randomOffViewPosition
{
    NSRect bounds = [self bounds];
    float radius = hypot(bounds.size.width, bounds.size.height);

    float angle = 2.0 * M_PI * (random() % 360 / 360.0);
    NSPoint p;
    p.x = radius * cos(angle);
    p.y = radius * sin(angle);
    return p;
}
```

Declare the method in `PolynomialView.h`.

Now, when the user asks for a new polynomial, you will also create a layer. You'll make the **Polynomial** object the delegate of the layer. Thus, you need to go into `Polynomial.m` and implement the method that will get called when the layer wants its delegate to draw it:

```
- (void)drawLayer:(CALayer *)layer
        inContext:(CGContextRef)ctx
{
    CGRect cgb = [layer bounds];
    [self drawInRect:cgb
           inContext:ctx];
}
```

Return to `PolynomialView.m`, and rewrite the method for creating new polynomials and animating them from the random point onto the view:

```
- (IBAction)createNewPolynomial:(id)sender
{
    // Create an instance of Polynomial
    Polynomial *p = [[Polynomial alloc] init];
    [polynomials addObject:p];

    // Create a layer
    CALayer *layer = [CALayer layer];
    CGRect b = [[self layer] bounds];
    b = CGRectInset(b, MARGIN, MARGIN);
    [layer setAnchorPoint:CGPointMake(0,0)];
    [layer setFrame:b];
    [layer setCornerRadius:12];
    [layer setBorderColor:[p color]];
    [layer setBorderWidth:3.5];

    // The instance of Polynomial will do the drawing
    [layer setDelegate:p];

    // Add the new layer to the base layer for the view
    [[self layer] addSublayer:layer];

    // Render the layer
    [layer display];

    // Make an animation that will move the layer on screen in 1 sec
    CABasicAnimation *anim
            = [CABasicAnimation animationWithKeyPath:@"position"];
    [anim setFromValue:
            [NSValue valueWithPoint:[self randomOffViewPosition]]];
    [anim setToValue:
            [NSValue valueWithPoint:NSMakePoint(MARGIN,MARGIN)]];
    [anim setDuration:1.0];
    CAMediaTimingFunction *f =
[CAMediaTimingFunction functionWithName:kCAMediaTimingFunctionLinear];
    [anim setTimingFunction:f];

    // Start the animation
    [layer addAnimation:anim forKey:@"whatever"];
}
```

Try it! Build and run the application. For now, simply click the Add Polynomial button. Pretty polynomials slide onto the screen? Excellent.

Removing Polynomials

Now we need to rewrite the **deleteRandomPolynomial:** method. This requires two methods: the method that starts the animation and the one that removes the layer when the animation is over:

```
- (IBAction)deleteRandomPolynomial:(id)sender
{
    // Get the array of CALayers that represent polynomials
    NSArray *polynomialLayers = [[self layer] sublayers];

    // Are there no polynomials to remove?
    if ([polynomialLayers count] == 0) {
        NSBeep();
        return;
    }

    // Pick a random layer
    int i = random() % [polynomialLayers count];
    CALayer *layerToPull = [polynomialLayers objectAtIndex:i];

    // Choose a point to drag it off to
    NSPoint randPoint = [self randomOffViewPosition];

    // Create the animation that will drive the motion offscreen
    CABasicAnimation *anim =
        [CABasicAnimation animationWithKeyPath:@"position"];

    // The animation will let you stuff anything you want into its
    // dictionary.  At the end of the animation, you will want to know
    // which polynomial was dragged off screen.
    [anim setValue:layerToPull forKey:@"representedPolynomialLayer"];
    [anim setFromValue:
                [NSValue valueWithPoint:NSMakePoint(MARGIN,MARGIN)]];
    [anim setToValue:
                [NSValue valueWithPoint:randPoint]];
    [anim setDuration:1.0];
    CAMediaTimingFunction *f =
[CAMediaTimingFunction functionWithName:kCAMediaTimingFunctionLinear];
    [anim setTimingFunction:f];

    // You need a callback when the animation is done
    [anim setDelegate:self];
    [layerToPull addAnimation:anim forKey:@"whatever"];

    // The position during the animation is temporary.  Without
    // next line, the deleted polynomial flashes before being removed
    [layerToPull setPosition:CGPointMake(randPoint.x, randPoint.y)];
}
- (void)animationDidStop:(CAAnimation *)anim finished:(BOOL)flag
{
    CALayer *layerToPull =
            [anim valueForKey:@"representedPolynomialLayer"];
```

```
    Polynomial *p = [layerToPull delegate];
    [polynomials removeObjectIdenticalTo:p];
    [layerToPull removeFromSuperlayer];
}
```

Build and run it. Now you can remove polynomials, right?

Moving Many Layers Simultaneously

The **blastem:** method will be moving many layers at the same time. To group many animations together, you will use **NSAnimationContext**:

```
- (IBAction)blastem:(id)sender
{
    [NSAnimationContext beginGrouping];
    [[NSAnimationContext currentContext] setDuration:3.0];
    NSArray *polynomialLayers = [[self layer] sublayers];

    for (CALayer *layer in polynomialLayers) {
        CGPoint p;
        if (blasted) {
            p = CGPointMake(MARGIN, MARGIN);
        } else {
            NSPoint r = [self randomOffViewPosition];
            // Convert from NSPoint to CGPoint
            p = *(CGPoint *)&r;
        }
        [layer setPosition:p];
    }
    [NSAnimationContext endGrouping];
    blasted = !blasted;
}
```

Build and run that. Try the Blast button. Nice?

Try resizing the window. Ugh!

Resizing and Redrawing the Layers

As a final enhancement, you are going to resize the base layer, but resize and redraw the polynomial layers only when the window resize is over:

```
- (void)resizeAndRedrawPolynomialLayers
{
    CGRect b = [[self layer] bounds];
    b = CGRectInset(b, MARGIN, MARGIN);

    NSArray *polynomialLayers = [[self layer] sublayers];
    [NSAnimationContext beginGrouping];
```

```
    [[NSAnimationContext currentContext] setDuration:0];
    for (CALayer *layer in polynomialLayers) {
        b.origin = [layer frame].origin;
        [layer setFrame:b];
        [layer setNeedsDisplay];
    }
    [NSAnimationContext endGrouping];
}

- (void)setFrameSize:(NSSize)newSize
{
    [super setFrameSize:newSize];
    if (![self inLiveResize]) {
        [self resizeAndRedrawPolynomialLayers];
    }
}

- (void)viewDidEndLiveResize
{
    [self resizeAndRedrawPolynomialLayers];
}
```

Build and run the app. Resize the window.

CALayer

In the exercise, you did explicit drawing on the CGContext of the **CALayer** in your **Polynomial** class. This mechanism allows you to do any sort of drawing that you can imagine on the **CALayer**.

However, much of the time, you will simply want to control a few common things:

- An image
- The background color
- Corner rounding
- A image filter to run the contents of the layer through

Instances of **CALayer** can handle all these things itself, with no delegate. (Once again, the Apple engineers deliver on the promise that common things are easy and uncommon things are possible.)

CALayer has subclasses to make particular kinds of drawing easier.

- Drawing text on a layer is easier if the layer is an instance of **CATextLayer**.

- Getting OpenGL calls onto a layer is easier if the layer is a subclass of **CAOpenGLLayer**.

- The base layer of a view is an instance of **_NSViewBackingLayer** (not a public class!) that knows to draw the contents of the view upon itself. In this exercise, your view-backing layer was simply painting itself white. (That is what you did in the view's **drawRect:** method.)

Chapter 33

A SIMPLE COCOA/OPENGL APPLICATION

This chapter is not designed to teach you OpenGL; if you want to learn OpenGL, read *The OpenGL Programming Guide*. This chapter is intended to show you how to do drawing with OpenGL in an application that is written using Cocoa. Like all other drawing in Cocoa, OpenGL rendering will be done in a view. Until now, all your views have used an **NSGraphicsContext** to do drawing with Quartz, via **NSImage**, **NSBezierPath**, and **NSAttributedString**.

Using NSOpenGLView

NSOpenGLView is an **NSView** subclass that has an OpenGL drawing context. Just as you needed the focus locked on a view to do drawing with Quartz, so the OpenGL drawing context must be active for any OpenGL drawing commands to have an effect.

Here are some important methods in **NSOpenGLView**:

```
- (id)initWithFrame:(NSRect)frameRect
        pixelFormat:(NSOpenGLPixelFormat *)format
```

The designated initializer.

```
- (NSOpenGLContext*)openGLContext
```

Returns the view's OpenGL context.

```
- (void)reshape
```

Called when the view is resized. The OpenGL context is active when this method is called.

```
- (void)drawRect:(NSRect)r
```

Called when the view needs to be redrawn. The OpenGL context is active when this method is called.

Writing the Application

Figure 33.1 shows the application that you will create.

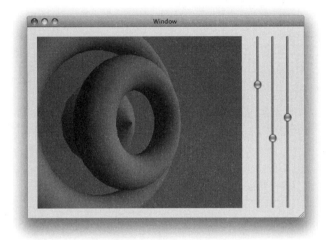

Figure 33.1 Completed Application

Create a new Cocoa application project, and call it Gliss (short for "GL Bliss"). Under the Project menu, use Add to Project... to add the frameworks OpenGL.framework and GLUT.framework—both in /System/Library/ Frameworks/—to the project. You will not be using the GLUT event model— just a couple of convenient functions.

Create a new Objective-C class, and name it **GlissView**. In the GlissView.h, change the superclass and declare an outlet and an action:

```
#import <Cocoa/Cocoa.h>

@interface GlissView : NSOpenGLView
{
    IBOutlet NSMatrix *sliderMatrix;
}
- (IBAction)changeParameter:(id)sender;
@end
```

Lay Out the Interface

Open MainMenu.nib.

In the Library window, drag an **NSOpenGLView** from Cocoa -> Views & Cells -> Data Views onto the window (Figure 33.2).

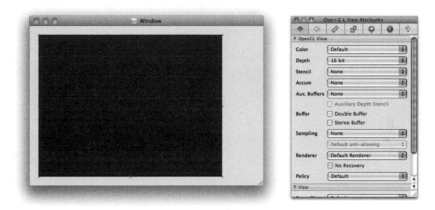

Figure 33.2   Drop an NSOpenGLView

In the Identity Inspector, set the class of the view to be **GlissView** (Figure 33.3)

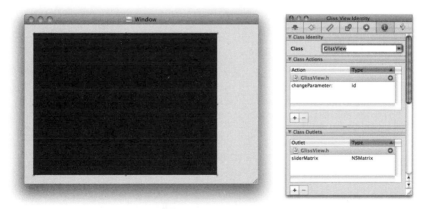

Figure 33.3   Set the Class

Drop an **NSSlider** on the window. Configure the slider to be continuous. In the Layout menu, choose Embed objects in -> Matrix. In the Inspector, set the matrix in Tracking mode, and give it three columns (Figure 33.4).

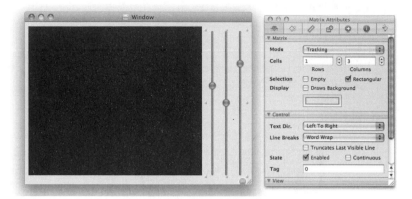

Figure 33.4   Matrix of Sliders

Set the target of the matrix to be the **GlissView**, and set the action to be **changeParameter:**. Set the sliderMatrix outlet of the the **GlissView** to point to the matrix. (Be sure to create connections in both directions.)

The first slider will control the X-coordinate of the light. Set its range from –4 to 4, and give it an initial value of 1. It should have a tag of 0. The Inspector should look like Figure 33.5.

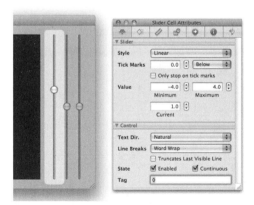

Figure 33.5   Set Limit, Initial Value, and Tag for First Slider Cell

The second slider will control the angle from which the scene is viewed. Set its range from –4 to 4, and give it an initial value of 0. It should have a tag of 1.

The third slider will control from how far the scene is viewed. Set its range from 0.3 to 5, and give it an initial value of 4. It should have a tag of 2.

Select the **GlissView**. In the Attributes Inspector, set the view to have a 16-bit depth buffer, as shown in Figure 33.6.

Figure 33.6   Create a 16-Bit Depth Buffer

In the Size Inspector, make the **GlissView** resize with the window.

Inspect the **NSMatrix**. Set it to autosize its cells. In the Size Inspector, make the matrix cling to the right edge of the window, as shown in Figure 33.7. Save the nib file.

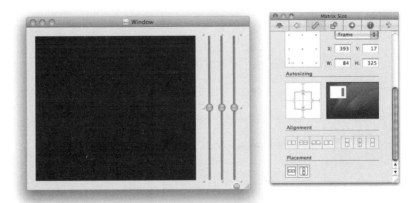

Figure 33.7   Matrix Size Inspector

Write Code

Edit GlissView.h as follows:

```
#import <Cocoa/Cocoa.h>

@interface GlissView : NSOpenGLView
{
    IBOutlet NSMatrix *sliderMatrix;
    float lightX, theta, radius;
    int displayList;
}
- (IBAction)changeParameter:(id)sender;
@end
```

Next, edit GlissView.m:

```
#import "GlissView.h"
#import <GLUT/glut.h>

#define LIGHT_X_TAG 0
#define THETA_TAG 1
#define RADIUS_TAG 2

@implementation GlissView
- (void)prepare
{
    NSLog(@"prepare");

    // The GL context must be active for these functions to have an effect
    NSOpenGLContext *glcontext = [self openGLContext];
    [glcontext makeCurrentContext];

    // Configure the view
    glShadeModel(GL_SMOOTH);
    glEnable(GL_LIGHTING);
    glEnable(GL_DEPTH_TEST);

    // Add some ambient lighting
    GLfloat ambient[] = {0.2, 0.2, 0.2, 1.0};
    glLightModelfv(GL_LIGHT_MODEL_AMBIENT, ambient);

    // Initialize the light
    GLfloat diffuse[] = {1.0, 1.0, 1.0, 1.0};
    glLightfv(GL_LIGHT0, GL_DIFFUSE, diffuse);
    // and switch it on.
    glEnable(GL_LIGHT0);

    // Set the properties of the material under ambient light
    GLfloat mat[] = {0.1, 0.1, 0.7, 1.0};
    glMaterialfv(GL_FRONT, GL_AMBIENT, mat);
```

```
    // Set the properties of the material under diffuse light
    glMaterialfv(GL_FRONT, GL_DIFFUSE, mat);
}


- (id)initWithCoder:(NSCoder *)c
{
    self = [super initWithCoder:c];
    [self prepare];
    return self;
}

// Called when the view resizes
- (void)reshape
{
    NSLog(@"reshaping");
    // Convert up to window space, which is in pixel units.
    NSRect baseRect = [self convertRectToBase:[self bounds]];
    // Now the result is glViewport()-compatible.
    glViewport(0, 0, baseRect.size.width, baseRect.size.height);
    glMatrixMode(GL_PROJECTION);
    glLoadIdentity();
    gluPerspective(60.0, baseRect.size.width/baseRect.size.height,
                   0.2, 7);
}

- (void)awakeFromNib
{
    [self changeParameter:self];
}

- (IBAction)changeParameter:(id)sender
{
    lightX = [[sliderMatrix cellWithTag:LIGHT_X_TAG] floatValue];
    theta = [[sliderMatrix cellWithTag:THETA_TAG] floatValue];
    radius = [[sliderMatrix cellWithTag:RADIUS_TAG] floatValue];
    [self setNeedsDisplay:YES];
}

- (void)drawRect:(NSRect)r
{
    // Clear the background
    glClearColor (0.2, 0.4, 0.1, 0.0);
    glClear(GL_COLOR_BUFFER_BIT |
            GL_DEPTH_BUFFER_BIT);

    // Set the view point
    glMatrixMode(GL_MODELVIEW);
    glLoadIdentity();
    gluLookAt(radius * sin(theta), 0,  radius * cos(theta),
              0, 0, 0,
              0, 1, 0);
```

```
    // Put the light in place
    GLfloat lightPosition[] = {lightX, 1, 3, 0.0};
    glLightfv(GL_LIGHT0, GL_POSITION, lightPosition);

    if (!displayList)
    {
        displayList = glGenLists(1);
        glNewList(displayList, GL_COMPILE_AND_EXECUTE);

        // Draw the stuff
        glTranslatef(0, 0, 0);
        glutSolidTorus(0.3, 0.9, 35, 31);
        glTranslatef(0, 0, -1.2);
        glutSolidCone(1, 1, 17, 17);
        glTranslatef(0, 0, 0.6);
        glutSolidTorus(0.3, 1.8, 35, 31);

        glEndList();
    } else {
        glCallList(displayList);
    }

    // Flush to screen
    glFinish();
}
@end
```

Note that the OpenGL calls are broken into three parts: **prepare**, all the calls to be sent initially; **reshape**, all the calls to be sent when the view resizes; and **drawRect:**, all the calls to be sent each time the view needs to be redrawn. Build and run the app.

Chapter 34
NSTASK

Each application that you have created is in fact a directory, and somewhere down in that directory is an executable file. To run an executable on a Unix machine, such as your Mac, a process is forked, and the new process executes the code in that file. Many executables are command line tools, and some are quite handy. This chapter shows you how to run command line tools from your Cocoa application by using the class **NSTask**.

NSTask is an easy-to-use wrapper for the Unix functions **fork()** and **exec()**. You give it a path to an executable and launch it. Many processes read data from standard-in and write to standard-out and standard-error. Your application can use **NSTask** to attach pipes to carry data to and from the external process. Pipes are represented by the class **NSPipe**.

Multithreading versus Multiprocessing

Multithreading gets a lot of hype because it enables you to take advantage of multiple processors and cores. Multithreading can also ensure that your application stays responsive while it is doing some sort of processing in the background. Multithreaded programming is, however, difficult: The activities of one thread often stomp on the data being used by another.

You can often use multiprocessing to get much of the benefit of multithreaded programming with few of the headaches. That is, instead of creating a new thread to do some sort of processing, simply create a whole new process.

Following are other benefits of multiprocessing over multithreading.

- Rewriting the capabilities of many command line tools would be very time consuming.
- If you have a memory leak in the external process, the operating system will clean up for you when the external process ends.

- The external process can run as a user other than the application. Thus, the external process can have a set of permissions completely different from those of the application.

Although not as glamorous as multithreading, multiprocessing is probably more useful in real life.

ZIPspector

You can use the /usr/bin/zipinfo tool for looking at the contents of a zip file. Find a zip file on your machine, and try running zipinfo in the Terminal like this (-1 is dash-one, not dash-el):

```
# /usr/bin/zipinfo -1 /Users/aaron/myfile.zip
greatfile.txt
swellfile.rtf
magnificent.pdf
```

You are going to create an application that uses zipinfo (Figure 34.1). Note that it will have to send some arguments and read from the process's standard-out.

Figure 34.1   Completed Application

In Xcode, create a new project of type Cocoa Document-based Application. Name the project ZIPspector. This program will only view zip files, not edit them. In the Info panel for the target, set ZIPspector to be a viewer for files with the UTI `com.pkware.zip-archive` (a system-defined UTI, so it will know the extension, icon, etc., for zip files). (See Figure 34.2).

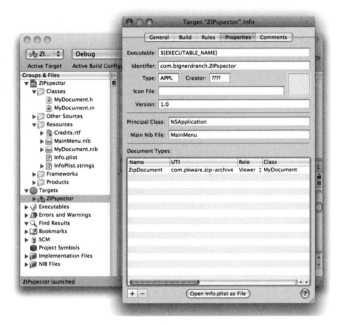

Figure 34.2   Setting UTI

In `MyDocument.h`, create outlets for an **NSTableView** and an **NSArray** for holding the filenames in the zip file:

```
@interface MyDocument : NSDocument
{
    IBOutlet NSTableView *tableView;
    NSArray *filenames;
}
@end
```

Open `MyDocument.nib`. Add a table view to the window, and set the view to have one uneditable column with the title Filenames. Control-click on the table view to bring up its Connection panel. Make the `dataSource` outlet point to File's Owner (Figure 34.3).

Control-click on File's Owner to bring up its connection window. Drag to set the `tableView` outlet (Figure 34.4).

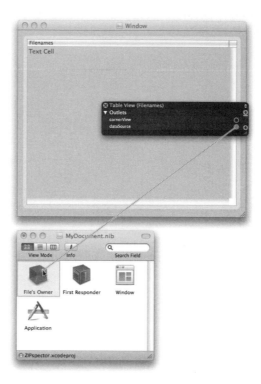

Figure 34.3   Set dataSource Outlet

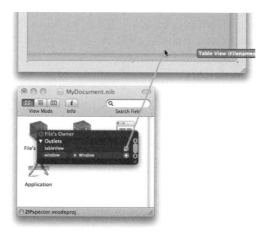

Figure 34.4   Set tableView Outlet

In MyDocument.m, you are going override **readFromURL:ofType:error:** to create an **NSTask** that executes zipinfo. Also, create an **NSPipe** and connect it to the standardOut of the **NSTask** (Figure 34.5).

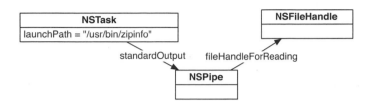

Figure 34.5   Object Diagram

Here is the code:

```
- (BOOL)readFromURL:(NSURL *)absoluteURL
            ofType:(NSString *)typeName
             error:(NSError **)outError
{
    // Which file are we getting the zipinfo for?
    NSString *filename = [absoluteURL path];

    // Prepare a task object
    NSTask *task = [[NSTask alloc] init];
    [task setLaunchPath:@"/usr/bin/zipinfo"];
    NSArray *args = [NSArray arrayWithObjects:@"-1", filename, nil];
    [task setArguments:args];

    // Create the pipe to read from
    NSPipe *outPipe = [[NSPipe alloc] init];
    [task setStandardOutput:outPipe];
    [outPipe release];

    // Start the process
    [task launch];

    // Read the output
    NSData *data = [[outPipe fileHandleForReading]
                                    readDataToEndOfFile];

    // Make sure the task terminates normally
    [task waitUntilExit];
    int status = [task terminationStatus];
    [task release];

    // Check status
    if (status != 0) {
        if (outError) {
            NSDictionary *eDict =
                    [NSDictionary dictionaryWithObject:@"zipinfo failed"
                            forKey:NSLocalizedFailureReasonErrorKey];
            *outError = [NSError errorWithDomain:NSOSStatusErrorDomain
                                        code:0
                                        userInfo:eDict];
        }
```

```
        return NO;
    }

    // Convert to a string
    NSString *aString = [[NSString alloc] initWithData:data
                                    encoding:NSUTF8StringEncoding];

    // Release the old filenames
    [filenames release];
    // Break the string into lines
    filenames = [[aString componentsSeparatedByString:@"\n"] retain];
    NSLog(@"filenames = %@", filenames);

    // Release the string
    [aString release];

    // In case of revert
    [tableView reloadData];

    return YES;
}
```

Now you need table view data source methods:

```
- (int)numberOfRowsInTableView:(NSTableView *)v
{
    return [filenames count];
}

- (id)tableView:(NSTableView *)tv
 objectValueForTableColumn:(NSTableColumn *)tc
                    row:(NSInteger)row
{
    return [filenames objectAtIndex:row];
}
```

Your application doesn't save, so if you wish, you can delete the method **dataOfType:error:**. Also, you can open up the MainMenu.nib file and delete any menu items that are concerned with saving.

Build and run your application. You should be able to see the contents of any zip file. (No Untitled document will appear—this is a viewer —you must open an existing .zip file.)

Asynchronous Reads

As mentioned in Chapter 24, the run loop is the object that waits for events. Those may be keyboard, mouse, or timer events. These are all run loop data sources. You can also make a file handle a run loop data source.

In this section, we are going to fork off a process that burps up data occasionally. We will attach a pipe to standardOut, but instead of trying to read all the data from the file handle immediately, we will ask it to read in the background and send a notification when data is ready.

To see whether you can make an IP connection to another machine, use /sbin/ping. Try running it in Terminal:

```
$ /sbin/ping -c10 www.bignerdranch.com
PING www.bignerdranch.com (69.39.89.150): 56 data bytes
64 bytes from 69.39.89.150: icmp_seq=0 ttl=50 time=35.579 ms
64 bytes from 69.39.89.150: icmp_seq=1 ttl=50 time=35.099 ms
64 bytes from 69.39.89.150: icmp_seq=2 ttl=50 time=34.546 ms
64 bytes from 69.39.89.150: icmp_seq=3 ttl=50 time=35.495 ms
64 bytes from 69.39.89.150: icmp_seq=4 ttl=50 time=35.685 ms
64 bytes from 69.39.89.150: icmp_seq=5 ttl=50 time=35.667 ms
64 bytes from 69.39.89.150: icmp_seq=6 ttl=50 time=36.435 ms
64 bytes from 69.39.89.150: icmp_seq=7 ttl=50 time=52.296 ms
64 bytes from 69.39.89.150: icmp_seq=8 ttl=50 time=36.142 ms
64 bytes from 69.39.89.150: icmp_seq=9 ttl=50 time=36.188 ms

--- www.bignerdranch.com ping statistics ---
10 packets transmitted, 10 packets received, 0% packet loss
round-trip min/avg/max/stddev = 34.546/37.313/52.296/5.021 ms
```

If you want to end the program prematurely, press Control-c to send it a sigint signal. This will cause it to write out the stats and terminate.

iPing

Now you are going to write a Cocoa app that uses **NSTask** to run ping (Figure 34.6).

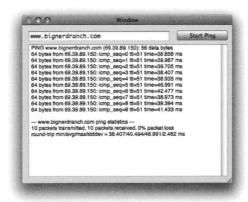

Figure 34.6   Completed Application

In Xcode, create a new project of type Cocoa Application named iPing. Create a new Objective-C class named **AppController**. **AppController** needs two outlets, a variable for the **NSTask**, and an action:

```
@interface AppController : NSObject
{
    IBOutlet NSTextView *outputView;
    IBOutlet NSTextField *hostField;
    IBOutlet NSButton *startButton;
    NSTask *task;
    NSPipe *pipe;
}
- (IBAction)startStopPing:(id)sender;
@end
```

Open MainMenu.nib and drop a text view, a text field, and a button on the window. The button should be put in Toggle mode. The title should be Start Ping; the alternate title, Stop Ping Figure 34.7).

Figure 34.7   Button Attributes

Drag an **NSObject** out of the library. In the Identity Inspector, set its class to **AppController** (Figure 34.8).

Make the **AppController** the target of the button; its action should be **startStopPing:**. Set the outputView, hostField, and startButton outlets to point to the text view, the text field, and the button, respectively(Figure 34.9).

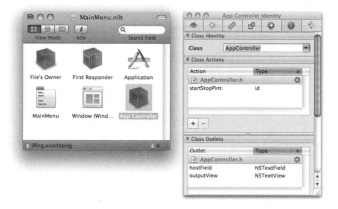

Figure 34.8 Create AppController

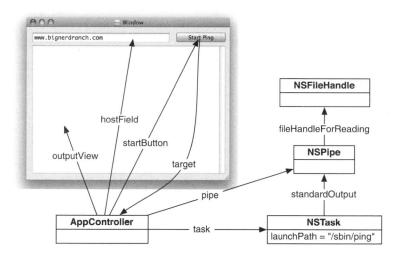

Figure 34.9 Object Diagram

In AppController.m, implement **startStopPing:**

```
- (IBAction)startStopPing:(id)sender
{
    // Is the task running?
    if (task) {
        [task interrupt];
    } else {
        task = [[NSTask alloc] init];
        [task setLaunchPath:@"/sbin/ping"];
```

```
            NSArray *args = [NSArray arrayWithObjects:@"-c10",
                                        [hostField stringValue], nil];
            [task setArguments:args];

            // Release the old pipe
            [pipe release];
            // Create a new pipe
            pipe = [[NSPipe alloc] init];
            [task setStandardOutput:pipe];

            NSFileHandle *fh = [pipe fileHandleForReading];

            NSNotificationCenter *nc;
            nc = [NSNotificationCenter defaultCenter];
            [nc removeObserver:self];
            [nc addObserver:self
                    selector:@selector(dataReady:)
                        name:NSFileHandleReadCompletionNotification
                      object:fh];
            [nc addObserver:self
                    selector:@selector(taskTerminated:)
                        name:NSTaskDidTerminateNotification
                      object:task];
            [task launch];
            [outputView setString:@""];

            [fh readInBackgroundAndNotify];
    }
}
```

While the task is running, the file handle will be posting notifications when data is ready. Implement the method that will get called:

```
- (void)appendData:(NSData *)d
{
    NSString *s = [[NSString alloc] initWithData:d
                                    encoding:NSUTF8StringEncoding];
    NSTextStorage *ts = [outputView textStorage];
    [ts replaceCharactersInRange:NSMakeRange([ts length], 0)
                    withString:s];
    [s release];
}

- (void)dataReady:(NSNotification *)n
{
    NSData *d;
    d = [[n userInfo] valueForKey:NSFileHandleNotificationDataItem];

    NSLog(@"dataReady:%d bytes", [d length]);

    if ([d length]) {
        [self appendData:d];
    }
```

```
    // If the task is running, start reading again
    if (task)
        [[pipe fileHandleForReading] readInBackgroundAndNotify];
}
```

When the process is done, we should do some cleanup:

```
- (void)taskTerminated:(NSNotification *)note
{
    NSLog(@"taskTerminated:");

    [task release];
    task = nil;

    [startButton setState:0];

}
```

Build and run the application.

Challenge: .tar and .tgz files

The `zipinfo` tool gives a listing of files in a zip file. You can get a similar listing for tar files by using the command line `tar`:

 # /usr/bin/tar tf MyFiles.tar

If the `tar` file is also compressed, add a z to the flags:

 # /usr/bin/tar tzf MyFiles.tgz

Extend ZIPspector to deal with `.tar` and `.tgz` files also.

Chapter 35
THE END

When I teach a class, it always ends with the "Feel-Good Talk," which delivers the following messages.

- The knowledge you have received from this experience never comes easy. You have learned a lot of stuff. Be proud.

- The only way to solidify what you have learned is to write applications. The sooner you start, the easier it will be.

- There is still much more to learn, but you have crossed the hump in the learning curve. Matters will be easier from here. Once again, the only way to progress is to write applications.

- As a speaker, I'm available for weddings, parties, bar mitzvahs, and other events. I also offer five-day classes at the Big Nerd Ranch. For a schedule, please see the Big Nerd Ranch Web site (`www.bignerdranch.com/`).

The final part of the "Feel-Good Talk" is a listing of resources that will help answer your questions as they arise. As with any programming topic, your answers will be found in a hodgepodge of online documentation, Web sites, and mailing lists.

- If you have a question about Cocoa, first check the reference documentation. All the classes, protocols, functions, and constants are listed there. Look in `/Developer/Documentation/Cocoa/Reference/`.

- If you have a question about Objective-C, first check is the Objective-C reference documentation. Use Xcode's Help menu to access the documentation.

- If you have a question about Xcode or Interface Builder, first check the developer tools reference documentation.

- Mark Dalrymple and I wrote a book on the plumbing of Mac OS X from a developer's point of view. If your code is going to do anything with the operating system (e.g., multithreading or networking), I strongly recommend that you pick up a copy of *Advanced Mac OS X Programming*.

- Don't be afraid to experiment—most questions can be answered by creating a tiny application. Creating this application will probably take you less than 15 minutes.

- The Web site for this book (`www.bignerdranch.com/products/cocoa1.shtml`) has the answers to many questions and several fun examples.

- The CocoaDev Wiki (`www.cocoadev.com/`) is a good place to learn new tricks.

- Apple also has a mailing list for Cocoa developers. You can join the mailing list at Apple's list server (`http://lists.apple.com/`). The list is archived at `www.cocoabuilder.com/`.

- Several Cocoa-related blogs (including the "Late Night Cocoa" podcast) are syndicated at `www.macdevnet.com/`.

- If you have exhausted all other possibilities, Apple's Developer Technical Support will answer your questions for a fee. I find the folks there consistently knowledgeable and helpful, and they have answered lots of questions for me.

- Join the Apple Developer Connection. It will give you access to the latest developer tools and documentation. The ADC Web site is `http://connect.apple.com/`.

Finally, try to be nice. Help beginners. Give away useful applications and their source code. Answer questions in a kind manner. It is a relatively small community, and few good deeds go forever unrewarded.

Thanks for reading my book!

Challenge

Write a Cocoa application and get someone (not yourself) to use it.

INDEX

Symbols

%@, 38, 41–42, 71–72, 231
$ (in tokens), 231
+ in method names, 52
@ symbol, 24, 38
.???? extension, 163
+ prefix, 203
: (in method name), 34

A

Abstract classes, 123, 154
Accented characters, 228, 284
acceptsFirstResponder, 265, 272–273
Accessor methods, 48, 74–77, 113, 117, 119,
    142–143
Action, 22, 80
    See also Target/action
Action methods, 19, 136
Active Build Configuration, 39
add:, 125, 130, 178, 370–372
addEmployeesObject:, 369
addObject:, 34, 44, 63
addObjectsFromArray:, 44
addObserver:, 121, 146, 210–214, 414
Adobe PDF, 2, 262, 283–285, 294, 339
Advanced Mac OS X Programming, 417
Affine transform, 239, 379–380
Alert panels
    confirm delete request, 218–219
    icon, 217
    modal operation, 218
    NSRunAlertPanel(), 217–218
    removeEmployee:, 218–220
    sheet, 218
allKeys, 199, 333

alloc, 33–34, 72
Amazon Web service, 346–349
AND (&), 250
Animation. *See* Core animation
AppController, 85–89, 185–186, 252–256, 412
appendData:, 414
AppKit framework, 6, 79, 107, 283
Apple, Inc.
    Cocoa developers mailing list, 418
    Copland, 3
    Developer Connection, 418
    Developer Technical Support, 418
    GUI guidelines, 16
    history, 1
    Mac OS X, 3
    and NeXT, 3
applicationShouldOpenUntitledFile:, 205
archivedDataWithRootObject:, 161
Archived (objects), 14
Archiving/unarchiving
    decoding, 156–157
    encoding, 154–155
    extension and icon, 163–165
    infinite loops, 165–166
    Info.plist, 157, 163–165, 168
    initWithCoder, 154–156
    NSCoder, 154–157, 166
    NSCoding, 154–157, 167
    NSDocument, 157–160, 168
    NSDocumentController, 157–158
    NSKeyedArchiver, 154, 161, 166
    NSKeyedUnarchiver, 161–163, 166
    NSWindowController, 157–160, 162
    universal type identifiers (UTIs), 168–169
    updateChangeCount:, 168
Arguments and methods, 34, 56, 201

more cocoa?

- Cocoa Bootcamp

- iPhone Bootcamp

- Advanced Cocoa Bootcamp

- Objective-C/Cocoa Bootcamp

- Advanced Mac OS X Bootcamp

BiG
nerD
ranch

www.bignerdranch.com

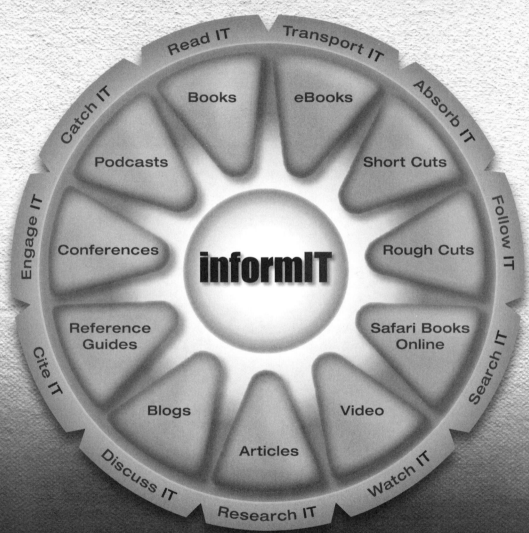